Wild Lime

Cooking from the bushfood garden

Dedicated to the memory of my late father for encouraging me
to always endeavour to do my best

Wild Lime

Cooking from the bushfood garden

JULEIGH ROBINS

Gardening notes: Rhys Freeman
Cookery consultant: Ian Robins

ALLEN & UNWIN

First published in 1996
This edition 1998
Allen & Unwin Pty Ltd
9 Atchison Street, St Leonards 2065, Australia
Phone: (61 2) 9901 4088
Fax: (61 2) 9906 2218
E-mail: frontdesk@allen-unwin.com.au
Web: http://www.allen-unwin.com.au

National Library of Australia
Cataloguing-in-Publication entry

Robins, Juleigh, 1952–
    Wild Lime: cooking from the bushfood garden.
    Bibliography.
    Includes index.
    ISBN 1 86448 082 3.
    1. Wild foods – Australia. 2. Cookery (Wild
    foods). I. Freeman, Rhys, 1970–. II. Title.
641.5994

Designed by Phil Campbell
Photography by Peter Rad
Typeset by Lynne Hamilton
Printed in Australia by McPherson's Printing
Group, Maryborough, Victoria

10 9 8 7 6 5 4 3 2

Front cover: Native peppermint leaf
Back cover, top right: Bush tomatoes (front),
dried quandong, native pepper leaves

Contents

Acknowledgments

Many people have contributed to *Wild Lime* over the years. I would like to thank Dr Beth Gott for her wonderful store of Aboriginal knowledge and generosity, Heather Hartshorne and Wendy Phelps for their time and botanical expertise in checking the manuscript.

Thank you to Rhys, Gil and Meredith Freeman, Janet Chisholm and the women of Napperby Station, David and Judith Thompson, Wendy and David Phelps, Rick McLeod and Micheal Dinoris for hunting out all those bushfood samples that we always had to have yesterday.

Thanks to the wonderful staff at Robins Bush Foods: Chris Wheelehouse, Nadia Mezzina, Di Ford and Colleen Huckvale, who weighed, measured, and test-cooked some of the recipes. Thanks to those individuals who have contributed their thoughts on bushfoods and for letting us see their depth of experience and the commitment that the bushfood industry is based on.

Thank you to Foong Ling Kong for editing, and Phil Campbell for designing, the book.

Thank you to Paul Donovan and Anna Dollard from Allen & Unwin. Anna was a most gracious and caring editor, who gently guided us, so that we hardly knew we were being shown a better way.

To Anton and Bram, two wonderful sons who have had to put up with a rather distracted mother for some time. To my mother, Nance, and stepfather, Kevin, for helping out so much. To Trevor for all the support and grammatical corrections. To Ian for working with me through all the years, and contributing his talent and skills to our business and expertise.

Why Bushfoods?

The first questions that people ask when they find out that we have a business based on indigenous foods is 'Why bushfoods? How did you ever get involved with that?' I suppose the answers to those questions lie at the very heart of this book. Ultimately, I believe that we cook with bushfoods because they taste wonderful. They excite our palates, and have led us into new and creative culinary paths as restaurateurs, caterers and now, bushfood manufacturers.

I derive enormous satisfaction from developing recipes that make use of indigenous foods, and having them become acceptable and desirable to people who may not have heard of them. A simple tart made of beautiful bush fruits, for example, helps reveal the bounty that this land offers, and continues to do so, despite the odds.

Being involved with bushfoods has really opened my eyes, and my family's, to the way we relate to our landscape. Despite being born in Australia, I was largely unaware of my own land. Here we are, surrounded by coasts, forests and plains that once supported large tribes of people and nurtured them, and yet, I was still ignorant of the food potential of many of our native plants.

It makes good sense to grow and eat our native plant foods. I doubt that I will ever come to grips with the dominance of European farming methods and crops in an environment that is so clearly alien to them. Doubtless, historians will have answers as to why our English colonists insisted on imposing their imported systems, crops and livestock to the absolute detriment of the Aboriginal peoples, indigenous plants and animals. As a cook, I prefer an agriculture based on the food plants which grow regionally and flourish naturally in the local environment, and don't require extensive irrigation or massive amounts of fertiliser or chemical sprays to repel pests. Like farmers, cooks are tied to the land. We want healthy plants that are juicy and full of flavour; we appreciate the seasonality and growing cycles of produce. I don't know anyone who cooks who is glad that tomatoes and strawberries are available all year round, especially since they bear little resemblance—in terms of taste and flavour—to when they are in season.

Learning about bushfoods can only teach us their value, and make them a part of our lives and the physical environment we live in. A simple walk along the beach or in the bush becomes an adventure.

These days, our sons look out for little fruits or interesting leaves when we're out in the bush and want to know their use. Sometimes I know, often I don't, and we try to identify them through books and other sources. I hope that our kids will grow up with the knowledge and expectation that Australian indigenous foods are not only available, but also desirable.

When we ran a little food shop and catering business in the Melbourne suburb of Toorak, cooking with bushfoods quickly became a normal part of our repertoire after we 'discovered' their exciting flavours. One of my favourite things to make was a bourdaloue, a classic French tart traditionally filled with almond cream and baked with apples or pears. Our customers loved it. After encountering bushfoods, I still kept my passion for European cakes, but began to introduce non-European fruits, seeds and nuts into their preparation. We were never cut out to be traditionalists! Thus the classic bourdaloue was filled with a macadamia nut cream and baked with the jewel-like Illawarra plums and riberries. Instead of an apricot glaze, we used one made from Kakadu plums. At first, our regular clients looked and politely enquired as to what on earth the tart was. To their credit, they were game to try anything at least once, and after a few weeks, we were getting more orders for the Illawarra bourdaloue. What was once strange slipped comfortably into the vernacular, and no-one thought twice about ordering bushfood cakes. So we went on from there, incorporating them into more cakes, breads, biscuits, sauces, jams and chutneys. Through these various products, people became more aware of bushfoods, and what great eating they were. Everyone wanted to know where they came from, what they looked like and how we found them. I couldn't answer them well back then, so what started as an interest quickly became a study, and, I must admit, a passion.

No knowledge about bushfoods can be gleaned without first learning about Aboriginal culture and practices. So much can be gleaned from books, but much more can be understood by talking to people who know. I have been fortunate to have met and spoken with some very generous Aboriginal people who have shared their knowledge and skills with us. Various Aboriginal communities from all over the country are keen to be involved in the developing bushfood industry, either through wild harvesting of seasonal products, or growing bushfoods with traditional Aboriginal land-management techniques with the incorporation of modern sustainable farming practices, where appropriate. As Colin Anderson from the Council of Aboriginal Reconciliation put it, 'Much of Australia's farmland needs restoration after more than 200 years of introduced, often inappropriate, farming practices. We have the opportunity to dove-tail indigenous vegetation management for restoration and land care with indigenous vegetation management for commercial production. Both objectives support the replanting and care of not only trees, but also the understorey of shrubs, herbs and grasses. In recreating whole ecosystems on marginal or degraded agricultural or under-utilised land, we will be providing the catalyst for a whole suite of macro and micro plant life and wildlife to return to and re-establish natural habitats.

'We need to change the way we look after this country and we need to look for world-wide niche markets for our products. This is why it is important that all the people of Australia, whether they be indigenous or non-indigenous, recognise the value of our own home-grown resources. The values to Australia can be measured in terms of cultural and social benefits, economic advances and, environmental gains.'

Many Aboriginal communities are exploring how they can not only continue to involve themselves in the bushfoods industry but also help its destiny. The Council for Aboriginal Reconciliation has identified a series of recommendations for all of us to follow towards a genuine celebration and utilisation of our cultural diversity. These include the application and teaching of land management techniques; plant identification and traditional plant usage; and awareness of the potential commercial values as well as medicinal, nutritional, aesthetic, environmental and spiritual value of indigenous plant foods.

Through my own study of bushfoods, I have learnt how, and how not to, handle some of the bushfoods mentioned in this book. More importantly, I have slowly come to understand much more of the cultural significance of food in Aboriginal life. These insights have left me wanting to know and understand more about bushfoods and broader Aboriginal culture. As I have come to enjoy learning about and appreciating Aboriginality, I hope that bushfoods can become one of the paths that will reconcile Australia's Aboriginal and non-Aboriginal cultures.

It's not so long ago that Chinese, Greek, Italian, and more recently, Thai and Vietnamese, migrants began to change the culinary map in Australia. Our exposure to these communities through the medium of food has contributed significantly to the acceptance in Australia of a multicultural society. From an English-based meat-and-three-veg nation, we now have in our shopping trolleys Thai fish sauce, fresh lemongrass and sun-dried tomatoes. Let's add to that bush tomato chutney, quandong jam, bunya nuts, fresh warrigal greens and a healthy appreciation of Aboriginal culture.

Bushfoods have a true flavour that hasn't been genetically manipulated or bred. Tests conducted by various agencies around the country have shown them to be highly nutritious, more so than their farmed European relatives. We have a chance to develop an exciting agriculture around these foods, and while farmers will need to select the best fruit-bearing strains and the most hardy specimens to grow, they will largely be left untampered compared to most of the common fruits, vegetables and grains available. With the emphasis in the bushfoods industry on clean foods, organic growing methods, the questioning of the principles of monocultural growing systems and the increasing interest in permaculture and 'polyculture', Australia may well have a unique and highly desirable future in food production based on bushfoods. Aboriginal and Torres Strait Islander peoples and many others share this long-term vision.

I have recently completed a year as an industry representative on the Australian Native Bushfood Industry Committee (ANBIC) steering committee, which was

Why Bushfoods?

established by the Rural Industries Research and Development Corporation. ANBIC was set up to assess the current status of the bushfoods industry, its size and scope, as well as identifying and potentially charting its future as a financially viable Australian industry. A major outcome of ANBIC's work was the staging of the inaugural Australian Native Bushfood Conference in Brisbane in May 1996, where there was agreement to form a national legal entity to represent the bushfoods industry with all its diverse components, from Aboriginal communities involved in bushfoods, to growers, wild harvesters, manufacturers and processors, to the hospitality industry.

The bushfood industry is, of course, still a fledgling one and is struggling to come to grips with the needs, wants and capabilities of its various parts. The transition from fragmented and often small, cottage businesses to a cohesive industry won't be an easy or rapid path, but with some sensitivity and thought, the future of the industry could be culturally, environmentally and financially enriching and rewarding. The term 'greenfield industry' never had a better application.

When we opened our first restaurant at the very end of the seventies, fresh herbs were only just becoming available, and supply wasn't guaranteed. The only way I could get the freshest herbs and salad greens for our restaurant was to grow them myself. This was my introduction to growing food plants until the dedicated herb growers appeared. I see great parallels with the emerging availability of bushfoods. Some are more readily available to consumers than others (a list of suppliers is included at the back of the book), and it will take time to bring these foods to the markets. Having bushfoods in the garden allows you to experiment with different foods, and there is a certain satisfaction in having grown something yourself, and being able to go into the garden to pick them fresh, as you need them.

Bushfoods add enormous interest to your garden, and can change the way you look at native plants, even the non-food varieties. They can be grown for their wonderful fragrance and visual beauty, and you do not necessarily need special little plots to nurture them. One of the loveliest aspects of growing bushfood plants is the variety of bird life and native creatures that will be attracted to your garden.

I hope that I have convinced you that you can't live without bushfoods! It was the spirit of adventure that led us to cook with bushfoods, and we have written *Wild Lime* in the same spirit. It is our hope that it will provide you with a framework within which to interpret bushfoods.

We have been highly selective with our choice of bushfoods, and have chosen those that we are most familiar and proficient with since we are on a learning curve ourselves! You'll find that many of the recipes are interpretations of the classics. Some recipes have manifest themselves as we tried to work out what on earth to do with a particular ingredient. All, however, are 'tried and true'. The nicest thing about cooking and gardening is sharing the knowledge with friends. Here are some of our best-ever tips and recipes. We hope you enjoy the result.

Fruit

Bush Tomato

Also known as the desert raisin and has various Aboriginal names according to the region

The experience of tasting our first bush tomato will long be remembered. This fruit remains one of our favourite bushfoods. What a wonderfully exciting flavour! We knew that we could really cook with them and have developed quite a repertoire of recipes.

The fruit was initially difficult to find in large amounts until we made the acquaintance of Janet and Roy Chisholm, third-generation owners of Napperby Station, an outback cattle station that lies 220 km north-west of Alice Springs. The Station is an important supplier of bush tomatoes as the plants grow in abundance over the 6500 square km property.

Three hundred Aboriginal people from the Anmatyerr group live on the station and some of the men from the community work as stockmen. The bush tomato was one of the most important and precious of the desert fruits and one of the desert peoples' staples. It was a prolific crop that the Anmatyerr people would harvest after fire and particularly after rains when the plants regenerated. The plants would grow vigorously for a few seasons and fruit prolifically, the crop eventually declining until the next fire.

The Anmatyerr women still gather bush tomatoes in large coolamons. Traditionally, the desert people would gather the bush tomatoes after they had dried on the bush and grind them with water to form a thick paste, mould them into large balls and dry them in the desert sun. These huge balls of dried bush tomato were then stored in tree forks, where they would keep for very long periods, and were used as needed.

Bush tomato plants usually provide an abundant harvest and the ripe fruit looks like a yellowish cherry tomato with a green tinge. The fruit needs to dry in the sun and, after this process, shrivels to a rich reddish-brown colour and looks much like a raisin. The process of drying the bush tomato is essential—it reduces the level of alkaloids in the fruit and also concentrates the existing intense flavour. Eating too many bush tomatoes fresh without drying them first can make you ill.

The edible bush tomatoes are generally a good source of carbohydrates and vitamin C. Some related species, however, are not edible and have toxic levels of the alkaloid *solanine*. Take care when choosing; these can be easily mistaken for the edible varieties.

TO GROW

Solanum centrale

Distribution: Widely dispersed throughout the outback, particularly the Central Australian desert, and inland Queensland, NSW, SA, WA and NT.

The shrubs are small (up to 30 cm), with grey to green leaves. They are in the same family as potatoes and tomatoes. The attractive flowers are large and purple with yellow centres, and reminiscent of traditional tomato flowers. The plants appreciate a sandy situation with low humidity. They may adapt to moist coastal conditions, but will not do well in wet summers. Cold winters cause these plants to die back, and if conditions are severe, they might not regrow.

The bush tomato is a fairly hardy shrub if conditions are to its liking and it may sucker in open areas. It would be suitable as a low specimen plant where there is lots of sun and good air movement. The plants are not long lived, perhaps up to two years, but new plants are hardy and grow rapidly.

Seeds should be extracted from the mature fruit before sowing.

Relations

Some species of the *Solanum* family are bitter and poisonous, so only grow those listed here. Edible desert *Solanum*s include *S. petrophilum*, *S. cleistogamum*, *S. chippendalei* and *S. ellipticum*. *S. orbiculatum* may be eaten, although it is very bitter. *S. esuriale* is a bush tomato that is found in south-eastern Australia and may suit cultivation in the southern temperate states. The seeds of the *S. esuriale* must be removed before use.

To harvest

The bush tomato ripens in the wild in the Central Desert, usually from July to August, although drought and rain can affect the growing cycle. In regions other than the Central Desert the ripening period is during high summer. Bush tomatoes need some rainfall or watering to develop the fruit, but require equally good strong sunlight and heat to dry the fruit. In the wild, the hot desert sun dries the fruit quickly and efficiently so that it remains on the bush until collected. In a good season bush tomatoes fruit abundantly.

STORING BUSH TOMATO

Sun-dried bush tomatoes will keep for up to a year if stored in a dry and well-ventilated area. It is important to dry the bush tomatoes well if you want to store them in a dried state. If the bush tomatoes still feel quite soft after harvesting and appear to hold some residual moisture, dry them by laying them on a clean sheet or cloth in full and direct sunlight until they become firm and raisin-like. Or dry them out very slowly and gently in a very low oven with the door slightly ajar. Bush tomatoes will freeze beautifully after drying and this method of storage can be easier if time or weather doesn't permit effective dry storage. Remember that for safe eating the bush tomato must be sun-dried to at least the 'raisin' stage.

TO COOK

The bush tomato has a spicy, piquant flavour and can be added to many standard savoury dishes to give a special tasty edge. Words such as piquant, curry and spicy come to mind when describing its taste. In its naturally dried state the fruit can taste quite bitter to the uninitiated palate, and this bitterness can detract from the savoury spiciness of the fruit. Don't be deterred from cooking with these fruits though—used judiciously, their wonderful pungency can add great depth of flavour to many dishes. It's useful to think of this fruit more as a spice or flavouring rather than as a tomato as we commonly know it.

The best way to use the bush tomatoes is to grind them in a food processor with a metal blade to a fine or coarse powder. If there is too much moisture left in the dried fruit they tend to form a paste during processing. If this happens, freeze the whole dried fruit until they are quite hard and then process in small amounts. Once the bush tomatoes are ground, they can be added directly to your recipe. No further processing is required.

The bush tomato is intensely flavoured and, if added too liberally to a dish, will add bitterness rather than flavour. Many people make the mistake of trying to use the fruit whole, or attempting to rehydrate the whole dried fruit and then adding it to a dish. This is not advisable, as the flavour tends to overwhelm the rest of the ingredients. As a guide, a ratio of one part bush tomato to ten parts other ingredients is usually appropriate to deliver the flavour without the bitterness. So, if you are making a bush tomato soup, perhaps use 1 kg fresh tomatoes to 100 g bush tomatoes. Despite the seemingly small amount of bush tomato to fresh, the dominant flavour will be bush tomato.

Bush tomatoes are a delicious addition to almost any recipe that is based on the traditional tomato. They're also a useful addition to slow-cooked dishes such as casseroles and soups—the bush tomato acts as a thickening agent besides seasoning the dish. The dried and ground bush tomato swells and absorbs liquid during the cooking process as rehydration occurs. This is ideal if you're health-conscious or would like to avoid flour-based thickeners.

Goes with

Bush tomato is a savoury-tasting fruit and very versatile in the kitchen. Use in marinades and sauces, soups and casseroles, savoury tarts and pies. Bushfoods that are suited to the bush tomato include native peppers, kurrajong, wattleseeds, tubers, native nuts, wild thyme and warrigal greens. Generally the softer-fleshed fruits such as lilly pillies, lemon aspen and limes don't complement the piquancy of the bush tomato.

Chilli, pepper, cheese, olives, garlic, capsicum, anchovies and tomatoes are perfect. Onions, eggplants, potatoes and most vegetables are enhanced by the gutsy flavour of the bush tomato.

Bush Tomato Soup

This soup may be reduced even further to form the basis of a pasta sauce. The bush tomato flavour will strengthen with time, so it's advisable and convenient to make this soup in advance and heat to serve.

To serve 6

1⅓ cups (200 g) bush tomatoes
10 dried native pepper leaves
20 very ripe, red tomatoes
2 large onions, finely diced
½ cup (125 ml) olive oil
1 teaspoon (5 g) salt
fresh basil leaves to taste

In a food processor, grind the bush tomatoes and native pepper leaves to a fine texture that resembles coffee grounds. You will find this easier if the bush tomatoes have been frozen before processing.

Bring a pot of water to the boil and immerse the fresh tomatoes for about 30 seconds. Lift out with a slotted spoon and peel. Chop coarsely.

Sauté the onions in the olive oil in a medium-sized saucepan over medium heat until soft and tender. Add the chopped tomatoes and cook for 10 minutes.

Add the ground bush tomatoes, native pepper and salt. Cook for 45 minutes over a low heat, stirring occasionally.

Add the fresh basil a few minutes before the end of the cooking time.

Remove from the heat and purée until smooth.

To serve, accompany the soup with a small pizza brushed with olive oil, and topped with goat's cheese, basil and a good sprinkling of ground bush tomato. Or twist some puff pastry into long sticks, brush with a little butter, parmesan and ground bush tomato.

SHORTS

- Add ground bush tomato to pizza, either sprinkled over the topping, or make a sauce seasoned with bush tomato to spread on the pizza base.

- Spread some bush tomato sauce on a pizza base and top with goat's cheese, mozzarella and basil.

- Add some ground bush tomato during the last stages of making a mayonnaise.

- Make a sweet potato and bush tomato risotto, adding the bush tomato with the last ladleful of stock.

- Bush tomato sauce...the ultimate Australian tomato sauce!

Bush Tomato Tart with Roasted Red Capsicums and Olives

This tart evokes the tastes of summer, so choose the most beautiful, ripe red tomatoes that you can find—hopefully direct from the garden alongside the bush tomatoes—and enjoy the rich, almost jam-like texture of this tart.

You will need a 23 cm (9 in) pizza tray.

To serve 6 to 8

250 g puff pastry
1 x 55 g egg, beaten with a little water for egg wash
1 medium onion, finely chopped
2 cloves garlic, minced
¼ cup (65 ml) olive oil
10 large ripe red tomatoes, coarsely chopped
½ cup (75 g) ground bush tomatoes
3 native pepper leaves, left whole
½ teaspoon (1 g) dried wild thyme or common thyme
salt to taste
½ tablespoon (12 ml) tomato paste
1 large red capsicum
pitted black olives and a little extra olive oil

Carefully roll out the puff pastry to fit the pizza tray. Roll out the additional puff pastry and cut into 2–3 cm wide strips. These strips are going to be placed around the edge of the pastry base to form a wide border, so estimate how many you'll need, cut them and rest the puff pastry to allow it to firm up a little.

With a pastry brush, paint a strip of egg wash around the perimeter of the base and place the pastry strips flat along this strip to make a border. Continue placing the strips until you have a border around the perimeter of the tart that is 2 strips high. Rest this pastry tart case for at least 20 minutes in the refrigerator.

In a large saucepan, sauté the onions and garlic in the olive oil until the onions are tender. Watch the heat so that the garlic doesn't burn.

Add the fresh tomatoes and cook for 20 minutes. Then add the bush tomatoes and the native pepper leaves, thyme, a little salt and the tomato paste. Let this cook and reduce for a further 30 minutes. This mixture should reduce to under half its original volume and become almost jam-like in texture. If the filling is still too soupy, cook for a further 10 minutes or until the texture firms up and the mixture is gooey.

Take the filling from the heat and quickly purée in a food processor until smooth. Refrigerate until cool. Spoon the filling into the chilled prepared pastry case, spreading almost to the edges. Leave the filling a little humped in the centre and away from the pastry edge—it will spill over the pastry edge if it's too close. As the pastry starts to rise you can spread the filling out more if needed.

Preheat the oven to 190°C (375°F).

Carefully brush egg wash on the surface of the pastry strips. Be careful not to drip it over the sides as this will inhibit level rising of the pastry. ➤

Bake in the preheated oven until the pastry is well cooked and golden (approximately 40–50 minutes). Ensure that the base of the tart is cooked through.

While the tart is cooking, roast the capsicums directly over a gas flame or under a griller until they are charred all over. When their skins have blackened, wrap them in a clean tea-towel until cool enough to handle. Peel away the skins, rinse briefly under cold water and cut into thin lengthwise strips.

Let the tart cool to room temperature. Place the strips of roasted capsicum carefully across the surface in a lattice pattern. Place a whole or halved olive in each lattice space and gently brush the whole surface with a little extra olive oil.

Beef with Bush Tomato and Red Wine Sauce

To serve 6

1½ tablespoons (22 g) finely ground bush tomatoes
a pinch of native (black) pepper
a pinch of salt
6 beef steaks (cut and size as preferred)
2 tablespoons (50 ml) olive oil for frying
1½ onions, finely chopped
1½ teaspoons (40 ml) tomato paste
3 cups (750 ml) pinot noir (or light-bodied red wine)
3 teaspoons (75 g) castor sugar
1½ teaspoons (20 g) unsalted butter

Combine the ground bush tomatoes, pepper and salt. Coat both sides of the steaks with the mixture.

Heat a large skillet and add the olive oil. Pan-fry the steaks until cooked to your liking (2 minutes each side for rare and longer for medium and well done). Keep the steaks warm.

In another pan gently cook the onions, tomato paste, red wine and sugar, and heat through until the sugar is dissolved. Increase the heat and simmer until the volume is reduced by half. Add the cooking juices from the steaks to the red wine sauce, remove from the heat and quickly whisk in the butter until it is melted. Pour over the steaks and serve.

This dish needs little else except some steamed new potatoes or maybe rice, a fresh green salad and a good bottle of red.

Bush Tomato and Chilli Salsa

Salsas are the cook's answer to producing a delicious sauce on the spur of the moment, and will dress up almost any grilled meat or vegetable dish. Try this over grilled chicken, with a steak, or tossed through pasta shells.

To make 2 cups (500 ml)

1/4 cup (60 ml) white vinegar
1 teaspoon (5 g) salt
1 tablespoon (25 g) castor sugar
3 small red chillis, finely chopped
2 teaspoons (10 g) ground bush tomatoes
10 large, ripe tomatoes, finely chopped (skinned if preferred)
2 onions, finely chopped
2 cloves garlic, chopped
2 tablespoons (50 ml) good-quality olive oil

In a medium-sized stainless-steel saucepan, bring the vinegar, salt, sugar and chillis to the boil. Add the ground bush tomatoes and cook for 10 minutes on a low heat. Remove from the heat.

Combine the tomatoes, onions and garlic in a large bowl. Add the saucepan ingredients to the bowl.

Let the salsa sit for an hour for the flavours to infuse before serving. Just before use, drain off any excess liquid that has collected and stir through the olive oil.

Eggplant Parmigiana with Bush Tomato Salsa

To serve 6

1 cup (100 g) almond meal
1/2 cup (40 g) dry bread crumbs
3 large, long eggplants
1/2 cup (70 g) plain flour
1/2 cup egg wash
1/2 cup (125 ml) olive oil
1 large onion, thinly sliced
1 1/4 cups (300 ml) Bush Tomato Salsa (see above)
2 1/2 cups (450 g) grated mozzarella

Preheat the oven to 160°C (325°F).

Combine the almond meal and bread crumbs. Cut each eggplant lengthwise into 4 thick slices. Dust each slice in the plain flour, then dip in the egg wash and lastly in the combined almond meal and bread crumbs.

Heat the oil in a shallow frying pan and gently sauté each eggplant slice for 2–3 minutes on each side until golden brown. Remove from the oil with a slotted spoon and drain on kitchen paper to remove the excess oil. When all the eggplant slices have been browned, lay them flat on a baking tray and scatter over the sliced onion. Spread the salsa generously over the onion and, finally, sprinkle the grated cheese on top.

Bake in the preheated oven for 10 minutes or until the cheese has cooked to a golden crust.

Wild Lime

*Also known as desert lime, native cumquat,
limebush, desert lemon*

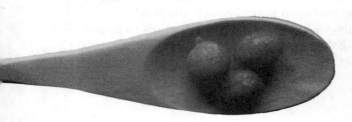

Wild lime—just the name of this fabulous little fruit is evocative and excites the cook's imagination. What can it be like? Out of a wonderful field of candidates, the wild lime is doubtless among the élite in terms of flavour and visual beauty. It resembles a perfect, miniature lime, and its flavour is closely aligned to the West Indian lime. It has a very thin, porous skin, and juicy segmented flesh like other citrus fruit. The skin and flesh are a yellowish lime-green in colour.

The wild lime is a true citrus. It is a very juicy little fruit, and it's quite surprising that the plant is described botanically as a xerophyte, that is, a drought-tolerant plant that actually thrives in hot and dry climates. The wild lime is the only member of the orange sub-family that is able to withstand severe drought and hot, dry winds. When these conditions occur the plant sheds its leaves and the leafless grey green twigs carry on photosynthesis at a reduced rate. When conditions ease, the leaves grow back. The wild lime also has a high tolerance of freezing temperatures; it can withstand, without injury, temperatures of 55°C (130°F) below zero. In this respect, the wild lime ranks a close second to the Chinese cumquat in its resistance to cold.

The wild lime is a small tree or large shrub usually found on clay or heavy clay soils, and grows in clumps or dense thickets. When young, the plant has blue-grey leaves, and spines or thorns growing along the branches. More mature plants lose their spines. They usually flower from July to September, and the wonderful fruits follow.

Wendy and David Phelps of Longreach Bush Tucker are largely responsible for the wild lime's popularity in the bushfood industry. They have pioneered its use, and have convinced many landholders who have it growing on their land, in western Queensland in particular, that the quickly spreading plant is more than just a nuisance. Wendy and David are now the largest single suppliers of wild lime to the bushfoods industry.

TO GROW

Eremocitrus glauca
Distribution: Inland, arid Queensland and NSW, parts of SA.

Clearly the plant favours arid and semi-arid inland areas and 200 to 500 mm rainfall regions. It's a very hardy plant that is tolerant of frost, drought and alkaline soil. It can be slow-growing to start with, but shoots up quickly. Under ideal conditions a mature tree can reach from 2 to 8 m. To hasten its growth, the wild lime can be grafted on to normal citrus rootstock. The plant responds very well to pruning and makes an interesting plant for the garden. If its spreading suckers are a concern, it can be grown in a tub.

Relations

The close relatives of the wild lime include the rainforest limes: the finger lime, *Microcitrus australasica*, the round lime, *M. australis*, the Mt White lime, *M. garrawayi*, and the Russell River lime, *M. inodora*.

To harvest

Wild limes flower in spring, and the fruit ripens in late spring and summer, approximately 10 to 12 weeks later. As the trees are usually not very tall, harvesting the fruit is not too onerous apart from avoiding the prickly thorns that grow along the stems. The fruit is ripe when it reaches an approximate length of 1 to 2 cm and is a lime green to bright yellow. It will be firm, juicy and not hard. The wild lime may start bearing about 2 to 3 kg of fruit about four years after planting.

STORING WILD LIME

If you don't use your harvest of wild limes immediately and need to store them, the best way is simply to freeze the cleaned fruit direct from the tree. They will keep for up to a year if frozen.

TO COOK

The wild lime is a deliciously tart and acidic fruit that tastes strongly of the true lime flavour that we associate with the West Indian lime (not the Tahitian lime, which is a hybrid and with nowhere as intense a flavour). The whole fruit may be used in cooking. Because of its miniature physiology the skin and pips are not intrusive, so no special preparation is needed. The lime has a great strength and depth of flavour. To give you some idea of its strength use a ratio of 10 whole (zest, flesh and juice) wild limes to 1 West Indian lime. That may not sound all that impressive, but there are, on average, 100 wild limes to 100 g; 10 g of wild lime gives the flavour effect of a whole West Indian lime and an average West Indian lime weighs about 35 to 40 g. Wild limes can be substituted for ordinary limes in many recipes. If the recipe uses only lime juice halve the ratio: 5 whole wild limes will equal the juice of an average West Indian lime.

As with most bushfoods, the wild lime is best added to a dish at the later stage of the cooking process. The flavour will be at its best and the colour will be retained beautifully. There are very few tricks to learn with the wild lime as it can be used with confidence in familiar citrus applications—marmalades, sauces, curd, brûlées, soufflés and so on. (The pectin level of wild limes varies according to the fruits and season, so you may need to adjust as necessary.) Just remember the flavour intensity, and to use the whole fruit.

Goes with

There are some bushfoods that will accompany wild limes successfully, primarily the bush 'herbs'. The limes may be seasoned with native pepper, lemon myrtle and native mint. Fruits such as lemon aspen, native tamarind, wild rosella and bush tomato will not complement the wild lime.

Chilli, ginger, coriander and lemongrass will all mix well with wild lime.

Wild Lime, Ginger and Coriander Butter

This is a simple butter, that is, a butter with the addition of few elements and one stage of preparation. A flavoured butter is traditionally made with a mortar and pestle, but using a food processor is much easier and more convenient.

Flavoured butters are a great standby at barbecues; try this one over freshly grilled salmon steak or chicken breast redolent of the smoky flavours of the fire.

To make about 2 cups (500 ml)

2 ½ cups (500 g) unsalted butter, at room temperature
2 tablespoons (15 g) wild limes, puréed and strained
2 teaspoons (10 g) freshly minced ginger
6–10 sprigs coriander, chopped (to taste)
a pinch of salt
pepper to taste

Combine all the ingredients in a food processor and blend until a smooth and silky butter is formed. The butter will be fairly loose at this stage so pat it into shape or press into a serving bowl and refrigerate until it firms up. Bring the butter back to room temperature before serving so that it melts easily over the food.

Wild Lime Marmalade

To make 6 cups (1½ litres)

1 cup (140 g) wild limes, sliced
1 lemon, sliced
8 cups (2 litres) water
castor sugar

Combine the wild limes, lemon and water in a large, heavy-based, stainless-steel saucepan and bring to the boil. Adjust the heat and allow to simmer briskly until the volume of liquid is reduced by half.

Remove from the heat and measure the volume of liquid in a measuring jug. Add an equal weight of sugar to the volume of water. (For example, use 1 kg sugar for 1 litre liquid, and so on.) Stir until the sugar dissolves.

Return to the heat and bring back to the boil. Continue to cook until the marmalade reaches its setting point. Test this by placing a teaspoon of the marmalade on a chilled saucer. If it's ready, the marmalade will form a skin and wrinkle when pushed with a finger. If it's not ready, it will still be runny on the saucer and will require additional cooking time.

Once the marmalade is ready, ladle into sterilised jars and seal. Refrigerate after opening.

Fresh Scallops with a Wild Lime and Lemon Myrtle Sauce

To serve 6 as a main course
(halve the recipe for an entrée)

1 tablespoon (25 g) unsalted
  butter
3 teaspoons (15 ml) canola
  oil
3 cloves garlic, crushed
1 onion, finely diced
36 fresh scallops
1½ teaspoons (3 g) dried
  and ground lemon myrtle
¾ cup (100 g) wild limes,
  coarsely chopped
a pinch of salt
3 teaspoons (15 g) castor
  sugar
½ teaspoon native pepper
3 cups (750 ml) cream

In a large skillet, heat the butter and oil, and cook the garlic and onion until the onion is tender but not brown.

Sprinkle the raw scallops with half the lemon myrtle and add them to the pan with the garlic and onion. Cook the scallops for 2–3 minutes (that's all, don't overcook), remove from pan, cover and keep warm. Scallops are best cooked until opaque.

Add the wild limes, salt, sugar, pepper and the rest of the lemon myrtle to the pan juices. Bring back to a simmer and continue to cook for a further 5 minutes. Add the cream and continue to simmer until the sauce reduces to a rich, thick consistency.

Toss the scallops through the sauce to heat through.

Serve in wide, flat bowls on a bed of lemon myrtle-scented rice.

SHORTS

- Preserve wild limes in brandy and, after some months of maceration, use the fruit and the lime-infused brandy as the base for a sauce to accompany a dish such as duckling. Prick the wild lime skins with a needle and place them in a brandy and sugar solution of 1 part sugar to 2 parts water. Gently cook for about 15–20 minutes and bottle them in very clean, sterile jars.

- Try making a wild lime curd and add a little native mint to taste. Use the Lemon Aspen Curd recipe (see page 36), replacing the lemon aspen with the wild lime in the same ratio, that is, for 100 g lemon aspen use 100 g wild lime.

- Make a refreshing sorbet with some finely chopped wild limes or use the brandied wild limes (above) as the basis of a sorbet.

Wild Lime Sauce for Squab

This is a quick and simple sauce that can be made in advance and kept refrigerated for up to a week. The tartness of the sauce is particularly delicious with poultry, so you could serve it over pan-fried chicken breasts, duck or poussin if you can't get squab. Squab are young pigeons bred for the table, and are available from specialist poultry shops and gourmet butchers. They are sold as whole birds and you will need one per serve.

To serve 6

6 x 300 g whole squab
½ teaspoon salt
½ teaspoon native pepper
1 tablespoon (25 ml) macadamia nut oil

Wild Lime Sauce
1 onion, finely diced
1 clove garlic, crushed or finely chopped
2 teaspoons (10 ml) macadamia nut oil
3 cups (750 ml) Chicken Stock (see page 182)
20 (about 20 g) desert or finger limes, chopped
6 mountain pepper leaves, crushed
2 teaspoons (10 g) castor sugar
desert limes for garnish (optional)

To make the Wild Lime Sauce, sauté the onion and the garlic in the oil in a large saucepan over medium heat. Add the chicken stock and simmer until the liquid is reduced by half. Add the desert limes, crushed pepper leaves and sugar.

Simmer until the sauce is reduced to the consistency of a glaze, that is, quite a thick, clear syrup. Remove from the heat and strain.

Preheat the oven to 190–200°C (375–400°F).

Season the squab by rubbing salt and pepper all over the bird. Heat the oil in a pan and brown the birds on all sides for about 5 minutes. Place the birds onto an oven tray and bake in the preheated oven for 10 minutes.

Remove the birds from the oven, cover with a clean tea-towel or foil and rest for approximately 15 minutes. When the birds are cool enough to handle, carefully remove the breast bones and the legs. Carefully remove the breast meat from the carcass.

To serve, gently warm the breasts, still covered with foil, in a 160°C (325°F) oven.

If you are making the sauce at this stage, add the breast and leg bones to the chicken stock and proceed. If you've made the sauce in advance, don't bother to add the bones, simply reheat.

Slice each squab breast into two large pieces and place the 4 slices of breast meat on the plate. Spoon over the hot sauce and scatter around the whole desert limes that have been warmed in the sauce.

Wild Lime and Ginger Tart Brûlée

To serve 6 to 8

300 g Sweetcrust Pastry (see
  page 184)
1¼ cups (300 ml) cream
1 tablespoon (15 g) chopped
  fresh ginger
4 teaspoons (20 g) wild
  limes, chopped (about
  15–20)
5 egg yolks
½ cup (100 g) castor sugar
1 teaspoon (5 g) powdered
  gelatine
1 cup (250 ml) hot water
icing sugar

Roll out the pastry to fit an 18 cm tart tin and bake
blind (see page 183).

In a small, stainless-steel saucepan, bring the cream,
ginger and wild limes to the boil.

While waiting for the cream to boil, place the egg
yolks and sugar into a bowl and whisk until creamy. Do
this by hand.

Take the cream off the heat and add the egg mixture
to the cream. Return to a medium heat and stir
constantly with a wooden spoon. Cook out the custard
until it coats the back of the spoon, then strain through
a fine sieve to remove any lumps.

Dissolve the gelatine in the hot water, stirring
occasionally until the mixture clears.

Add a little of the custard to the gelatine mix and
stir through. Then gently whisk the gelatine mixture
back into the wild lime and ginger custard while it is
still warm. Allow to cool a little.

Pour the custard into the prepared tart case and
place in the refrigerator to set firm.

About 30 minutes before serving, sprinkle the top of
the tart liberally with icing sugar. Put under a griller
until the sugar is caramelised.

Once the sugar is caramelised and the tart has a
lovely toffee top, place it very carefully (as the custard
will have melted a little under the heat and may wobble
with quick movements and ruin all your hard work) in
the coldest part of the refrigerator to reset.

This visually stunning tart needs no decoration.
Simply serve it on a platter, cut into thin wedges and
accompany with fresh sliced fruit such as mango, Kiwi
fruit and strawberries.

Wild
Orange

*Also known as native pomegranate, bumble tree, mpultjati
(other Aboriginal names depending on locale)*

The wild orange, or *Capparis mitchellii*, was named after the explorer Major Mitchell, the first white man to see the tree. He recorded that the fruit 'had an agreeable perfume'. The fruit that we know as the wild orange is well regarded by the Aboriginal people as a fresh fruit, and is a good source of vitamin C and thiamine. The bark from the base or root of the tree is also used to make a lotion that relieves headache.

Wild oranges are related to the caper bush that originated in Africa and Asia, but which the Mediterranean peoples have made their own. Other near relatives of the wild orange and the caper are plants in the mustard family. In Australia we have at least seventeen native capers, all fruit-bearing and edible, although some may not be overly palatable. All were, and some still are, important Aboriginal foods. Early botanists were surprised to find what they thought was the Mediterranean caper growing in northern Australia. We now know that *C. spinosa* var. *nummularia* is a native variety; its buds make an excellent pickled caper, which we have yet to develop as a commercially viable bushfood.

Another native caper, *C. canescens*, has mustard oils in its rind and was used as a mustard substitute last century.

Wild orange trees grow in arid and semi-arid country, in scattered woodlands and grassy plains, largely throughout western Queensland. The tree is small with a dense crown and spectacular, large flowers with creamy petals and up to fifty long, elegant, drooping stamens. While it flowers most of the year, the flowers peak for fruit in late winter to early spring. White butterflies can be seen clustered around these flowers when they are in bloom—a most spectacular sight. The fruit that follows in summer is globular and green, and hangs from the tree in distinctively curved stalks. The ripe fruit is yellow-green, and usually about the size of a ping pong ball, but can grow larger. It is soft to the touch and sweet-smelling. The skin is inedible, and the pulpy flesh is scooped out from inside the fruit. A good, ripe fruit, however, is excellent eating.

TO GROW

Capparis mitchellii
Distribution: Outback Queensland, northern NSW and parts of NT and WA.

A large bush or small tree, the wild orange has a dark trunk, large, showy, creamy flowers and stiff, dull-green leaves. The leaves are often used as stock fodder. The shoots and branches often have many sharp thorns, although older plants seem to be less spiky. Due to this feature of the plants, they should be planted away from paths and walkways.

The plant is very slow-growing, but should adapt well to most arid or semi-arid conditions under cultivation. Avoid planting in climates with excessive humidity. The wild orange likes heavy soils but will adapt to a variety of soil conditions and is drought and frost tolerant. Due to the variable nature of the fruit, there is considerable opportunity for plant selection and improvement in cultivated specimens.

Propagation is both from seeds and cuttings. Seeds can be extracted from the fruit and sown, and cuttings can be taken at most times of the year from firm, healthy growth.

Relations

Apart from the plants mentioned, *C. lasiantha*, also known as nepine or split-jack, and from drier climates, has a smaller, yellowish fruit that splits open when ripe. It has a sweet custard flavour, with skin similar to a dried peach or pear, and peppery seeds. Spread talcum powder at the base of the plant to stop ants getting to the fruit. The fruit needs to be picked while still slightly green and just splitting, and stored away to ripen. Unlike the wild orange's the skin of this ripe fruit is edible. *C. lucida, C. arborea, C. unmbanata* (northern wild orange) and *C. loranthifolia* are all related and edible species.

To harvest

The wild orange fruits ripen over summer and they are ready when they start to develop a brownish colour on the skin. Green fruits can be ripened in the sand. A fully grown tree will yield around 3 kg of fruit in the wild. This may improve with some expert work on plant selection, but such work is in its infancy as the wild orange is rarely seen under cultivation.

STORING WILD ORANGE
Wild oranges will keep for a week in their fresh state. If you wish to store the fruit for extended periods, it may be frozen. Scoop out the flesh from the wild orange, discard the skins, and place the pulp in a container suitable for freezer storage.

TO COOK

Use only the pulpy flesh of the wild orange; the skin is bitter and inedible. The flesh is a mustard yellow in colour, and the hot, peppery seeds are well enmeshed in the flesh and difficult to remove. The best way is to push the wild orange pulp through a sieve rather than to try to remove them manually.

The wild orange is similar to the Kakadu plum in that the flesh is mucilaginous when cooked, that is, the fruit pulp will absorb the liquid it is cooked in, and the resulting fruit and cooking juices become quite viscous and almost jelly-like when cooled. This characteristic makes the wild orange a useful thickening agent and flavouring in casseroles and other slow-cooked dishes— it will absorb much of the vegetable liquids and cooking juices.

The wild orange is an intriguing fruit. It is an odd blend of sweet and bitter, and each fruit can vary in the proportion of these flavours. The taste is like a cross between mango, pawpaw and passionfruit with an astringent aftertaste like bitter orange. The seeds have a hot peppery taste. Even in savoury applications you will need to soften the bitterness of the fruit with the careful use of a sweetener. Sugar may be used, but much nicer is the addition of honey and a little cinnamon. Wild orange will add an interesting dimension to lamb, pork and chicken dishes, and will also work well in curries, rice dishes and couscous.

I recommend that you try wild orange in desserts too, especially in ice-cream. Wild oranges give ice-creams, sorbets and mousses a most interesting flavour and edge; their natural astringency, moderated with sugar or honey and cream, coupled with the complex fruit flavours, creates quite an unusual but very luscious dessert. Wild oranges don't require cooking for these desserts. Just use the seeded flesh fresh, or thawed if the fruits have been frozen.

Goes with

Wild oranges may be complemented by a number of bushfood seasonings. Depending on the recipe, native cinnamon, native nutmeg, native pepper, lemon myrtle and native mint can all play their part with the wild orange. Not many fruits sit well next to wild orange, but the native tamarind, despite its tartness, is a good partner. Honey is a complementary flavour, and so is curry, Indian- or Asian-style. Wild orange lends itself to Morroccan-style dishes, and cardamom and saffron will be great co-flavourings.

Wild Orange and Lamb Casserole

To serve 6

2 wild oranges, halved and with flesh removed

2 cups (500 ml) water

1 tablespoon (25 g) castor sugar

2.5 kg diced lamb (ask your butcher to do this)

1 tablespoon (20 g) plain flour

¼ cup (60 ml) oil

3 onions, diced

3 parsnips, diced

3 carrots, diced

3 potatoes, diced

3 cloves garlic, crushed

3 fresh oranges, peeled and diced

2 cinnamon sticks

1 teaspoon (5 g) salt

1 teaspoon (2 g) native pepper

1 teaspoon (2 g) wild or common thyme

Preheat the oven to 160°C (325°F).

In a saucepan, bring the wild oranges, water and sugar to the boil and keep boiling for 2–3 minutes. The seeds will loosen from the wild oranges, so strain the fruit to remove them. Retain the pulp and cooking juices.

Dust the diced lamb with the flour. Heat the oil in a heavy-based skillet, and brown the lamb in batches. Return the lamb to the skillet, add the diced vegetables, garlic, oranges, cinnamon sticks and seasonings. Ensure that all the ingredients are well mixed together and transfer the mixture to a suitable casserole dish. Cover with the wild orange pulp and juices, and cook in the preheated oven for 1½–2 hours.

To complement the dish's Middle Eastern overtones, serve on a bed of couscous seasoned with native mint.

SHORTS

• Add some chopped wild orange to spice up your next lentil soup.

• Use wild orange in a chicken curry.

• Add some finely chopped wild orange to an ice-cream base just before churning.

Quandong

Also known as desert peach, native peach, bidjigal, gudi gudi and other Aboriginal names depending on the region

In the days of the early European settlers the quandong was given the name of wild or desert peach, although it bears little resemblance to the fruit in taste and appearance. When compared to a European fruit, its taste is closer to that of an apricot crossed with rhubarb with a slight touch of cinnamon.

Fresh quandong

The quandong is certainly a visually beautiful and striking tree, reaching heights of up to 7 m in ideal conditions. Its globular, bright red fruits (some trees bear white ones) hang down elegantly from olive-leafed branches. The deliciously tart flesh has quite a dry texture and encircles a large, hard, pitted kernel. Quandong kernels were often more valued by the early European settlers as components of beaded jewellery than the fruit itself!

Extensive research has been conducted on the quandong's viability as a commercial crop. The CSIRO division in Adelaide began studying the quandong in 1973, with a large contribution from Brian Powell, who has championed the fruit as an ideal crop for arid and poor or degraded soil areas. There are now many quandong trees in plantations around the country, but they have yet to reach their potential due to inferior plant stock and the invasion of the quandong moth, which can virtually wipe out a crop. Quandong

growers have recently formed the Australian Quandong Industry Association to promote the use of quandong as a commercial crop and assist in the marketing of the fruit as a quality product.

The quandong was, and still is, an important staple food in the outback in the seasons that it fruited prolifically. The fruit, which is very high in vitamin C (about twice that of oranges), was eaten fresh or dried (the form we are most familiar with today), or made into cakes that were dried and stored.

The seed kernel has a strong flavour, not unlike wintergreen oil (Denco-rub), and a high oil content (75 per cent of kernel). It is also a good source of protein (25 per cent of kernel), and varies in flavour from sweet to bitter. The Aboriginal peoples were known to eat the kernel but valued it even more as a medicine. Many Aboriginal communities today harvest the quandong for commercial sale to restaurants and the bushfoods processing industry.

TO GROW

Santalum acuminatum

Distribution: Widespread in semi-arid to arid environments over most of southern Australia from WA, SA, Victoria, NSW and also enters Queensland and NT.

Quandongs are a parasitic species, and obtain nutrients through the roots of nearby plants, particularly when they are young. This makes it a challenging but interesting plant to cultivate. The quandong grows in many soils—sand, clay, even rocky situations and in poor soils, but generally prefers the sandy soils. Good drainage is essential for success. It tolerates full sun and droughts, although watering is advisable in very dry years. The tree is highly tolerant of salinity and is frost resistant but, on the whole, doesn't do as well in the cooler climates. The plant is widespread in the wild, but many young trees are destroyed by cattle or rabbits.

The quandong is suitable as a plantation or garden plant along the drier areas of the Murray River in south-eastern Australia, and, other drier parts of all the mainland states. The species is well suited as a specimen plant in drier gardens.

Germination from seed is not for the inexperienced propagator. Do not extract the seed from the stone, but store the whole fruit in slightly damp potting mix in a dark place. If you are using the seed, place in a plastic bag with the mix and keep the medium damp (but not too wet) and warm (18°C) for several weeks. Germination can begin after one or two months, although it may take much longer, even up to two years, so be patient. Germination is most successful in autumn. Plants grown from seed don't seem to yield good-quality fruit, and, the harvest may be poor.

The new plants should be repotted into ordinary potting mix. They should have a host plant, perhaps clover or lucern, growing in the same pot. Plant them into their permanent positions as soon as possible, near a suitable host shrub or tree (perhaps an exotic fruit tree, gum or wattle). Grafting is currently used to obtain quality plants. It has also been suggested that sterilising the seed may assist germination. Soak the seed for 30 minutes in a bleach like White King, diluted to ten parts water to one of bleach, before placing in the potting mix.

Relations

S. lanceolatum, known as plumwood or bush plum, is prevalent in every mainland state. It is a parasitic species that has palatable blue-coloured fruits with good levels of vitamin C. The wood from *S. spicatum*, also known as sandalwood, is aromatic, and the leaves from the tree can also be used to wrap food before cooking.

To harvest

Quandong fruit usually ripens in spring, from September to October. An average tree should provide a harvest of at least 2 kg of fresh fruit, although there are trees that will produce up to 30 kg. The quandong tree takes up to four years to yield its first good crop of fruit, but, once established, will continue to fruit for some time, being a long-lived tree. There are anecdotes that describe trees fruiting for sixty years, making them worth the first few years' wait. The fruit is very easy to harvest from the tree as it hangs from long stems. When ripe, the fruit will fall from the tree.

TO COOK

Have a good repertoire of quandong recipes in your file as you're bound to need them if you have a good fruiting tree in your backyard! This fruit is very versatile, and may be used successfully in sauces, cakes, pies, tarts and to make quandong jam.

The best way to store quandong (or buy it) is in its dried form. The fruit will need reconstituting before use unless you're cooking in a casserole or using a slow-cook method where the fruit can absorb the liquid it requires over time. To reconstitute the fruits and leave the natural flavour unadulterated, immerse them in cold water, bring to a simmer and continue simmering for about 2 minutes. Take the quandongs and water off the heat and place a lid on the saucepan and allow to cool completely in the water. The dried quandongs need to steep in this liquid for at least a couple of hours and, for the best results, overnight in the refrigerator for them to really plump up. With this treatment, the quandongs will swell to 2 to 2.5 times their dried weight and size.

As a rule of thumb, a good working ratio for quandong rehydration is 1 cup of dried quandong (about 50 dried quandong halves) to 1 litre of liquid. After soaking overnight, the quandongs will have absorbed well over half of the liquid. The remaining liquid will be well coloured and flavoured by the quandongs. Don't discard it—measure, add an equal weight of sugar, and bring the mixture to a boil. Cook until it has reduced by a third to make a quandong syrup, and use it to accompany your quandong pie, ice-cream or tart. This is one of the most satisfying features of bushfoods; so often you can get more than one use and yield from the product. In restaurants in particular this makes bushfoods much more economical than perhaps first realised.

I tend to use water as the rehydrating liquid as we prefer to highlight the natural flavours of the bush fruits. If preferred, a good-quality white wine, champagne, apple cider or juice may be used. Keep the liquid light so that the quandong flavour is not swamped.

Goes with

Quandong has a delicate flavour, so be careful not to overwhelm it with bushfoods that are strongly flavoured or acidic. Keep away from bush tomatoes, wild rosella and lemon aspen. Quandong will combine with muntries, lady apple (but riberry is too strong), bunya nuts, macadamias, wattleseed and kurrajong. Quandong can also be seasoned with the native peppers, native mint and wild thyme. Lemon myrtle is not a very good match.

Quandong will be complemented by peaches, apricots, figs, bananas, apples and pears. Fresh ginger, garlic and chilli (in moderation) go well with quandong, as do cardamom, cinnamon and nutmeg.

STORING QUANDONG

By far the most popular way of storing quandong is to follow the Aboriginal method of first drying out the fruit. Remove the flesh from the kernel in two neat halves and allow to air- or sun-dry. The firm structure of the flesh and its non-adherence to the kernel make the halves easy to separate. Once the fruit has completely dried, keep it sealed and away from potential insect infestation. It will keep for a very long time, with no deterioration, for up to a year. Quandong flesh also freezes well. Just freeze the fruit whole.

The kernel may be used dried or frozen. There has been some question as to its toxicity and the advisability of eating the fresh kernels. So perhaps use them as a decorative item rather than as a food. Tasting one or two probably won't hurt, but err on the side of caution.

Quandong Jam

To make 8 x 250 ml jars

10 cups (1 kg) fresh
   quandong
1 kg castor sugar
100 ml water

Coarsely chop the quandong and combine with sugar and water in a large saucepan. Place the saucepan over a moderate heat, stirring constantly, as it comes to the boil. Adjust the heat so that the jam simmers. Cook until the jam reaches setting point, stirring occasionally, about 45 minutes.

Test that the jam is ready by dropping a teaspoon of it on a chilled saucer and cool. If set, the jam should wrinkle when touched. If it is too loose, cook a little longer. Be careful, however, not to overcook and caramelise the sugar, as this will alter both the colour and flavour of the jam.

Once the jam is ready, pour into sterilised jars and seal. The unopened jars will keep for up to a year in the pantry. Refrigerate once opened.

Quandong, Port and Chilli Sauce

This rich and flavoursome sauce calls for a meat dish with some character; roasted duck or pheasant would be perfect, as would a lean cut of pork.

To make 3 cups (750 ml)

½ cup (50 g) dried quandong or 1 cup (100 g) fresh quandong
2 cups (500 ml) apple juice
1 cup (250 ml) port
½ teaspoon chilli powder
a pinch of salt
2 teaspoons (10 g) cornflour, dissolved in a little cold water

If the quandong is dried, place in a saucepan with the apple juice and bring to a simmer. Cook for 10 minutes, turn off the heat, and allow them to cool and stand for at least 2 hours to rehydrate.

If the quandongs are fresh, cut away the flesh from the stone in halves. Place the quandongs and apple juice in a saucepan and bring to a gentle boil.

Add the port, chilli powder and salt, and simmer for 5 minutes. Thicken the sauce slightly by briskly stirring in the dissolved cornflour before removing from the heat.

SHORTS

- Put quandong in couscous or polenta to accompany kangaroo, beef or lamb.

- Quickly pan-fry some butterflied pork steaks or roast a loin of pork with Native Mint and Muntries Stuffing (see page 99) and serve with some Quandong, Port and Chilli Sauce (see above).

- Macerate quandongs in sugar and liqueur and use as a centre for chocolates.

- Cook polenta in your favourite way, adding cheese, ginger, chives and chopped, drained quandongs. Smooth into a pan, and bake in a 160°C (325°F) oven until brown.

- Add chopped quandongs that have been marinated in Grand Marnier to an ice-cream base just before churning.

- Use quandong syrup over fruits, ice-cream and crepes.

Quandong Lattice Pie

If you don't have the full amount of quandongs for this recipe, try adding apricots to the mix as they complement the quandong flavour very well. The reserved liquid kept from soaking the quandongs can be boiled with an equal volume of sugar and reduced to make a quandong-flavoured syrup to pour over the pie.

To make a 20 cm (9 in) pie

300 g Sweetcrust Pastry (see page 184)
2 cups (500 ml) water
2 cups (500 ml) unsweetened apple juice
2 cups (200 g) dried quandong or 4 cups (400 g) fresh (about 55 fruit)
1¼ cups (250 g) castor sugar
½ cup (50 g) almond meal
1½ tablespoons (35 g) unsalted butter
egg wash
extra castor sugar for sprinkling

Roll out the pastry and line the tart case. Refrigerate until needed. Roll out some additional pastry and cut into uniform-sized strips for making the lattice top. Chill with the tart case until needed.

If using dried quandong: Bring the water to the boil in a saucepan. Add the apple juice and dried quandongs to the liquid. Remove from the heat and leave the quandongs for at least 2 hours to reconstitute. If you can do this overnight the result will be even better as the dried fruits will plump up to 3 times their dried size. Strain the quandongs once they are nice and fleshy.

Preheat the oven to 180°C (360°F).

Place the drained or fresh quandongs, sugar and almond meal in a bowl and mix so that the quandongs are thoroughly coated with the dry ingredients. Spread this mixture evenly into the tart case.

Break the butter into small knobs and dot the surface of the filling. With a pastry brush, brush egg wash along the outer pastry rim of the pie and make a lattice pattern on the top with the reserved strips of pastry, making sure to brush some egg wash carefully on the surface of each strip as it is laid across the pie. Weave the lattice strips evenly over the filling and secure them carefully to the pastry rim with egg wash. Crimp the edges to seal.

Finally, apply a light egg wash to all the outer pastry surfaces and sprinkle liberally with sugar.

Place the pie on a baking tray, preferably lined with silicon or baking paper (it drips as it cooks) and bake in the preheated oven for 1–1½ hours until the pastry is golden and the juices are bubbling.

Let the pie cool a little before attempting to remove it from the tart case. The butter, sugar and fruit juices caramelise during cooking and can be difficult to handle when hot. Serve warm or at room temperature.

Bush Cucumber

Also known as wild cucumber, ulcardo melon, smooth cucumber, native gooseberry, ilkurta

We owe a debt of gratitude to Wendy and David Phelps from Longreach Bush Tucker at Longreach in outback Queensland for introducing this wonderful cucumber to us. They had been growing them to assess their suitability as a potential crop for a sustainable bushfood agricultural industry in the largely arid Queensland rangelands.

The bush cucumber, while certainly showing promise as a short-term cash crop within a bushfood plantation, is yet to enjoy the commercial success of some of the other rangeland foods, such as wild limes and native thyme. It is a direct relative of the cantaloupe and is actually from the same wild ancestral stock from which many of the Asian melons have been bred. In the wild the *Cucumis melo* ssp. *agrestis* is a fast-growing, creeping vine that spreads along flat ground or over small logs or in clumps of tall grass, and grows well in the sheltered areas of grassy plainlands following good summer rains. The vine flowers prolifically in early summer and produces a pretty little fruit. The globular-shaped cucumbers are tiny, about 2 to 5 cm in length, fresh green in colour with a slight speckle or faint stripe marking their skins. The skin is quite bitter, but the ripe flesh inside is sweet and has a refreshing flavour of cucumber with distinct mint overtones.

Be careful not to confuse the bush cucumber with the paddy melon (*C. myriocarpus*) as this melon is poisonous. Visually, the two fruits are quite different. Although they are about the same size, the skin of the bush cucumber is smooth and shiny; the paddy melon has bristles and bands of dark green on a yellowish rind.

The Aboriginal people of the arid outback regions have long valued the bush cucumber as a food plant. They used to harvest the fruits, which were usually abundant after the rains, and prepare them by wrapping the fruits in paperbark and cooking them in sand heated with hot rocks, or even in ground ovens. Since the moisture content of the bush cucumbers is high, the fruit was usually steamed rather than baked, and eaten hot. Today they have largely chosen to boil the fruits rather than cook them in paperbark.

TO GROW

Cucumis melo ssp. *agrestis*

Distribution: Grows extensively in the wild throughout the outback in all states except Victoria and Tasmania. Can be grown as an annual in the southern states.

The bush cucumber is a fleshy, sprawling groundcover plant with short, wide and coarse leaves, and thick succulent stems. It loves plenty of sunshine and water, and in the wild, appears in vast numbers after good rains. In the garden this species does best in deep soils and, unusually for a semi-arid species, appreciates regular watering. It can be readily grown in the southern states and in the more arid zones.

Like tomatoes, capsicums and eggplants, the plants thrive during the warmer months and die off in cold winters, particularly in the south. The plant is extremely frost sensitive, and is best grown as an annual in the vegetable patch for its cucumbers rather than as a long-term creeper or groundcover. It can be very readily re-propagated as necessary; the seeds from the bush cucumber germinate very easily in warm moist soil.

The parent of melons, cantaloupes and cucumbers is *C. melo* ssp. *melo*. This plant still grows naturally in Europe and Asia; in fact the bush cucumber and the northern hemisphere sub-species look very much alike.

To harvest

The vines grow rapidly over summer and fruit abundantly when well watered. In the wild they favour the rich alluvial flood plains or along stream banks where the water supply is good. The vines tend to die off as the fruit forms and ripens. In the garden the vines must be protected from frost to ensure a good crop. The vines will be a generous provider of fruit throughout the summer months.

STORING BUSH CUCUMBER

The bush cucumber should be treated as any cucumber bought from the greengrocer. Keep it in the vegetable compartment of your refrigerator and it will stay fresh for a few days. If eating the cucumbers fresh, pick them as they ripen on the vine; they are best eaten immediately. The bush cucumber is a high-yielding vine, and any extra fruit will freeze if left whole with its skin intact. Don't wash or prepare the fruit in any way for freezing—it is best frozen straight from the vine.

TO COOK

Goes with

Bush cucumbers are a delightful smaller version of the traditional cucumbers found in all fruit shops and supermarkets. They form similar flowers, leaves and fruit, only much smaller in size. The average size of the bush cucumber fruit is approximately 4 to 5 cm long, and they are quite fat and rounded, almost globular in shape. They are a very attractive little cucumber to serve. The skin of the bush cucumber is slightly lighter in colour than that of the standard cucumber.

When ripe, the flesh tastes similar to a common cucumber: refreshing, juicy and sweet, but with distinct mint characteristics. The skin is bitter, however, so if the cucumber is cooked with its skin intact the moderating influence of sugar will be needed. Alternatively, the bush cucumber can be peeled, but be careful not to take off too much of the flesh.

Cooking the bush cucumber as a vegetable may seem appealing, but this isn't recommended because the bitterness is still dominant after steaming or sautéing whole. Salsas, chutneys or relishes seem to be the more appropriate vehicles for the bush cucumber; they make the most of its flavour and the sugar and vinegar components soften the bitterness. These sauces or relishes suit fish or chicken dishes, and allow the cucumber's mint flavour to come forward.

While this little cucumber is also very seedy, if making a sauce, salsa or chutney, don't bother removing the seeds as it is quite a tedious and unnecessary exercise.

Be guided by the typical characteristics of the cucumber flavour when combining bush cucumbers with other bushfoods. It is perhaps unsuited to the sweeter fruits such as the native raspberry and quandong, and its texture will not stand up to the fibrous tubers and stems of some bushfood plants such as the lily tubers (*Arthropodium* etc.) or cumbungi. The inherent bitterness of the bush tomato is not recommended for combination with the bush cucumber. Most of the leaf foods would suit, especially the native mints, peppers, lemon myrtle, native thyme and the peppermints.

Herbs such as borage, mint, basil, coriander and chervil work well. Pepper, fresh ginger, onion, chives and celery are successful partners, as are the fresh flavours of yoghurt or crème fraîche.

Bush Cucumber Raita

Raitas are traditionally served as an accompaniment to curries. This raita may also be served with grilled lamb, chicken or fish. The fresh, minty, cucumber taste of the bush cucumber is well partnered by the yoghurt and native mint.

To make 3 cups (750 ml)

1 cup (125 g) bush
   cucumbers, peeled and
   finely diced (about 20)
juice of 1 lemon
2 teaspoons (10 g) castor
   sugar
2 teaspoons (5 g) fresh
   native mint, chopped or
   1 teaspoon (2 g) dried
   native mint, crushed
a pinch of salt
2 cups (500 ml) natural
   yoghurt

Remove as many seeds from the diced cucumber as is practical and place in a bowl. Sprinkle the lemon juice, sugar, fresh or dried mint and salt over the cucumber and mix well to distribute the seasonings.

Allow the seasoned cucumber to rest for about 15 minutes for the flavours to infuse and to allow the sugar and salt to dissolve.

After resting, drain away any excess liquid from the cucumber and fold through the yoghurt.

This raita will develop its full flavour over time, so prepare it well in advance.

SHORTS

- For an elegant dish, try the peeled and seeded bush cucumber as a light soup, chilled or hot, perfumed with fresh borage. Float some borage flowers on the surface to contrast against the pale green of the soup.

- Bush cucumbers are fabulous in a light pickle to serve as antipasto. I can imagine lots of jars of pickled bush cucumbers lining pantry cupboards by summer's end and served as an alternative to the dill cucumber. Use sprigs of native mint and native pepper in the pickle instead of dill.

- Pickled cucumbers can be served whole or sliced into salads. Peel the smaller bush cucumbers and leave them whole (or halved). Toss them with the tiny tomatoes that are now widely available (e.g. cherry tomatoes, yellow pear tomatoes) and finish with a Lemon Myrtle Dressing (see page 143).

- Choose large bush cucumbers and peel them carefully. Wrap them in paperbark and bake them in the traditional way (lay them on a warrigal green or spinach leaf first). When just cooked, serve them with melted Wild Lime, Coriander and Ginger Butter (see page 11).

Bush Cucumber and Native Mint Salsa

This salsa falls somewhere between a chunky fresh sauce and a dressing. Its blend of clean flavours is particularly good with fish, poultry or cold vegetable dishes. Make it when the bush cucumbers ripen in early summer.

To make about 3 cups (750 ml)

½ cup (50 g) bush cucumbers, washed and diced (about 10)
1 small onion, finely chopped
¼ teaspoon ground lemon myrtle
¼ teaspoon finely minced garlic
½ teaspoon finely minced fresh ginger
½ teaspoon castor sugar
¼ teaspoon native pepper or ½ teaspoon cracked black pepper
½ teaspoon salt
⅓ cup (80 ml) olive oil
½ teaspoon fresh mint bush or river mint leaves, finely chopped
¼ cup (60 ml) fresh lemon or lime juice

Put the bush cucumbers in a mixing bowl.

Mix the onion, lemon myrtle, garlic, ginger, sugar, native pepper and salt in a pot with the oil and cook over a very low heat until the onion becomes transparent (about 10 minutes). Don't let the mixture brown. When the onion is transparent, cool the mixture and add to the bush cucumbers.

Add the mint and fresh lemon or lime juice. Let this sit for at least an hour before serving to allow the flavours to fully develop.

Serve on grilled fish or with Lemon Myrtle Fish Cakes (see page 140).

Lemon
Aspen

Many of the indigenous fruits bear unlikely names given to them by European settlers who struggled to come to terms with their environment by calling the new fruits and trees by old familiar names. The lemon aspen is not an aspen at all, but probably reminded some of the early settlers of the American aspens. It is actually a rainforest tree bearing clusters of delicious fruit and is one of a number of rainforest *Acronychia* that have edible fruit.

The lemon aspen has an amazing flavour. I love to watch people when they first taste it. Their first reaction is surprise at the strength and tartness of the fruit, and then there's a struggle to further categorise the taste. The lemon aspen is distinctly lemon or citrus, but there are other subtle, special aftertastes that demand attention. After the initial intense acidic lemon hit, complex secondary flavours of eucalypt and honey creep in and surprise the palate. The taste of the fruit is not purely lemon, but an amalgam

of intriguing, familiar tastes that are difficult to define. How convenient it would be if bushfoods would fall into neat, familiar flavour categories! Our indigenous foods, while sometimes reminiscent of European foods, have their own particular characteristics that we need to learn to accept and value. Although we may use the fruit of the lemon aspen in place of a traditional lemon, bear in mind that this fruit will bring its own unique qualities of taste and texture to the dish, and subtly alter it and claim it as its own.

Lemon aspen fruit has a distinctively different appearance and taste to a lemon. They are a pale greenish to lemon-coloured fruit about the size of a Waltham grape, rounded, but with a crenulated top where the fruit joins the stalk. It grows in small clusters on the tree. Lemon aspens have a very thin, edible outer skin and firm, but juicy, almost underripe grape-like flesh that surrounds a hard inner core, not unlike an apple, with tiny black seeds.

This is an exciting fruit to eat and to cook with. While the flavour is intense and acidic, it is also deliciously refreshing and evocative.

TO GROW

Acronychia acidula
Distribution: Tropical north east, eastern and far north Queensland.

The lemon aspen is a medium-to-tall tropical rainforest tree but will grow fairly successfully, though not as tall, further south. In its natural environment it can reach approximately 20 m. It occurs naturally in high-altitude parts of north-eastern Queensland.

The tree has dark-green, oval-shaped leaves and masses of creamy yellow flowers. The flowers are quite small, but attractively scented and profuse. The tree appreciates a sunny well-drained position and, due to its tropical origins, needs regular and substantial watering. The soil around the tree should not be allowed to dry out. As it is a tall tree, plant it in a position that will allow the canopy to develop without restriction.

The lemon aspen can be propagated from seed. If you can obtain the fruit fresh, sow it whole. Caterpillars particularly enjoy lemon aspens and often destroy the seeds, so be sure to protect your seeds and seedlings from them.

Relations

Other related edible *Acronychia*s include *A. wilcoxiana*, the coast aspen *A. imperforata* and *A. suberosa*. *A. imperforata* has an edible fruit that is also quite tasty. This species is also adaptable to cooler climates, perhaps more than the lemon aspen itself. It grows well in windy coastal sites, but is very difficult to propagate. For this reason, plants may not be easy to find. Try a nursery that specialises in rainforest plants.

A. oblongifolia (yellow wood) inhabits coastal forests from northern NSW to eastern Victoria, and also has a fruit with a rather acidic, lemon taste. It is a useful plant for cooler climates.

To harvest

Lemon aspen is ready to harvest, depending on the climatic conditions, from April through to July. The trees can grow very tall in a rainforest environment, and the fruit is high up on the mature trees. In a drier environment the trees are shorter, and therefore are easier to harvest. The fruit grows in small clusters and, ideally, must be just under-ripe for harvesting. The fruit very quickly rots if allowed to fall from the large trees in the steamy rainforest environment. Lemon aspen is typical of many bushfoods: it fruits abundantly every second year with the alternating year's harvest being very light. Climatic conditions can also affect the harvest.

STORING LEMON ASPEN

As lemon aspen is a seasonal fruiting tree it is best to harvest the ripe fruit and freeze it immediately for long-term storage. No special preparation is needed before freezing—simply place whole, clean fruit without their stems in a freezer bag and freeze. Lemon aspen fruit can also be preserved in a light sugar syrup for up to a year.

TO COOK

Lemon aspens are very tart, acidic and intensely flavoured. They may be used successfully in most recipes where lemons or limes are called for, and add a twist in place of lemongrass. Use with confidence in all fish and seafood dishes. They are equally at home with poultry such as chicken, duck and turkey and are fabulous in cakes and biscuits.

However, the strength of the lemon aspen's flavour should never be underestimated. Too much lemon aspen will overwhelm the flavours of the other ingredients. How to judge the appropriate amount of lemon aspen if you want to experiment? A good rule of thumb is 100 g of lemon aspen equals the juice, pulp and the zest of 6 whole medium to large lemons. Depending on its seasonal variability, 100 g of lemon aspen equals about 20 fruit.

Use the whole fruit. It is extremely versatile and, depending on its use, the best flavour results are achieved by processing in a cyclonic food processor until the fruit is very finely chopped. It can also be puréed with the addition of a little water (lemon juice may be used, but it's really unnecessary). Before incorporating the lemon aspen into the recipe, you may wish to strain and, if appropriate, remove the fine black seeds and the core.

Lemon aspen retains its flavour if added to cold sauces or dressings, and also if heated, if sugar is added. Only a small amount of sugar is needed to stabilise the tart flavour. If adding lemon aspen to a hot sauce such as a butter sauce, the best result will be obtained if it is added towards the end of the recipe and heated through. If the lemon aspen is added at the initial reduction stage of most sauces, it fades in flavour and gives only a hint of its true character.

To achieve the best results with lemon aspen in desserts, try sprinkling the fruit liberally with sugar and leaving it overnight if possible to intensify the flavour. Retain any juice that gathers in the bowl overnight and incorporate in the recipe.

Goes with

Lemon myrtle, native pepper, native ginger, the native mints and lilly pilly will all work extremely well with lemon aspen. Wild rosella will fight the lemon aspen as they are both very tart flavours, except in desserts with the moderating influence of sugar. Keep lemon aspen right away from bush tomatoes, Illawarra plums and the figs.

Lemon aspen will overwhelm delicate fruits such as the Kakadu plum. The native limes, both arid and tropical varieties, are too similar in acidity and in the citrus quality of the fruit.

Other fruits that complement lemon aspen particularly well are raspberry, mango and rhubarb.

Lemongrass, ginger and radish (especially the Japanese variety) work very well with it, too.

Lemon Aspen Mayonnaise

Try this with salads, fresh asparagus spears, over freshly cooked prawns or yabbies, with crudites and so on. This mayonnaise will keep in the refrigerator for up to 5 days.

To make 4 cups (1 litre)

¾ cup (75g) lemon aspen
(about 15 fruits)
¼ cup (50 ml) white wine
vinegar
5 egg yolks
1 teaspoon (5 g) salt
1 teaspoon (2 g) ground
mountain pepper
3½ cups (900 ml) olive oil

Process the lemon aspen with the vinegar in a blender or food processor to a purée.

In a medium-sized bowl, whisk the egg yolks until thick. Whisk in the salt and pepper, and continue beating until the mixture is smooth and thick.

Gradually add a few drops of oil, whisking steadily until all the oil is incorporated. Do not add too much oil at the start or the mixture will split. Once the mayonnaise begins to thicken, add the rest of the oil in a slow and steady stream, whisking all the time.

Whisk in the vinegar and lemon aspen, and taste to adjust the seasonings.

Lemon Aspen Dressing

With a few good basics, the simplest ingredients can be transformed into a feast. This dressing is one of those culinary resources that can be made and kept for months in the refrigerator, ready to enliven a vegetable or salad. Give the dressing a good shake to emulsify the ingredients before using.

To make 4 cups (1 litre)

2¾ cups (680 ml) light
olive oil
1¼ cups (300 ml) white
wine vinegar
4 tablespoons (100 g)
puréed lemon aspen
2 teaspoons (10 g) salt
½ teaspoon crushed or
ground mountain pepper
1 tablespoon (25 g) castor
sugar
2 cloves garlic, crushed

Combine all the ingredients in a covered container (a large screwtop jar is ideal) and shake until well blended. Always shake the jar or bottle well before using.

Lemon Aspen Marinade

This marinade is very versatile. Use it with chicken and fish or even with stronger meats like lamb or kangaroo. The tang of lemon aspen gently permeates the meat or fish, and is a great way of adding interest to barbecues.

To make 4 cups (1 litre)

1 cup (100 g) lemon aspen (about 20 fruit)
3¾ cup (900 ml) macadamia nut oil
1 teaspoon (2 g) or 10 dried mountain pepper leaves, finely crushed

Process the lemon aspen berries in a food processor or vitamiser until coarsely chopped.

Whisk together the oil, lemon aspen and mountain pepper leaves.

This marinade is perfect for fresh fish, baby octopus, calamari or chicken and is sufficient for 1 kg of raw fish or meat. Try marinating baby octopus for 3–4 hours and then grill on a very hot barbecue for about 1½–2 minutes on each side, turning as necessary. When cooked, drizzle over a little Lemon Myrtle Dressing (see page 143), ground sea salt and a sprinkle of mountain pepper to taste. Serve on a bed of roasted red capsicum.

Lemon Aspen Butter Sauce

This sauce is ideal to use with fish and seafood. Pool the sauce on a plate and place some pan-fried fish fillets on the sauce.

To make 4 cups (1 litre)

1½ cups (400 ml) white wine
3 whole lemon myrtle leaves
3¼ cups (800 ml) cream
4 tablespoons (100 g) lemon aspen, crushed
1 cup (200 g) unsalted butter
1 teaspoon (5 g) salt
½ teaspoon ground mountain pepper

Combine the wine and lemon myrtle leaves in a saucepan over medium heat and reduce until about a quarter of the liquid remains.

Add the cream and lemon aspen at this stage and let the sauce come back to the boil. Lower the heat to a simmer and quickly stir in the butter, salt and pepper until the butter melts completely. Remove from the heat imediately. Try to complete this stage as quickly as possible to avoid dissipating the lemon aspen flavour.

Strain the sauce through a fine sieve and serve immediately.

Lemon Aspen Shortbread

To make about 45 biscuits

2 cups (400 g) unsalted
   butter
1 cup (150 g) icing sugar
3½ cups (500 g) plain flour
1 cup (100 g) almond meal
3 teaspoons (15 g) lemon
   aspen, seeded and puréed

In an electric mixer, combine the butter and icing sugar. Lower the speed of the mixer and add the plain flour, almond meal and lemon aspen. Mix until well combined.

Chill the shortbread mix and rest until it is quite cold and firm. This will take about half an hour.

Preheat the oven to 160°C (325°F). Line a tray with silicon or baking paper.

Roll out the dough on a lightly floured surface and cut into rounds or triangles and place on the prepared tray. Place on the top shelf of the preheated oven and bake until a light golden colour, about 20 minutes.

SHORTS

- Blend lemon aspen and strain the fruit to obtain the juice, then sprinkle over lightly steamed vegetables. Stir the remaining pulp through crème fraîche, sour cream or yoghurt to accompany sweet or ordinary potatoes, smoked salmon or freshly opened oysters.

- Cook green prawns and dip them into Lemon Aspen Mayonnaise (see page 33). Or use fresh artichoke hearts. Use the mayonnaise to make a summer salad of sliced chicken breasts, riberries, cubed mango or cantaloupe, chopped river mint and fresh baby lettuce leaves.

- Lemon Aspen Dressing (see page 33) may be used to enliven any salad, from simple greens to fresh asparagus spears. Try it over some very thin slices of raw tuna or serve warm with fillets of poached or chargrilled Tasmanian ocean trout. Nestle the fish on some Asian cress leaves that are now readily available in the larger supermarkets. Use it on a leek and avocado terrine.

- Barbecue, chargrill or pan-fry prawns that have been marinated in lemon aspen and ginger.

- Use lemon aspen in place of lemongrass in a Thai-style tom yum soup—add it towards the end of cooking.

- The fruits may be used whole as a garnish, or chopped into large pieces. Despite its attractive appearance on the plate, the whole fruit is usually too tart for most palates.

Lemon Aspen Curd

To make 4 cups (1 litre)

4 tablespoons (100 g) lemon aspen, finely chopped or puréed
6 x 55 g eggs
9 egg yolks
1 ½ cups (300 g) castor sugar
¼ cup (60 ml) milk
1 cups (400 g) unsalted butter

Place all the ingredients in a heavy-based saucepan (stainless steel is ideal, do not use aluminium) over medium heat, stirring constantly. The mixture will look curdled at this stage, but when the curd cooks out, it will have a smooth texture.

Keep stirring until the butter has completely melted, then lower the heat and stir until the curd begins to thicken and coats the back of the spoon. Don't allow the curd to overheat as this will cause the egg whites to cook, and the result will be a grainy texture.

When the curd is ready, take it immediately off the heat and strain through a sieve into sterilised jars. Don't leave it in the pot to strain later as the heat from the pot will continue to cook the curd. The curd will thicken considerably once it cools.

To make a lemon aspen curd tart, spoon the curd into a lightly baked tart shell, and cook in an oven preheated to 130°C (300°F) until the curd begins to set, about 30 minutes. Chill and serve with a riberry and red berry salad and pure or clotted cream.

Lemon Aspen Ice-cream

To make 4 cups (1 litre)

4 tablespoons (100 g) lemon aspen, finely chopped or puréed
1 ¼ cups (250 g) castor sugar
6 egg yolks
2 cups (500 ml) milk
2 cups (500 ml) cream
2 tablespoons (100 g) glucose

Sprinkle the lemon aspen with the sugar and leave overnight or for at least 2 hours.

To make the ice-cream, whisk the egg yolks and the milk together, and add the sugared lemon aspen. Place the mixture over a medium heat, stirring constantly, until it starts to coat the back of a spoon. Strain.

When completely cool, fold in the cream and glucose. You can wash the leavings from the custard and reserve the lemon aspen pieces to return to the mixture for texture. Pick through the lemon aspen and discard the hard core pieces. Chill the mixture in the refrigerator.

Using an ice-cream machine, churn following the manufacturer's instructions.

Yabby Ravioli with Lemon Aspen Butter Sauce

This makes a delicious and light entrée.

To serve 6

Pasta

3 x 55 g eggs
1 tablespoon (25 ml) olive oil
1¾ cups (250 g) plain flour
(this could be a blend of
plain flour with a small
amount of kurrajong or
wattleseed to flavour...but
not too much! These are
delicate flavours.)
egg wash

Yabby Mousse Filling

12–15 yabbies, boiled and
shelled
1 onion, diced
1 tablespoon (25 g) unsalted
butter
2 x 55 g eggs
salt and pepper to taste
2 teaspoons (10 ml) lemon
aspen juice or juice from
a lemon
⅓ cup (80 ml) cream
macadamia oil
180 g warrigal greens or
spinach
¾ cup (180 ml) Lemon Aspen
Butter Sauce (see page 34)

To make the Pasta, lightly beat the eggs and oil with a fork. Place the flour into a food-processor bowl and slowly add the egg mixture while processing to form a dough. Remove the dough when it forms a ball, and wrap in a towel or with plastic wrap. Rest in the refrigerator for an hour.

To make the Yabby Mousse Filling, blend the yabby tails in the food processor. Sauté the onion in the butter and add to the yabby meat. Add the remaining ingredients and blend to a smooth paste. Chill the mixture until it is quite cold.

Roll out the pasta to about 2 mm thickness and cut out rounds that are 8 cm in diameter. Brush the outside edge of the pasta round with the egg wash. Place a teaspoonful of the yabby mousse on one half of the pasta round and carefully fold the other half over the top to form a semi-circle. Press the pasta edges together firmly and crimp with a fork.

Bring a pot of salted water to the boil. Drop in the ravioli carefully and cook until they float to the surface, or until tender.

Drain and toss the ravioli gently in some macadamia oil.

To serve, blanch some warrigal greens (or spinach) to form a bed for the ravioli pillows. Just before serving, pour a generous amount of the hot lemon aspen butter sauce over the ravioli.

Rosella

Rosella is the common name of two species of hibiscus currently being used as food plants in Australia today. One is the native rosella, which is an indigenous species, and the other is the wild rosella, an introduced and naturalised species that grows as a weed, largely in coastal areas in the far north. Hibiscus species occur naturally in the South-east Asian and Pacific regions and in the West Indies and Mexico. There are no known poisonous hibiscus, and many indigenous peoples throughout these regions use them as medicinal plants.

The hibiscus found in Australia are useful and delicious food plants. The wild rosella, while not a truly indigenous food but a wild food, has become part of the bushfood cornucopia, as it shares similar qualities with the native species.

The rosellas mentioned here are plants and the scrumptious treats that can be made are definitely not from the rosella birds! How often people have looked at me askance when I offered them a wild rosella dish, especially when made from the wild rosella with its brilliant red hue that does not diminish in cooking. One can only wonder at the rationale behind the English naming of so many of our bushfoods!

Native
Rosella

Also known as native sorrel and native hibiscus

The native rosella is an attractive small tree or large spreading bush which can grow from 3 to 6 m, often on coastal foreshores or behind mangrove swamps as well as in rainforest gullies and edges. The plant has edible leaves, flower petals and calyxes. The calyx of the native rosella flower is the closed sepals of the hibiscus flower in seed, and it is this part of the plant that is most widely used in cooking today. In culinary circles the calyx is commonly referred to as the 'fruit' of the native rosella or the native rosella 'flower'. This may not be botanically correct, but for cooking purposes is descriptive and useful terminology. The calyx is fibrous and crisp in texture, and cooks well in sauces and preserves. There are historical accounts that the Aboriginal people ate the very young shoots and the roots of young plants, but there is some debate as to the safety of doing so.

The bush has vivid yellow, pink or white flowers with deep maroon bases, stamens and stigmas. The dark emerald-green leaves have three lobes and a coarse texture. The taste of the leaves and calyx is quite sour and acidic. The petals are pretty and add a tart note to salads.

The native rosella was, and continues to be, a very useful plant for the Aboriginal people of the tropical north. The leaves, calyxes and flowers are eaten raw or cooked as vegetables. The stem of the native rosella is very fibrous, and was used to make string. A number of hibiscus species are used as food plants; some are also very important medicinal plants. The close relative of the native hibiscus is *Hibiscus tiliaceus*, commonly known as Yal, cottonwood or yellow hibiscus. The stringy bark from this bush is removed in long strips and squeezed to force out the liquid or sap in the inner bark. This liquid is used as is or diluted with a little water for the treatment of boils and as an antiseptic wash for wounds. Strips of the bark are also used as a bandage to bind and close wounds.

TO GROW

Hibiscus heterophyllus

Distribution: Native rosella is usually found from north Queensland down into subtropical NSW.

The native rosella is a lovely garden plant grown successfully in suburban gardens even as far south as Victoria. It is an adaptable, fast-growing large shrub (or small tree) and a popular ornamental plant, due to its large showy flowers which can be white or bright yellow, and sometimes pink. The plant adapts to many soil types but, being a tropical and subtropical species, does require moisture and good drainage. It likes either full sun or light shade, but isn't frost tolerant.

Propagate from cuttings or, in warmer climates, sow seeds from the plants. Fresh seeds should be lightly scarified with sandpaper before sowing. Take cuttings from recently hardened new growth, and ensure that they are planted in a well-drained medium; if the cuttings become too moist the stems may rot.

Relations

H. tiliaceus is another good food plant that makes a fine garden specimen. Other related species with similar requirements are *H. sabdariffa*, the wild rosella, or *Abelmoschus moschatus*, the climbing hibiscus.

To harvest

The younger leaves of the native rosella are the most palatable and may be harvested at almost any time of the year, although spring and summer will produce the most prolific growth. The native rosella blooms from summer through to autumn, with a few flowers in the cooler months, in protected positions. The petals can enliven a salad when the garden is not offering many other colourful alternatives. The tart calyx should be harvested after the petals of the flower fall and the sepals close around the forming seed pod. The seed pod has to be removed before you cook with the calyx.

STORING NATIVE ROSELLA

The leaves of the native rosella may be kept in the vegetable crisper of the refrigerator. If you have a tree in the garden it seems a much more attractive option to simply harvest what you need at the time of use. The calyx is most abundant during the late spring and autumn months, and may be frozen, either whole or after the seed pod has been removed. There is no need to prepare the calyxes, just freeze them immediately after harvesting. Once the calyxes have been picked, don't let them sit for more than a day as they deteriorate quite quickly. You'll obtain the best results if they are picked, cleaned and harvested on the same day.

For cooking ideas, complementary flavours and recipes, see wild rosella (pages 43–47).

Wild
Rosella

The wild rosella is an introduced species that has become a naturalised plant over a long period of time. The wild rosella was probably introduced to Australian shores by early visitors from South-east Asia. There is evidence of Indonesian fishermen from the eighteenth century until the early years of this century visiting the northern coastal regions to fish for, and process, sea slugs or bêche-de-mer. The Indonesians would stay along the coastal areas of Arnhem land and the Kimberley. Traces of their visits still exist today, from bits of broken pottery and glass to introduced plants such as the Indonesian tamarind trees that grew from the discarded seeds of the tamarind fruit they brought with them. The wild rosella was probably introduced by these fishermen, and has become naturalised in the coastal regions behind the mangrove swamps.

The wild rosella is commonly grown by Queenslanders and Territorians. Wild rosella jam is a famous country Queensland product, a testament of its popularity.

The wild rosella has a very tart flavour like the native rosella, but with a raspberry–rhubarb–plum quality that makes it a very palatable fruit. The calyx, also commonly called the 'fruit', is large,

The Wild Rosella 'flower'

fibrous and a brilliant magenta. Visually it's a stunning fruit. The paramount culinary bounty of the wild rosella is indisputably its calyx, often referred to as a wild rosella 'flower'.

The fruit of the wild rosella is ideal in preserves such as jam and relishes, and suits both savoury and sweet applications. Wild rosella sauce is delectable with all sorts of meats and seafood. Try wild rosella in a mousse with a little yoghurt and coconut, or make a wild rosella syrup and splash it in champagne or pour it over some fine French-style crêpes.

The leaves are tart, with a hint of the fruit flavours. They make a good vegetable, and can be substituted for spinach. The tender new leaves are also ideal in salads. The leaves and fruits can be dried and used as seasoning or tea.

As wild rosella is an introduced and naturalised hibiscus, there is no traditional use of this particular plant.

TO GROW

Hibiscus sabdariffa

Distribution: Coastal and rainforest edge areas in NT and Queensland.

The wild rosella in its wild state is classified as a weed in the north and is now widespread in some parts of coastal Queensland, where it has invaded rainforest host sites. Care should be taken when planting this species to contain it. It is a fast-growing plant and produces large, delicate, yellow flowers about 10 cm across. The wild rosella can adapt to many different soil types and its ideal growing conditions—moisture, good drainage and full sun or part shade—reflect that of the native rosella. It is best grown as an annual. For best results, a long, hot summer is required. The wild rosella will seed readily and germinate best in warmer temperatures. Fresh seed should be lightly scarified with sandpaper before sowing. Cuttings may be taken from recently hardened new growth.

Relations

As for native rosella (see page 40).

To harvest

The calyx of the wild rosella should be harvested after the sepals close and the seed pod is formed. In most climates this occurs during autumn, around April and May. The tender young leaves should be harvested for salads, and older or larger leaves used for vegetable dishes. In the tropics the plant is treated largely as an annual and planted at different times to provide an ongoing supply of wild rosella calyxes. The calyx takes about 6 weeks to grow to maturity after the petals have fallen, and should measure approximately 3–4 cm in length.

STORING WILD ROSELLA

As for native rosella (see page 40).

TO COOK

Wild rosella flowers (or calyxes) are about 3–4 cm in length, with a rounded base that holds the internal seed pod. Around the perimeter of this base is a spiky crown that cradles the sepals and provides an attractive visual balance. Once harvested, the seed pod needs to be removed. Cut off the very bottom of the calyx and, using your finger, push the visible pod up through the top, where the sepals are close together. After the seed pod is removed, the sepals will close back and the wild rosella will keep its attractive shape. For most recipes this isn't very important but if you want to use the flower for a garnish clean it with care. If the wild rosellas are frozen whole, remove the seed pods while they are still frozen and not thawed, as they become difficult to handle and won't retain their shape. For most recipes, the wild rosella will need to be chopped fairly finely with a large, sharp knife as it has a fibrous texture, but a food processor works as well. This will be efficiently done if the wild rosella has been frozen first. The natural water content in the fruit means that if processed fresh or thawed they become messy and you won't achieve a standard-size cut.

If you are making wild rosella jam or relish, a rough chop with a knife may suffice as the fibre strands will break down more readily with a long, slow-cooking process. Wild rosella retains its strong colour during cooking, but I have noticed that in uncooked dairy-based desserts, the colour can fade to a dull brown if exposed to the air, which will then be retained in the body of the dessert. To avoid this, seal the top of mousses and bavarois, for example, with a miroir top made from gelatine and wild rosella syrup (see page 44), or cover with finely grated chocolate.

The rosella requires some sugar to sweeten it in almost all applications, even savoury sauces. Its deep, complex flavour and sharpness lends itself to rich meats such as emu, lamb, pork and game. It is equally at home with poultry and fish.

Goes with

Wild rosellas harmonise well with the lilly pillies, Illawarra plum, appleberry and, to a degree, lemon aspen. Bush 'herbs' that complement wild rosella include native pepper, wild thyme and native mint.

Due largely to their acidity wild rosellas are best not combined with Kakadu plums, the wild limes (various), Burdekin or Davidson's plums. The obvious savoury flavours of bush tomatoes, warrigal greens, cheesefruits and bush cucumbers are not suited to the wild rosella either. The tartness of the wild rosella will swamp the delicate flavours of the quandong and white elderberry.

Wild rosella is favourably accented by ginger, chilli and sugar. Its tartness is a good contrast for fruits such as peaches, pears, nectarines and berries. Apple is also a good foil. Coconut, banana and mango are pleasing partners, as are some nuts and cream desserts. Avoid using wild rosella with most vegetables such as the greens, root vegetables, and tomatoes—they just don't work.

Wild Rosella Syrup

This syrup is delicious over crêpes, drizzled over fresh fruit, particularly berries and soft fruits. Poach fresh peaches in the syrup for a summer dessert and serve chilled.

To make 8 cups (2 litres)

5 cups (1 kg) castor sugar
4 cups (1 litre) water
4 cups (200 g) wild rosella
   flowers, chopped

Heat the sugar and water in a large saucepan until the sugar is completely dissolved. Add the wild rosella flowers and bring to the boil. Lower the heat and simmer gently until the volume of liquid is reduced by a third. This will produce a rich, thick syrup of magnificent colour.

Remove the syrup from the heat and strain through a very fine sieve to remove all the wild rosella fruit. Bottle the syrup while still hot into clean bottles and seal. This syrup will keep for at least a year in the pantry. Once opened, it will keep for months if refrigerated.

SHORTS

- For a dessert garnish, candy the wild rosella flowers in a strong sugar syrup of 2 parts sugar and 1 part water. A small amount of crushed wild rosella can be added into the syrup while it is cooking for an even deeper, more lustrous colour. Place the perfectly clean flowers into the hot syrup after it has been removed from the heat. Cool the wild rosellas in the sugar solution, preferably overnight. Remove and place them bottom down on a rack to drain away excess liquid and allow to air dry. The finished candied rosella will be a beautiful, clear rich red in colour and quite firm to handle. Once these wild rosellas are dried, they may be stored in an airtight container for months and used as required. This process makes the wild rosella sweet enough to eat and softens the texture of the flesh.

- Instead of offering a kir royale, which marries blackcurrant syrup or cassis and champagne, try a rosella royale. Place a clean wild rosella in the bottom of a champagne flute. Pour in 15 ml Wild Rosella Syrup (see above) and gently fill with champagne. The wild rosella will eventually lift and move up the glass.

Wild Rosella Sauce

This particular recipe has been made with chicken stock, which marries it to poultry and white meat dishes. Try it with Chicken Breasts with Bunya Nut and Bacon Stuffing (see page 106).

To make 3 cups (for 6)

4 cups (200 g) wild rosella flowers, fresh or frozen
2 teaspoons (10 ml) olive oil
1 clove garlic, finely chopped
1 onion, finely chopped
½ cup (125 ml) port
a pinch of salt
1 teaspoon (5 g) castor sugar
a pinch of native (black) pepper
2 cups (500 ml) Chicken Demi-glace (see page 183)

Purée the wild rosella flowers in a blender or food processor. If the flowers are fresh, you'll need up to half a cup of water to form a purée. If the flowers are frozen, allow them to partly thaw so that they begin to soften before processing. The liquid from the thawing should be sufficient to form the purée. Set aside.

In a medium-sized saucepan, heat the oil over a moderate heat and cook the garlic and onion until soft and tender. Add the port, salt, sugar and pepper to the saucepan. Stir to dissolve the sugar, then stir in the wild rosella purée.

Add the demi-glace and bring the sauce to the boil. Lower the heat and allow the sauce to simmer gently for at least 10 minutes. The sauce may be served as it is with the wild rosellas, or strained if preferred.

Prawns in Wild Rosella and Ginger Sauce

To serve 6

¼ cup (60 ml) canola or vegetable oil
1.2 kg green prawns, shelled and cleaned for 30 tails
1 red onion
1 small red capsicum
30 snowpeas
16 wild rosella flowers, finely chopped, fresh or frozen
3 teaspoons (15 g) finely grated fresh ginger
scant ½ teaspoon salt
scant ½ teaspoon native pepper
1 ½ teaspoons (8 g) castor sugar

In a wok or large skillet, heat half the oil over a high heat. When hot, add the prawn tails and cook by tossing frequently. This should take no more than 2–3 minutes, depending on the size of the prawns. Remove the prawns from the wok, cover and keep warm.

Thinly slice the onion and capsicum and top and tail the snowpeas.

Add the remainder of the oil to the wok and heat. Toss the onion, capsicum and snowpeas in the oil and cook for 2–3 minutes. Add the wild rosella and ginger, and season with salt, native pepper and sugar. Toss through the vegetables, then return the prawns to the pan and cook for a further minute to heat through.

Serve immediately on a bed of rice.

Wild Rosella Cheesecake

To make a 23 cm (9 in) cake

1¾ cups (330 g) cream
  cheese or neufchâtel
¾ cup (170 g) castor sugar
2 egg yolks
2½ cups (670 ml) cream
3 teaspoons (15 g) powdered
  gelatine
3 cups (150 g) very finely
  chopped or lightly puréed
  wild rosella flowers, fresh or
  frozen

Biscuit Base
1 cup (125 g) crushed sweet
  biscuits
½ cup (90 g) unsalted butter,
  melted

Miroir
1 cup (250 ml) water
½ cup (100 g) castor sugar
2 cups (100 g) wild rosella,
  roughly chopped
2 teaspoons (10 g) powdered
  gelatine

To make the Biscuit Base, combine the biscuits and melted butter in a bowl. Press evenly into the base of a lightly greased 23 cm (9 in) springform tin. Refrigerate until firm.

Using the paddle attachment of your electric mixer if you have one (if not, a whisk will do) cream the cheese and sugar until light and runny in texture with NO lumps. Slowly add the eggs, one at a time, adding the second egg only when the first is fully incorporated. Place this mixture into a large bowl.

In a large, clean bowl, lightly whip the cream until the whisk leaves trails in the cream, and fold this through the cheese mix.

Dissolve the powdered gelatine in very hot (just boiled water) and sit to completely melt through.

When the gelatine is dissolved take a spoonful of the cheese cream mix and mix into the melted gelatine, then whisk the gelatine into the main mix with a balloon whisk. This step is designed to bring the temperature of the gelatine mixture down to the level of the main mixture for a smooth blending of the two.

Immediately fold through the finely chopped wild rosella. You will notice a wonderful marbling effect if you don't overblend. If you prefer a more uniform pink, by all means fold the wild rosella through more thoroughly.

At this stage the mix should still be at pouring texture. Pour into the prepared tin, smoothing the top to ensure an even surface.

Let the cheesecake set in the refrigerator for at least an hour before pouring on the miroir top.

To make the Miroir, bring the water, sugar and wild rosella flowers to the boil. Strain and discard the flowers. The sugar syrup should be a deep red colour. Let the syrup cool to room temperature before adding the gelatine (see above for instructions).

Before pouring onto the cake, test a very small amount on a saucer in your refrigerator to make sure the jelly will set well. If it's not setting, perhaps add another ½ teaspoon (2–3 g) gelatine. Remember that it continues to set firmer the longer it's refrigerated.

Once you are satisfied that the jelly will be perfect, carefully pour over the chilled cake. The cake must be well chilled when this procedure takes place or else the cream will melt and stain or blur the miroir.

Let the miroir set for at least 1–2 hours before serving. This cake freezes very well, even with the miroir.

Wild Rosella Relish

This relish complements almost anything, particularly rich meats; the sharp tang of the wild rosella helps cut the richness or fattiness of meats such as pork, lamb or duck.

To make 2 cups (500 ml)

4 cups (200 g) fresh or
frozen wild rosella, coarsely
chopped
1 Granny Smith or Jonathan
apple, cored, peeled and
chopped
⅓ cup (75 g) sultanas
1 onion, chopped
½ cup (125 ml) white vinegar
1 teaspoon (5 g) salt
1 cup (200 g) castor sugar
¼ teaspoon native (black)
pepper
a pinch of powdered ginger
1 cup (250 ml) water

Place all the ingredients into a medium-sized, stainless-steel saucepan over a high heat and bring to the boil. Stir constantly to dissolve the sugar, then lower the heat and simmer until the relish thickens. This should take about 45 minutes. Stir the relish occasionally, and adjust the heat if it starts to catch on the bottom of the saucepan. Once the relish is ready, pour into sterilised jars. It will keep for 6 months in the pantry. Refrigerate after opening.

Kakadu
Plum

*Also known as billygoat plum, green plum, wild plum and,
in East Arnhem land, murunga*

The Kakadu plum is common in the open forest areas at the Top End, from Darwin westwards to Arnhem land and the Kimberley region of northern WA. The trees are tall and slender, with grey-coloured bark that is rough to the touch. The light-green leaves are large, broad and long-stalked. The tree has small creamy flowers followed by fruits that ripen from around March to June. The Kakadu plum looks nothing like a plum; this remarkable fruit resembles an immature olive more than anything else—it's small, oval, a light olive to lime green with a thin skin and a very large stone to which the fibrous flesh adheres very strongly.

The Kakadu plum is recognised as having the highest content of vitamin C of all fruits. Testing has indicated that the Kakadu plum has approximately 3000 mg of vitamin C per 100 g of fruit, which is far in excess of citrus fruits—oranges, for example, have about 50 mg vitamin C per 100 g of fruit. Apart from this, the fruit is fairly typical of most fruits as it is low in fat, and has a reasonable level of soluble fibre and carbohydrates.

The taste of the uncooked Kakadu plum is acidic and refreshing, with a slight citrus aftertaste. Its flavour has been likened to English gooseberries. It is a bushfood that is probably better appreciated cooked rather than in its natural state. The fruit is eminently suited to jam, sauce and chutney-making, where its high level of fruit acid will act as a natural preservative. The resulting flavour of the Kakadu plum in these forms is very pleasant—the tartness of the fruit is retained, but it adopts an almost honey-like quality as it is tempered by sugar.

The soft and sticky inner bark of the tree was also used as a medicinal lotion by the Aboriginal people of the northern regions. It was pounded, added to water and applied directly to open sores and also used as a type of antiseptic wash. The lotion is also suitable as a soothing bath for aching limbs or feet.

TO GROW

Terminalia ferdinandiana
Distribution: North-western Australia to eastern Arnhem land.

This shade tree is suitable for seasonally dry tropical areas, and should grow well across most of northern Australia. A medium-sized tree, it will grow to 10 m, and has an attractive spreading habit. The tree is deciduous, and loses its leaves in spring.

During early summer it has many showy flower spikes followed by oval, green fruit. The Kakadu plum is suitable as a shade tree and as an ornamental specimen in sandy to loamy soils. It appreciates high summer rainfall and a dry winter, and grows well in full sun. Being very frost sensitive, it will not succeed in cooler districts.

Propagate new trees from seed. Germination can take from 6 to 12 weeks, and requires warm and moist conditions. One method is to dry the fruit and sow it whole. Removing the fleshy layer and scratching the seed casing may also give good results.

Relations

T. carpentariae, also known as wild peach, has similar looks with similar requirements and edible fruit. *T. seriocarpa*, the damson or dead dog tree, is a fast-growing, hardy deciduous tree from northern Australia. The edible blue-coloured fruits are small, profuse and quite sweet, compared to the Kakadu plum. The solid timber of this tree is suitable as building material. *T. catappa*, or the beach almond tree, also occurs in the tropics. It produces fruit that is quite large, but it is the inner seed, with its delicious almond-flavoured kernel, that is valued as food.

To harvest

Kakadu plums are usually ready for harvest from March until early June. The tree can be a prolific bearer, yielding up to 50 kg fruit in a good season. Like many bush fruits, however, the yield may vary from year to year. The fruits grow in clustered groups and are easy to pick.

STORING KAKADU PLUM

The Kakadu plum will keep well for at least a week after harvesting. It is wise to freeze the plums as soon as they are picked until you are ready to cook with them. Freezing will not adversely affect their nutritional properties; in fact, it will preserve them. The plums need no preparation for freezing. Kakadu plums may also be pickled and kept for up to a year in a sealed jar.

TO COOK

The Kakadu plum has some peculiar features that you need to understand to obtain the best results. On average, an individual Kakadu plum weighs around 3 g, of which 12 per cent is the seed. There are approximately 300 Kakadu plums per kilogram (30 per 100 g) or about 40 plums per metric cup. The flesh of the plum is extremely fibrous, and it adheres tenaciously to the stone. The stone is long and oval, and reminiscent of an olive pip in shape and in its woody feel in the mouth. Once cooked, the fruit becomes gelatinous but the fibrous strands are still evident as they don't break down easily. If used like this, the plum feels unpleasant in the mouth. The skin of the Kakadu plum is very thin in relation to the flesh.

All this means that the amount of usable fruit flesh from the Kakadu plum is severely restricted. When cooking with the plum you may lose up to 50 per cent of its original weight.

So, how do you get the most from the Kakadu plum with the minimum of fuss? The most effective method of obtaining usable fruit to incorporate into almost any recipe is to make a strained purée from the fruit. To make a purée, treat the Kakadu plum as you would a mango. Cut two large cheeks from each broad side of the fruit, and pare away the flesh. Cut off the flesh left on the stone. The flesh needs to be gently cooked, then puréed and passed through a fine sieve.

An easier and equally acceptable method of removing the flesh is to poach the whole plums in water to soften the flesh, and then push the fruit through a fine sieve, discarding the stones and fibrous strands.

The Kakadu plum has a strange texture. It is quite gelatinous, almost gummy. When making a purée, you can increase the yield and reduce the gumminess by incorporating some of the poaching liquid from the plums (if you use the easy method above) back into the purée. The fruit mass will absorb much of its cooking juices before it reaches a critical mass and breaks down into a slurry. Pass the purée through a fine sieve again.

Goes with

The Kakadu plum is a subtle and delicately flavoured fruit, and care needs to be taken not to swamp it with stronger flavours. It can be seasoned with native pepper, native mint and lemon myrtle, but is best kept away from strong-tasting bushfoods such as bush tomatoes and riberries. The acidic fruits will certainly overwhelm the Kakadu plum, so keep it away from wild lime, finger lime and lemon aspen. Kakadu plums can be blended with reasonably bland fruits such as apples, pears and even guavas, which is useful in preserve and sauce making if you only have limited supplies of the Kakadu plum.

Pickled Kakadu Plums

These pickled Kakadu plums can be used in savoury dishes as an alternative to olives, with cheese, in cold salads, antipasto platters or as a garnish for grilled fish and seafood.

To make 4 x 250 ml jars

2 cups (500 ml) white wine
   vinegar
¼ cup (50 g) castor sugar
2 teaspoons (5 g) ground
   native pepper leaves, or
   50 dried leaves
2 teaspoons (5 g) ground
   lemon myrtle leaves
1 onion, sliced
4 cups (500 g) Kakadu
   plums, whole

Bring the vinegar to a boil with the sugar, native pepper, lemon myrtle and onion in a stainless-steel pot. Boil for 10 minutes, remove from the heat, and add the Kakadu plums.

Leave the plums in the vinegar pickle as it cools and, when completely cool, bottle them in a sterile jar with an airtight lid. Sealed pickled Kakadu plums will keep for up to a year, and for some months if refrigerated after opening.

Fresh Sardines with Pickled Kakadu Plums

To serve 6

18 fresh sardines
1 tablespoon (40 ml)
   macadamia or vegetable oil
   for frying
250 ml (1 cup) Lemon Myrtle
   Vinegar (see page 139)
24 Pickled Kakadu Plums (see
   above)

Quickly pan-fry the fish in the oil in batches, taking care not to overcook. Each should take only 2–3 minutes. When ready, remove from the pan and keep warm.

Add the vinegar to the pan and gently heat through. Add the pickled Kakadu plums and let them completely heat through. Pour the deglazed pan juices and pickled plums over the warm fish and serve at once.

Duck Breast with Kakadu Plum Glaze

To serve 6

1¼ cups (150 g) Kakadu
plums, stones removed

1⅕ cups (300 ml) sweetened
apple juice

1 tablespoon (25 ml) canola
oil

6 x 200 g duck breasts

1 clove garlic, crushed

1¼ cups (300 ml) Chicken
Stock (see page 182)

½ teaspoon salt

½ teaspoon native (black)
pepper

Place the Kakadu plums and apple juice in a medium-sized saucepan and bring to the boil. Adjust the heat and simmer for 15 minutes, or until the fruit swells and the outer skins split. Remove from the heat and leave until cool enough to handle.

Strain the plums, pressing the plums against the sieve to push through as much flesh as possible. Reserve the strained juices and the pulp.

In a heavy skillet over a medium flame, heat the oil and add the duck breast, skin-side down, and cook for 3–4 minutes. Turn the breast over and cook the other side for 1–2 minutes. Don't overcook. Remove the duck breast, cover and keep warm while you cook the rest of them.

Drain as much oil as you can from the cooking juices and return the skillet to the heat. Cook the garlic until it just starts to brown. Add the stock, salt, native pepper and the Kakadu plum pulp and juices. Stir well and lower the heat to a simmer. Reduce the sauce until it forms a thick glaze, about 10 minutes.

Slice the duck breasts lengthwise and place the meat on serving plates. Return any juices from the duck to the Kakadu plum glaze, stir and spoon over the duck breasts.

As Kakadu plums have a delicate and subtle flavour, keep the accompanying vegetables simple and non-intrusive. Steamed new potatoes and asparagus work well.

SHORTS

- Use the Quandong Jam recipe (see page 22), replacing the quandongs with 5 cups of fresh Kakadu plums to make a jam. The Kakadu plum has a very high acid level but also a very low pH level, so it needs no additional preservative and will keep for a long time once cooked and sealed. The fruit is difficult to set, however, and will require the addition of pectin or jam setter for a good result.

Kakadu Plum Sauce

This sauce is well suited to white meats, particularly to fish.

To make 2 cups (500 ml)

1½ cups (200 g) Kakadu
  plums, stones removed
1 lemon, quartered
1 onion, chopped
2 cups (500 ml) water
scant ½ cup (100 ml)
  sweetened apple juice
scant ½ cup (100 ml) riesling
1 teaspoon (5 g) salt
½ teaspoon native (black)
  pepper
2 sprigs fresh coriander,
  chopped

In a medium-sized saucepan, place the Kakadu plums, lemon, onion and water over a medium heat and bring to the boil. Adjust the heat and simmer for 15 minutes until the outer skins of the fruit start to split.

Strain the plums, pressing the flesh against the sieve to push as much of the flesh through as possible. Discard the stones, lemon and onion.

In a clean, larger saucepan, combine the fruit pulp with the apple juice, riesling, salt and native pepper. Bring to the boil and reduce to a smooth sauce. This should take about 15 minutes.

Stir in the chopped coriander and mix well. Simmer for a further minute. Remove from the heat, strain and serve.

Lilly Pilly

Australia has more than sixty different lilly pillies, and all appear to bear edible fruit. They range from the large red or white bush apples from the tropical NT, to the tiny riberry of the eastern seaboard through to the stately trees of the southern states that bear, variously, white, pink and purple fruits. Some, like the bush apple, have large seeds, and some have tiny ones. Their tastes also vary markedly from the intense aromatic flavour of the riberry to the almost nashi pear taste and texture of the common lilly pilly (Acmena smithii). All seem to have some culinary application. Most fruits will suit jams, jellies, chutneys and sauces, and can be baked in biscuits, pies, tarts and cakes.

Lilly pillies are beautiful trees with waxy, dark-green leaves and clusters of vivid or soft-coloured fruit. They are found in many home gardens all over the country and are frequently grown as ornamentals. Sadly, most people don't realise that the fruit is edible and usually consider the falling ripe fruit a nuisance. Instead of cursing the falling fruit, harvest and eat it fresh, or make a big batch of lilly pilly jam or jelly.

Lilly pillies are ideal to preserve, usually being high in acid, and they set naturally with their own pectin, particularly if they are picked early before they ripen completely and fall.

Lilly pillies were one of the first fruits eaten by the very first European visitors. Joseph Banks wrote in his diary on 3 May 1770, 'we eat with much pleasure, tho they had little to recommend them but a slight acid'. In colonial society, lilly pillies were used to make jellies and a fruit wine. The fruits were eaten by the Aborigines as a refreshing 'snack' food, and were highly sought after.

Lady Apple

Also known as red apple, bush apple, wild apple

Lady apple is such a romantic name for this lovely fruit that comes from the tropical forests, rivers and coastal regions of the far north of Australia. It is a member of the lilly pilly family, but is distinctly different to the lilly pillies that are familiar to most Australians. Visually, it is reminiscent of the common eating apple with its bright rose-coloured skin, but the fruit has a rather bumpy bottom or tip, where the flesh divides into four lobes. The body of the fruit has vertical ribs. Where the riberry and the magenta lilly pilly are small, compact fruits, the lady apple is about the size of a Red Delicious apple.

You can bite into a lady apple, but it has an enormous single seed that looks like a large apricot stone. The flesh is a pale beige tinged with an almost rhubarb blush, and is crisp and crunchy.

The flavour of the lady apple is sweet, juicy and a little apple-ish, with overtones of riberry and nutmeg. It has a very refreshing finish on the palate, and an aromatic aftertaste. These qualities make lady apples highly prized by the Aboriginal people of the far north, particularly the coastal regions. The fruit is high in vitamin C—up to 17 mg per 100 g—and also has a high water content and some carbohydrate.

Lady apples are delicious just picked from the tree but are also good to cook with. Like all lilly pillies we have tried, they are well suited to sauces, relishes and chutneys.

The lady apple fruits during the wet season from December to early March, and is one of the few fruiting trees at this time, providing a welcome addition to the daily fare. When lady apples are in season, the Aborigines will harvest them in great quantities. They are usually eaten fresh, and the large seeds would be tossed to the side of the camp. Stands of these trees have sprung up over time from discarded seeds at old campsites. The discarded seeds and their consequent growth into groves of trees is a passive style of gardening, and may act as a horticultural indicator of previous campsites.

TO GROW

Syzygium suborbiculare

Distribution: Found in the far north from Cape York through to the top end of WA.

The lady apple is a medium-sized tree that will grow at best to 10 m. Most specimens are smaller, and may vary in size, shape and width, depending on growing conditions and their locale. Under cultivation, it is a very attractive ornamental tree with large, wide, rounded dark-green leaves. The flowers are colourful and fluffy, followed by spectacular large, red fruit that is visible from quite a distance.

Because the tree is native to coastal areas it tolerates salty winds. Although it prefers sandy soils, it will adapt well to many soil types, as long as they are well drained. It is doubtful that this tree will grow south of subtropical environments as it doesn't appreciate dry soil, cool climates or frost. In tropical and subtropical areas, it should be well watered, especially when the fruit is forming.

This species is best grown from seed. Extract the large single seed from the fresh fruit and sow immediately—it germinates readily.

To harvest

The lady apple ripens during the wet season monsoons, usually from December to late March, though the fruit may ripen earlier. The fruit needs to be harvested quickly as it ripens before it drops. In tropical regions, harvest from the tree—don't let the fruit ripen and fall as it will deteriorate in the high humidity. The low spread of the branches makes harvesting easy.

STORING LADY APPLE

Lady apples will keep for about a week in the refrigerator crisper. If kept in a fruit bowl out of the fridge they will deteriorate more quickly. They also freeze very well. Wipe the fruit clean and freeze whole. If you like, remove the central seed first and pack the halves into freezer bags.

TO COOK

Obviously, the large central seed needs to be removed from the lady apples, but for cooking or eating fresh the fruit need not be peeled. Clean the exterior well, and cut away any blemishes. The flesh of the lady apple is on average about 1 cm thick. This isn't much when you consider that the fruit can be as large as a tennis ball, but the large seed constitutes nearly three-quarters of the total fruit, and as yet we are unaware of any culinary use for it.

The fleshy lobes that extend from the tip of the fruit may need to be trimmed if the fruit is particularly large, as they can be a bit fibrous. On the smaller specimens (about golf-ball size), this isn't necessary.

The flesh is easy to handle and prepare for cooking. It will cut easily with a sharp knife and you could liken its texture to that of a persimmon—firm but not pulpy.

Unlike many of the other bush fruits, the flavour of the lady apple is delicate rather than intense. It suits white meats such as pork and chicken. Lady apples make great sauces, relishes and chutneys, particularly if seasoned with either the native or common nutmeg to highlight their own aromatic nutmeg nuances.

In dessert cooking, lady apples may be used in place of cooking apples. Try them in pies and tarts, and serve them fresh as an accompaniment to cheese.

Goes with

Lady apples and muntries are a winning combination, and lady apples will also be happy with riberry, Illawarra plum and wild rosella. Native nutmeg, native pepper and native mint are all suitable seasonings for lady apple dishes. The highly acidic fruits such as lemon aspen, Kakadu plums and wild limes are not compatible. Neither are bush tomatoes nor native cucumbers.

The lady apple is not really suited to vegetables in general, but will work very well with rhubarb, quince, berries, apples and pears.

Slow-cooked Pork Casserole with Lady Apples

Lovely slow-cooked, casserole-style dishes are back in style. So much emphasis recently has been on the quick, the easy and the simple in modern cooking that the virtues of the casserole, the stew and the ragout have been overlooked. This is a dish to make you fall in love with slow-cooked dishes all over again.

To serve 6

1½ kg pork leg or shoulder
1 tablespoon (20 g) plain flour
2 teaspoons (10 ml) olive oil
8 large lady apples, stones removed and diced
2 onions, coarsely chopped
2 parsnips, coarsely chopped
2 carrots, coarsely chopped
2 potatoes, coarsely chopped
a pinch of salt
a pinch of native (black) pepper
generous ¾ cup (200 ml) brandy
2 cups (500 ml) Chicken Stock (see page 182)
1 ½ cups (375 ml) cream

Preheat the oven to 160°C (325°F).

Ask your butcher to bone the pork and cut the meat into 3 cm dice for you. If this isn't possible, carefully trim the meat of excess fat, remove the meat from the bone and dice accordingly. Dust the meat with the plain flour and set aside while you prepare the vegetables.

Using a large, deep flame-proof casserole dish or pan, heat the oil, add the floured pork pieces and brown on all sides. This should take about 5 minutes. Add the chopped lady apples and vegetables to the pan and season with salt and pepper. Add the brandy and stir through. Finally, add the chicken stock and cream, stirring to ensure that all ingredients are well mixed. Put a lid on the casserole dish (or transfer to a lidded casserole dish if necessary) and place on the middle shelf of the preheated oven. Bake in the preheated oven until the meat is very tender, approximately 1½ hours. Serve with steamed rice or couscous.

SHORTS

- Place two or three stoned sweet lady apple halves with nutmeg, sugar and butter in puff pastry parcels and bake until golden brown in a 200°C (400°F) oven for 25 minutes.

- Make a salad of lady apple, chicken, nuts, sultanas and yoghurt.

- Purée some lady apples that have been cooked in sugar syrup until soft. Add some calvados and serve hot or cold with puddings or crêpes.

Lady Apple and Native Nutmeg Sauce

This is a very versatile sauce, suitable for serving with most meats, particularly with poultry and pork. It is very easy to prepare, and can be made in advance and gently reheated.

To make 3 cups (750 ml)

6 large lady apples, stones removed
2 cups (500 ml) unsweetened apple juice
a pinch of salt
a pinch of native (black) pepper
1 onion, finely diced
2 cups (500 ml) Chicken Stock (see page 182)
½ cup (100 g) sultanas
½ teaspoon dried and ground native nutmeg

Finely chop the flesh of the lady apple and combine with all the other ingredients, except the native nutmeg, in a large, heavy-based saucepan. Bring to the boil, then reduce the heat and simmer for 20 minutes.

Remove the sauce from the saucepan and purée to remove all lumps. Return the sauce to the saucepan and to the heat. At this stage, add the ground native nutmeg and allow the sauce to simmer for a further 5 minutes. Remove from the heat and serve with chicken or roast pork.

Lady Apple Chutney

To make 6 x 250 ml jars

10 lady apples, stones removed
2 onions, chopped
4 Granny Smith apples, peeled, cored and chopped
1 cup (200 g) sultanas
2 cups (400 g) castor sugar
1 teaspoon (5 g) salt
½ teaspoon native pepper (black pepper)
2–3 cloves
1½ cups (375 ml) white vinegar
1 cup (250 ml) water

Coarsely chop the lady apples and place in a large, heavy-based, stainless-steel saucepan with the chopped onions and apples. Add the sultanas, sugar, seasonings and liquids, and, stirring constantly, bring to the boil. Stop stirring once the mixture has come to the boil, and reduce the heat to a simmer.

Continue simmering until the chutney thickens, stirring occasionally.

After an hour, remove the chutney from the heat and pour immediately into clean, sterilised jars. Seal while still very hot. The sealed jars of chutney will keep for up to a year away from direct heat or light, but are probably best refrigerated once opened.

Riberry

Also known as clove lilly pilly and cherry alder

Riberries, or clove lilly pillies, as their name suggests, are delectable little fruits with a distinct clove-like flavour. They are tiny, pear-shaped berries, varying in colour from the softest pinks through to the more commonly seen bright purples and magentas. The riberry has a marvellous aromatic flavour and, while it is intense as most bush fruits are, is quite palatable to Western-trained tastes as a fresh fruit. The fruit is juicy, but only mildly sweet, with a gentle acidic finish with a dominant clove flavour on the palate. It seems surprising that such a tiny and pretty berry can pack such a powerful flavour punch.

Riberries contain the essential oils myrcene (as in nutmeg), pinene (found in many cooking herbs) and limonene (found in bay leaves), so although the clove flavour is potent, other subtle, complex flavours develop on the palate and contribute to the riberry's versatility and adaptability.

The planting of riberries in the garden is a time-honoured practice, if the high incidence of their appearance in suburban gardens is anything to go by. Many local councils have used the riberry extensively, making it one of the most common street, park and garden trees in the north-eastern states. If you know of a good fruiting tree in a public park, however, permission must be obtained from the local council before gathering. Take only the small amount that you will actually use, remembering that the riberry is intensely flavoured, and small amounts go a long way.

Once your own tree is established and fruiting well, pick and snack on the fruit and introduce them to your children. Most children seem to love riberries; I remember our sons' first encounter—they were initially hesitant, since it was a fruit they had never seen before, but today, they look on a bowl of fresh or frozen riberries as a special treat.

Riberries were widely appreciated primarily by the east-coast Aboriginal people from NSW right up into northern Queensland. They were normally eaten raw when in season, when they fruited prolifically. The riberries would often be eaten by the tribes as an invigorating delicacy—they contain a high proportion of water and essential minerals—while gathering food.

TO GROW

Syzygium luehmanii
Distribution: Widely distributed, from southern NSW through to northern Queensland.

Riberries will thrive along the eastern seaboard and are well worth trying as far south as Melbourne. In their natural rainforest environment they will grow to about 20 m; in gardens out of rainforest conditions they will probably reach heights of about 8 m, which is still substantial. They are an attractive garden specimen with pretty pinkish-coloured new foliage, and colourful flowers and fruit. Many plant nurseries will recommend riberry trees as an ornamental for the garden, without realising their culinary worth. Although riberry trees originally inhabited eastern coastal rainforests, they have been widely planted in Sydney and Melbourne as street and park trees as they are hardy and only slightly frost tender.

Naturally, given its rainforest origins, the riberry appreciates lots of water and rich soil for the best crops. Although the mature tree can withstand some mild frost, protect the young ones in particular from exposure to frost for successful growth. They will tolerate full sun to part shade.

The tree can be propagated by seed or from cuttings. If using seed, the fruit must first be macerated in water to remove the flesh from the seed, which can then be sown. Germination can be unreliable, and it's wise to sow seeds from a couple of different trees to maximise results. Cuttings will strike, but they can be slow to develop and have a high failure rate.

Relations

There are many different lilly pillies well worth trying. *Syzygium australe* (creek lilly pilly) has a refreshing taste, as does *S. paniculatum* (magenta lilly pilly). *S. oleosum* (blue lilly pilly) is slightly more unusual—its fruit starts off a reddish colour, changing to blue as it ripens. *Acmena smithii* is another very well-known lilly pilly that occurs as far south as Victoria, and produces a pleasant, if slightly bland, eating fruit.

To harvest

Depending on the area, riberries can be harvested from mid to late summer, from January to March. A fully mature tree will yield an enormous amount of fruit in a good year, up to 80 kg. Once the fruit starts to ripen on the tree, harvest it quickly before it falls or before the birds beat you to it!

STORING RIBERRY

As you will no doubt have lots of riberry fruit piled up in your kitchen after harvesting, you will be delighted to know that it freezes beautifully with no special preparation required. Pick over the fruit, discarding the stems and any bruised fruit, and place in airtight freezer bags before freezing. Riberries can also be preserved in syrup and stored in glass jars.

TO COOK

Because of their aromatic qualities, riberries are particularly suited to rich meats such as game. They are ideal with Australia's indigenous game meats such as emu, kangaroo and wallaby, and are equally at home with traditional game poultry, including quail, squab and pheasant. Use riberry with venison instead of the traditional juniper berry as a variation. Riberry is also delicious served with chicken, lamb or pork. It doesn't seem to suit beef or fish quite as well, but can be successful with seafood such as prawns or crayfish.

Riberry is delicious in many vegetable and salad dishes and with desserts. Try muffins or scones with riberry, and use them to make jams, jellies and sauces.

The riberry in its raw state varies in colour from purple to deep pink. Once cooked it tends to fade to a uniform soft pink. Cooking doesn't change the flavour, though, and it can be used in many recipes in place of the traditional clove. Besides imparting a clove-like flavour, the riberry will give the dish an interesting and subtle difference. It is also delicious to eat, giving little flavour bursts and providing a colour counterpoint to other ingredients.

Use riberries whole. The seedless variety produces fruit that can be fully used. If, however, the fruit you have is seedy, pass it through a fine sieve, and remove the seeds before adding the purée to a recipe. This won't be suitable for all recipes, but can be used in sauces or for preparing flavour bases for sweet mousses, sorbets or ice-creams.

For best results, use riberries fresh where possible. It is best to add them to a recipe while they are frozen, rather than thawed, as they will deteriorate less in the cooking process. This applies in particular to recipes for oven-baked dishes, such as cakes or puddings, where the oven heat is intense.

As with most bush fruits, remember that the flavour of the riberry is quite strong. Try to balance its intense flavours against the other ingredients. With most bush fruits too much is usually not better, but bitter!

Goes with

Bushfoods that complement riberries are Illawarra plums, native raspberries, lemon aspen, native ginger, the native peppers and the native mints.

Avoid piquant fruits such as the bush tomato and the highly acidic Davidson's and Kakadu plums. The strong flavour of the riberry can overwhelm the more subtle flavours of the white elderberry, dianella berry and quandong if used too liberally.

Other fruits and seasonings that can be used with success with riberries include most soft fruits such as berries, peaches, plums, apricots, mangoes, bananas, coconuts and rhubarb. Fresh ginger is delicious with riberry, and the judicious use of chilli (so as not to take away from the unique riberry characteristics) is fine. Apples, oranges and pears provide a perfect partnership with riberry. Perhaps not as obvious is the suitability of potato and pumpkin. Chocolate also works very well with riberry. Riberry is, however, unsuitable for cooking with tomatoes, celery and zucchini.

Boned Quail with Riberry Glaze

To serve 6

6 x 180 g quail, partly boned
    (remove the ribcage but
    leave the legs and wings
    intact)
salt and native pepper
300 g fresh warrigal greens,
    blanched
2 tablespoons (50 ml)
    macadamia oil
1 large onion, finely diced
2½ cups (625 ml) stock,
    made from the quail bones
    or Chicken Stock (see
    page 182)
2 cups (200g) whole riberries

Preheat the oven to 180°C (360°F).

Season the inside and outside of each quail with the salt and native pepper.

Stuff the boned-out chest cavity with the blanched warrigal greens. Rub the outside of the quails with the macadamia oil. Tie the legs together and place the quails on a baking dish in the preheated oven for approximately 20 minutes.

Remove from the oven and cover with foil. Rest in a warm place.

Add the onion to the pan juices and fry until translucent and soft. Add the stock and simmer until the volume is reduced by half.

Crush most of the riberries, reserving a handful for garnishing. Add the crushed berries to the stock, cover the pan and reduce until it forms a glaze. Remove from the heat and strain. Add the reserved riberries and serve over the quails.

SHORTS

- Toss riberries through a red berry salad and add a dash of Cointreau.

- Add riberries to a traditional summer pudding to provide the palate with a contrast to the berry flavours. In this dish riberries act both as a complementary and contrasting flavour.

- Add riberries with the last ladleful of stock to a pumpkin risotto.

- Use riberries in place of cloves in apple pie or pear crumble.

- Melt riberry jelly into a sauce for poultry.

- Put 100 to 200 g riberries per litre of vodka and bottle for a few months for the flavours and colour to infuse.

- Stuff apples with riberries, butter and almonds and bake in a moderate oven until the apples are soft.

- Add puréed riberries to a sorbet.

- If you have a small food-drying unit, dry the riberries out—they are delicious to nibble on or reconstitute for cooking.

Riberry Fritters

To serve 8

Fritters

2 medium-sized sweet
  potatoes or 3 large
  potatoes, peeled and
  roughly sliced
¼ cup (60 ml) milk
½ cup (70 g) plain flour
3 x 55 g eggs
3 egg whites
1 tablespoon (25 ml)
  thickened cream
salt and native pepper
1 cup (250 ml) macadamia
  or vegetable oil or clarified
  butter for frying
1½ cups (160 g) riberries

Riberry Butter Sauce

1 cup (250 ml) dry white
  wine
2 shallots or 2 good-sized
  spring onions, white part
  only, minced
½ cup (100g) unsalted butter
½ cup (50 g) riberries,
  puréed
riberries for garnish

To make the Fritters, cook the potatoes in boiling water until tender. Drain well, and return to the pot with the milk. Mash them until soft and creamy. Pass the mashed potatoes through a fine sieve or purée in a food processor to remove any lumps. Add the eggs, one at a time, to the potatoes and mix well between each addition.

Sift the plain flour into the mixture and stir vigorously or process until well incorporated. Add the egg whites and cream, and mix well into the potato batter. The batter should be the consistency of a thick custard. Season with salt and native pepper.

Heat a small amount of oil over medium heat in a heavy-based frying pan (cast iron is perfect).

Pour in a tablespoon of the batter. Immediately scatter approximately 10 riberries over the batter. As soon as the riberries have penetrated the batter, and the fritters start to cook around the edges, turn them over with a spatula to cook on the other side. Be careful when doing this—this batter has a delicate structure and can break apart. Once turned, press lightly on the fritter with a spatula.

These fritters cook very quickly, so be careful not to burn them. When the fritters are cooked, you will notice that the riberries show through attractively on one side. Drain on kitchen paper to absorb the excess oil and keep them warm in a low oven until the batter is finished. Lightly season the finished fritters with salt.

To make the Riberry Butter Sauce, combine the wine and the minced shallots in a non-reactive small saucepan (stainless steel is best). Cook over a medium heat and reduce until a tablespoon of liquid remains.

Whisk the butter into the liquid, little piece by little piece, until it is fully incorporated. A balloon whisk is ideal for this, but a fork will do. Avoid overheating the sauce or the butter will separate. You can tell if this has happened if the butter forms a yellowish, oily sheen on the surface. If you find yourself in this pickle, take the saucepan from the heat and whisk vigorously, or use a Bamix, to remix the butter.

Return to the heat, add the puréed riberries, salt and native pepper to taste, and stir briefly until the sauce has a consistent silky texture. Strain through a fine sieve and discard the leavings. If you make this sauce in advance, don't overheat it or let it come to the boil.

For an entrée, place 3 fritters on each plate, riberry-side up, and surround with a small amount of the butter sauce. Scatter a few riberries around them.

Crayfish, Riberry and Mango Salad

To serve 6

2 x 3 kg or 3 x 1.5 kg
 crayfish (fresh or cooked)
3 large mangoes, peeled and
 cut into 18 even slices
riberries for garnish

Riberry Vinaigrette
1 cup (100 g) riberries
1 cup (250 ml) white vinegar
salt and ground native pepper
a pinch of mustard powder
2 cups (500 ml) canola oil

Dispose of the crayfish by placing it in the freezer for 30 minutes. Bring a large pot of salted water to the boil and plunge in the crayfish. Remove once the shells turn red, about 3 minutes. Refresh. Crack the shells and remove the tail in one piece. Slice into even medallions of about 1 cm thickness. Set aside until ready to use.

To make the Riberry Vinaigrette, combine the riberries and white vinegar in a medium-sized saucepan. Add the salt, pepper and mustard powder, and bring to the boil. Cook until the riberries have infused their flavour. Remove from the heat and cool. Whisk in the oil to combine, then transfer to a screwtop jar and shake well to emulsify.

Place 3 slices of mango in the middle of each plate. Place 3 crayfish medallions on top of the mango, and dress lightly with the vinaigrette. Scatter the riberries over and around the plate and serve immediately.

Riberry Vinegar

To make 4 cups (1 litre)

½ cup (100 g) castor sugar
4 cups (1 litre) white vinegar
6 mountain pepper leaves,
 whole
2 cups (200 g) riberries
1 onion, chopped

Dissolve the sugar in the vinegar and bring to the boil. Add the pepper leaves, riberries and onion, and simmer for 10 minutes. Strain into a sterilised bottle and seal. The vinegar will keep for up to a year in a dark place.

Riberry Marmalade

Steven Pashley, the talented Executive Chef from Brisbane's Gazebo Hotel, introduced us to this riberry marmalade. It is an easy recipe to follow, and gives a great result; the limes in this marmalade really give it a zing. It makes a perfect breakfast condiment, especially on fresh home-made Wattleseed Bread (page 171). It is also an ideal glaze for pork or chicken dishes.

To make 6 x 250 ml jars

4 limes, seeded and finely sliced
2 lemons, seeded and finely sliced
5 cups (1.25 litres) water
8 cups (800 g) fresh or frozen riberries
1.5 kg sugar

Preheat the oven to 130°C (300°F).

Simmer the sliced limes and lemons in the water for 30 minutes. Add the riberries.

Heat the sugar on a tray in the preheated oven for 10 minutes and then add to the fruit mixture. Simmer rapidly for an hour.

Test the marmalade by spooning a small amount of jam onto a chilled saucer, and placing it in the refrigerator for a few minutes. The marmalade is ready when it holds its shape on the saucer and doesn't run.

Pour the marmalade into sterilised jars while it is still hot and seal. It will keep for 6 months. Refrigerate once opened.

Riberry Glazed Chicken

To serve 6

6 x 200 g chicken breasts (skinned)
scant 1 cup (225 ml) Riberry Vinegar (see page 65)
⅔ cup (150 ml) macadamia oil
1½ teaspoons (3 g) dried wild thyme
salt and native pepper
1¼ cups (300 g) Riberry Marmalade (see above)
fresh or frozen riberries for garnish
fine julienne of lime zest

Marinate the chicken in the vinegar, oil and wild thyme for at least 2 hours.

Preheat the oven to 180°C (360°F).

Take the chicken from the marinade (keep the juices) and place in a deep oven dish. Season the breasts with salt and native pepper to taste, and coat them with the riberry marmalade.

Place the baking dish in the middle rack of the preheated oven and bake for 30 minutes, or until done to your liking. Transfer the chicken breasts on to a serving platter, cover and keep warm.

Skim off any fat from the pan juices and set the baking dish over a medium heat. Add the remaining marinade to the dish and bring to the boil, stirring and scraping up any brown bits in the pan. Keep simmering until the volume is reduced by a third. Strain the sauce and pour over the breasts. Garnish the dish with riberries and the lime zest.

Riberry and Raspberry Strudel

This is a great twist to a European classic and makes a good summer dessert marrying the flavours of seasonal fresh raspberries and the riberry. For a truly Australian dessert, use native raspberries. Raspberries are a well-loved fruit, and they perfectly complement the riberry in colour and texture.

To serve 8

1 tablespoon (20 g) icing sugar
2 tablespoons (50 ml) warm water
225 g filo pastry
2 generous tablespoons (50 g) unsalted butter, cut into 8 pieces
extra melted butter
castor sugar
fine julienne of orange zest
double cream for serving

Filling
1 cup (100 g) riberries, fresh or frozen
450 g fresh native or European raspberries or good quality frozen raspberries
½ cup (50 g) castor sugar
1 cup (100 g) toasted macadamias, ground

Riberry and Raspberry Sauce
1 generous tablespoon (30 g) castor sugar
¼ cup (50 ml) water
½ cup (50 g) riberries, puréed
150 g raspberries, puréed

To make the Riberry and Raspberry Sauce, bring the sugar and water to the boil and remove from the heat. Purée the riberries and raspberries in a food processor or blender while slowly adding the sugar syrup. Refrigerate until needed and whisk briefly before serving to make sure the fruit has not separated from the syrup.

Preheat the oven to 220°C (425°F).

Make a light sugar syrup by dissolving the icing sugar in the warm water. Layer 4–5 sheets of filo pastry, brushing each sheet lightly all over with the warm syrup. Cut the filo into 8 squares.

To prepare the Filling, toss the riberries and raspberries in the castor sugar and ground macadamia until the fruits are thoroughly coated.

Portion the fruit mix equally between the 8 squares of filo pastry and daub the top of each fruit mound with a piece of butter.

Brush the edges of the pastry with some of the melted butter, fold the pastry into a roll, tuck in the ends and seal all the edges carefully. Lightly brush the top of the strudel with melted butter and sprinkle with castor sugar.

Place the strudels on the top shelf of the preheated oven and cook until they are golden brown.

To serve, gently warm the Riberry and Raspberry Sauce. Pool a small amount of sauce on the side of a white plate and place so that the strudel half sits on it. Sprinkle a few riberries and orange zest over the top of the strudel, and add some double cream on the side if you like.

Creek
Lilly Pilly

Also known as brush cherry, scrub cherry or lilly pilly

To most urban dwellers and gardeners, the creek lilly pilly (*Sygyium australe*) is probably the most well known of the lilly pillies after the common lilly pilly (*Acmena smithii*). May Gibbs incorporated many Australian flowers in her writing, and probably created her character Lilly Pilly while looking at the creek lilly pilly tree in her garden in the Blue Mountains, where it grows prolifically.

The tree grows naturally in rainforests and coastal rainforest or scrub areas, and extends from Queensland to the Victorian border. Despite its natural distribution, the creek lilly pilly can be found almost anywhere in WA, SA, Victoria and NSW, where it is a very popular garden plant and used as an ornamental in many streetscapes and public gardens.

The lilly pilly grows to quite a height if in a favourable position, and is often maligned because of the quantity of fruit it bears and

drops on domestic gardens. The fruit of the creek lilly pilly is rounded or slightly elongated, and usually about 2 cm long. Typically, it has the knobbly tip of most lilly pillies and grows in small clusters. The fruit is usually a deep pink, magenta or even dark purple, and has a small central seed. The creek lilly pilly and common lilly pilly are often confused with each other, as both are such common and well-known trees. The fruit of the creek lilly pilly, however, is much more palatable and interesting to eat than the common lilly pilly. The common lilly pilly is usually pale pink, white or mauve and after the stem has been removed the tip of the fruit has a small depression rather like a mushroom cap.

The texture of the creek lilly pilly is reminiscent of a nashi pear—crunchy, crisp and quite cool and refreshing on the palate. The fruit is good eaten fresh from the tree, or added to a fruit salad, especially a red berry salad, or baked in pies, tarts and puddings.

The creek lilly pillies were widely eaten by the Aboriginal people as a refreshing seasonal addition to their diet. The fruit doesn't have any startling nutritional qualities, but is high in water and has some carbohydrate content.

TO GROW

Syzygium australe
Distribution: Coastal and highland rainforests along the eastern seaboard.

The creek lilly pilly is a rainforest tree growing to at least 10 m, though often taller. It occurs naturally in subtropical and tropical coastal rainforests, in warm mild localities near rivers. In these situations, it can grow very large, sometimes to 30 m. The canopy is dense and a rich dark green, with short, fat, rounded leaves. Though this species originates from warm climates, the creek lilly pilly can also be grown almost anywhere, even in SA and WA. It likes most well-drained, humus-rich soils and will adapt to dappled shade or full sun. A steady water supply will plump up the berries. A dwarf form of creek lilly pilly is also available. *S.* 'Blaze' is a compact form growing to 2 m and would suit a small garden or even a large tub.

As with other lilly pilly species, germination is best from seed, though cuttings are sometimes successful. The fruit may be sown whole, or the flesh removed first. Soak the fruit in water for several days and, before sowing, remove the soft flesh from the seed. Seeds germinate slowly, often spasmodically.

To Harvest

The creek lilly pilly is a prolifically fruiting tree. Much of the fruit can be gathered from low branches, but if you don't want to leave any to the birds you will need to employ a ladder and a few helpers to bag the fruit. I would imagine that for most people the tree will produce fruit far in excess of the amount needed, even if you decide to preserve them in some way. The tree flowers in late autumn and the fruit is ready to harvest during the winter months and, in some areas, even later in the spring.

STORING CREEK LILLY PILLY

The creek lilly pilly is a tasty fresh fruit and will keep in the crisper of the refrigerator for up to a week. As with the other lilly pilly varieties, the fruit of the creek lilly pilly may be frozen whole. Pick through the lilly pillies, discarding any stems or twigs, and place in a freezer bag and freeze. The lilly pilly fruit can be preserved in a light sugar syrup and kept for months in a dark place.

TO COOK

The creek lilly pilly has a central seed which seems quite hard when eating fresh. However, when cooked, the seed softens and is not noticeable. The fruit is attractive whole, and is probably best used in this way. This lilly pilly is not suited to many savoury applications and is at its best in dessert cooking and preserves. The flavour is pleasant, and only slightly acidic, so you can be generous with the amounts used. Try the lilly pilly in a pie, either on its own or perhaps together with other soft fruits such as pears or plums. When baking with lilly pillies, it is best to use them frozen—their colour and flavour will be more effectively retained. Some colour loss during cooking will occur with this lilly pilly, although by comparison it is less marked than the fading of the riberry with heat.

Goes with

Creek lilly pillies have a subtle and delicate flavour. Use them judiciously with the flavour combinations suggested for the other lilly pilly varieties.

Creek Lilly Pilly Syrup

This syrup is good served over fruit or dessert crêpes. The recipe also works with the riberry.

To make 2 cups (500 ml)

1 cup (100 g) creek lilly pillies
2 cups (500 ml) water
2½ cups (500 g) castor sugar

Combine all the ingredients in a medium-sized saucepan. Bring to the boil, stirring constantly to dissolve the sugar. Adjust the heat and simmer for a further 20 minutes. Remove from the heat and strain.

The resulting syrup should be a clear, deep pink colour. The syrup may be sealed in jars or bottles and will keep for at least 6 months in a cool, dark place.

SHORTS

- Bake the lilly pillies in an open tart with a nut cream filling (see Bourdaloue, page 79).

- Make a syrup from the lilly pillies and poach both lilly pillies and white summer peaches in some Creek Lilly Pilly Syrup (above). Cool and chill. Serve in large glass goblets and just before serving or at the table top with chilled champagne.

- Make some lilly pilly jelly. The colour will be a dark wine to purple, and can be incorporated into sauces to serve with lamb. For a dessert jelly that will also appeal to children, prepare a light lilly pilly syrup and add some gelatine. Fresh or lightly poached lilly pillies can be suspended in the jelly, and, if set in a clear glass dish, look very attractive.

Creek Lilly Pilly and Nectarine Cobbler

A cobbler is cooked fruit with a sweet batter-like crust. We've combined creek lilly pillies with nectarines, but you could combine them with berries, any soft fruit or leave them solo.

To serve 6

3½ cups (350 g) creek lilly
    pilly
6 nectarines, sliced
1½ cups (250 g) castor sugar
juice of 1 lemon
generous tablespoon (30 g)
    unsalted butter

Topping
2 x 55 g eggs
⅓ cup (80 g) castor sugar
generous ⅓ cup (90 ml) milk
generous ⅓ cup (80 g)
    unsalted butter, softened
1 ¼ cups (170 g) plain flour,
    sifted
3 level teaspoons (12 g)
    baking powder
1 scant teaspoon (5g) salt

Toss the fruits in the sugar and spread in a lightly greased baking dish. Sprinkle with the lemon juice and dab the butter over the surface. Set aside while making the topping.

Preheat the oven to 180°C (360°F).

To make the Topping, whisk the eggs and sugar together. Whisk in the milk and melted butter, and gradually stir in the dry ingredients, beating well to form a smooth batter. Pour this batter over the prepared fruit, and place the dish on the middle rack of the preheated oven and bake for 30–35 minutes. The batter should be golden and the fruits should be bubbling under their crust.

Serve hot with pure cream.

Illawarra
Plum

Also known as brown pine, she pine

The fruit of the Illawarra plum tree is one of the most highly regarded in the bushfood industry today, largely due to the efforts of a number of innovative chefs such as Jean-Paul Bruneteau from Riberries restaurant in Sydney and Steven Pashley, the Executive Chef of the Gazebo Hotel in Brisbane.

According to Steven, 'Some of the problems associated with the Illawarra plum were similar to those with most of the other types of bushfoods available...What the hell do we do with these things? Then normal experimentation would begin. The first major lesson that most of us learned in a hurry was to cook the Illawarra plum only in stainless steel or ceramic cookware. The plum is highly astringent and therefore has a tendency to adopt a horrible lingering aftertaste...Of course many of the early European settlers paid little attention to the importance of cookware and this flavour-problem has caused the humble plum to be a much maligned and harshly criticised bushfood.'

Thanks to Steven's work, and that of other chefs committed to the use of bushfoods, the Illawarra plum has earned its rightful place as one of Australia's premier bush fruits. People like Steven and his wife, Leonie, have invested more than

their skills in the development of bushfoods as legitimate ingredients. The Pashleys have also established a bushfood plantation west of Brisbane, which includes Illawarra plums, riberries and lemon myrtle.

The fresh Illawarra plum is delicious, with definite plum characteristics and also a slight resinous quality that imparts an unusual and quite refreshing aftertaste. This resinous quality is from the inner 'core' of the fruit and sometimes from the outer skin, which can cause the bitter aftertaste that Pashley mentions. The fruit has good nutritional properties and is particularly high in vitamin C.

Illawarra plum trees have been embraced enthusiastically by many shires and councils as street plantings and park specimens, particularly in Sydney and Brisbane, where they are valued for their appearance and easy maintenance.

TO GROW

Podocarpus elatus

Distribution: Eastern seaboard rainforest from Queensland to southern NSW.

The Illawarra plum tree is a handsome evergreen rainforest tree with a dense canopy, and reaches a maximum size of 30 m. The narrow dark-green leaves are about 7 cm long. The tree likes moisture and rich soils, although it is reasonably adaptable and will grow in many soil types. It is largely frost resistant and adapts well to southern Australian climatic conditions if grown in full sun to part shade. The tree is rather slow-growing, particularly in the south. It can be heavily pruned and makes a successful container plant. Once out of its natural environment, it is doubtful that the Illawarra plum will reach its maximum height in domestic gardens, but it will still grow to a considerable size.

You'll need both male and female trees for fruit, but a male tree can fertilise many female ones. Seeds or cuttings are both suitable methods of propagation. The seed can be removed from the fleshy stalk and sown immediately, but germination is unreliable. Take cuttings when the new growth has hardened off. Cuttings are useful when you're growing trees of a particular sex, or for propagating superior forms. These are not difficult to strike.

Relations

P. lawrencii, or the mountain plum pine from the alpine regions of Victoria and NSW, is a large shrub with edible red fruit on the female plants. *P. spinulosus* from NSW and Queensland also have edible fruit.

To harvest

The Illawarra plum is a high-yielding tree that has fruit ready to pick from May through to June. In a cultivated environment the fruits can be harvested easily from low branches. Birds love the Illawarra plum, so harvest what you can, and then let the wildlife enjoy the rest.

The fruit is a rich, deep purple-black, and the inedible seed actually grows outside and sits at the end of the fruit. This makes the Illawarra plum a most convenient fruit—simply pull the seed away from the flesh, and you're left with a completely usable fruit.

STORING ILLAWARRA PLUM

The Illawarra plum freezes beautifully and, once frozen, will not deteriorate or lose flavour. It is best to remove the seed from the fruit before freezing—simply snap off where it joins the flesh. Seal the plums in freezer bags and freeze until ready to use. The plums may also be preserved in a light sugar syrup.

TO COOK

The Illawarra plum is a very convenient and delicious bushfood to cook with. It is a good-sized fruit about the size of a Waltham grape, and, on average, there are about 300 plums to a kilogram (or 30 per 100 g), which is about 40 plums (130 g) per metric cup.

While the plum has a resinous core which can add bitterness to cooked sauces, chutneys and jams, this can be overcome by removing the core as you would an olive stone. An olive corer does the trick very well. I have noticed, though, that this core is not always intrusive, and its bitterness certainly isn't evident if you're baking the fruit. Taste the Illawarra plum first before preparing the sauce to determine the intensity of the resin flavour. If in doubt, simply core the fruit.

It is important that you cook the Illawarra plums in stainless steel or ceramic cookware. The bitterness in them intensifies when they are cooked in aluminium.

Illawarra plums make wonderful sauces for meats of all kinds, including game such as kangaroo, emu and venison. They are delicious with lamb and all kinds of poultry, and surprisingly good with seafood. Illawarra plums perform extremely well when baked. Put them in scones or muffins, cakes and pastries.

Goes with

My favourite fruits to complement the Illawarra plum are without doubt the lilly pilly and the riberry. Baking them together in a tart (see page 79) is a joy—the rich, dark purples of the Illawarra plums contrast so beautifully against the pinks and reds of the riberries.

Appleberries, lemon myrtle, native mints and the native peppers mix well with Illawarra plums.

Macadamias and bunya nuts can be used with the plums, particularly in desserts. Avoid highly acidic fruits such as the limes and lemon aspen, and also the piquant fruits such as bush tomatoes and cheesefruit. Delicate-flavoured fruits such as white elderberries, dianella berries and quandong may work with the Illawarra plum, but the Kakadu plum will not.

Other fruits and seasonings that will complement the Illawarra plum include apricots, peaches, nectarines, rhubarb, coconut, ginger and chilli. Chocolate, almond and hazelnut are successful when teamed with the plums in desserts.

Illawarra Plum Marinade

This marinade is particularly suited to emu but can be used with poultry and lamb. Place the meat (for example a 1 kg fan fillet of emu) in a suitable container, pour over the marinade, and leave for 24 hours. This is very effective both as a flavour base and also as a meat tenderiser. Once the meat is cooked, garnish the dish with Pickled Illawarra Plums (see page 77). This recipe is enough to marinate 1 kg of meat or poultry.

To make 3 cups (750 ml)

¾ cup (200 ml) red wine
¾ cup (100 g) chopped
 Illawarra plums
1 onion, sliced
3 cloves fresh garlic, minced
1 tablespoon (10 g) ground
 mountain pepper
1 tablespoon (10 g) ground
 lemon myrtle
2 cups (500 ml) macadamia
 oil

In a stainless-steel pot, bring the red wine to the boil with the Illawarra plums, onion, garlic, mountain pepper and lemon myrtle. Boil for about 5 minutes and then cool. When completely cooled, mix well with the macadamia oil.

SHORTS

• Pan-fry prawn tails, or pieces of firm fish fillets that have been coated with shredded coconut. Serve with an Illawarra plum and chilli sauce. The wonderful colour of the Illawarra plum contrasts with the pale gold of the cooked fish.

• Chop Illawarra plums into a marinade and use it for meats that require some tenderising, such as emu. The high fruit acid of the plum will help tenderise and flavour the meat.

• Try an Illawarra plum pudding next Christmas. Substitute a large portion of the traditional dried fruits with Illawarra plums. It's usually best when baking to add the plums frozen or fresh, rather than thawed.

• Make a richly coloured Illawarra plum syrup to pour over fresh fruit.

Pickled Illawarra Plums

These plums make an interesting addition to an antipasto platter or can be served as an accompaniment to lamb or poultry dishes.

To make 6 x 250 ml jars

2 cups (500 ml) white wine vinegar
1 teaspoon (5 g) salt
2 tablespoons (50 g) castor sugar
2 teaspoons (5 g) ground lemon myrtle leaves
2 teaspoons (5 g) ground mountain pepper leaves
1 onion, sliced
3 cloves garlic, minced
10 cloves
4 cups (500 g) Illawarra plums, fresh or frozen, left whole

In a stainless-steel pot bring the vinegar and seasonings to the boil, and let boil for 10 minutes. Add the Illawarra plums and remove from the heat.

Let the plums cool completely in the pickle, and bottle in sterile, airtight jars. These pickled Illawarra plums will keep for up to a year unopened, and for some months after opening if refrigerated.

Illawarra Plum Scones

Many of the bush fruits can be put through a standard scone mix. Fruits such as riberries, muntries and dianella berries work well, but a favourite of ours is made from Illawarra plums; the deep purple of the plums in the creamy scone dough looks wonderful.

To make 12 scones

1 tablespoon (25 g) unsalted butter
2 cups (280 g) self-raising flour
½ teaspoon salt
½ cup (125 ml) milk
⅓ cup (50 g) Illawarra plums, halved

Preheat the oven to 210°C (410°F). Lightly grease a baking tray.

Rub the butter through the flour and salt until crumbs form. Make a well in the middle and pour in most of the milk. A little milk should be reserved for brushing the surface of the scones before baking.

Add the plums and quickly mix from the outside to the inside until a dough forms. Traditionalists insist a knife be used for this process and it seems to work well.

Roll the dough lightly and cut into rounds with a scone cutter or glass. Place the scones on the prepared tray and brush the tops with the reserved milk.

Bake the scones in the preheated oven for about 10–12 minutes.

Illawarra Plum and Chocolate Pudding

This combination of rich chocolate with the slight tartness of Illawarra plums is quite simple and the Wild Rosella and Raspberry Sauce (see page 45) is a lovely contrast against the richness of the pudding. Equally delicious would be a hot chocolate sauce or some lightly whipped cream. You'll need a tall fluted mould of about 1–1.5 litre capacity or 10 individual moulds.

To serve 8 to 10

100 g dark cooking chocolate
6 x 55 g eggs, separated
1 tablespoon (50 ml) honey
100 g finely chopped macadamias or almonds
⅓ cup (50 g) soft bread crumbs (not dried packaged crumbs)
¼ cup (50 g) castor sugar
⅓ cup (50 g) chopped Illawarra plums
canola spray or Pure and Simple or butter for greasing moulds
generous ¾ cup (200 ml) Rosella and Raspberry Sauce (see page 45)

Melt the chocolate in a double boiler, or simply place the chocolate in a small heatproof bowl that sits snugly over the top of a pot with simmering water, stirring occasionally.

Using the paddle attachment of your mixer, or briskly by hand, beat the egg yolks and honey until they start to become creamy. Add the melted chocolate at this stage, and keep beating until the mixture is foamy.

Preheat the oven to 180°C (360°F).

Toss the chopped macadamias with the bread crumbs.

Beat the egg whites with the 50 g of castor sugar until it forms stiff peaks.

Whisk about a third of the stiffened egg white into the chocolate mix. This will make the mixture softer and easier to work with. Gently fold the Illawarra plums through.

Carefully fold the rest of the egg whites and the nut and bread crumbs alternately into the mix in two parts.

Spray or grease the mould/s. Fill with the pudding mix and stand in a deep baking tray in enough hot water to come to within 3 cm of the rim(s). Bake the puddings in the preheated oven for about 35–40 minutes.

The secret to cooking this type of pudding successfully is to keep the water in the baking tray to just under boiling to provide a constant and gentle heat. This ensures that the finished desserts will have an excellent texture. Test if they are cooked by inserting a skewer in the centre—it should come out clean. When cooked, remove from the tray and stand for 5 minutes before unmoulding.

To serve, pour over some Rosella and Raspberry Sauce.

Illawarra Plum and Riberry Bourdaloue

This bourdaloue is a twist on the classic French tart, and a perfect example of the successful melding of traditional cuisine with highly unconventional ingredients. M. Escoffier would need to find a new culinary name for this delicious dessert. In France, apples or even pears would be used, and the nut cream would be almond-based, not macadamia.

However, this dish will delight even the most rigid traditionalist. It tastes divine, and is truly a visually beautiful tart. The deep black purple of the Illawarra plums are contrasted against the delicate pink hues of the riberries, and both are cradled in the golden nut cream that glistens under the finishing glaze.

This bourdaloue is best eaten at room temperature or gently warmed. It can be made well ahead of serving, even the day before. To warm, place on the low shelf of your oven which has been heated to 85°C (200°F) for about 20 minutes. It doesn't need to be hot. It is perfectly complemented by some of the wonderful double creams that are produced in various parts of the country.

To make 1 x 25 cm (10 in) tart, serving 8

200 g Sweetcrust Pastry (see page 184)
1 cup (130 g) frozen Illawarra plums
1 cup (110 g) frozen riberries
½ cup (100 g) Robins Kakadu Plum Jelly or apricot conserve

Macadamia Nut Cream
1½ cups (300 g) unsalted butter
1 cup (150 g) icing sugar
5 egg yolks
1½ cups (150 g) macadamia nut meal (grind whole nuts to a fine texture in food-processor if necessary)
¼ cup (40 g) cornflour

Line the tart case with the sweetcrust pastry. Do not blind bake the pastry as it will cook perfectly raw once filled.

To make the Macadamia Nut Cream, cream the butter and icing sugar using the paddle attachment on your mixer (if possible) until light and creamy. Start off slowly at first, but once the sugar is loosely mixed in with the butter, increase the speed until the colour of the butter mix changes from yellow to a very pale cream. Reduce the speed of the mixer again, and add the egg yolks, one at a time, until completely mixed.

Finally, add the macadamia nut meal and cornflour, and make sure it is well mixed in, but be careful not to overbeat. (Keep the speed of the mixer on low or the mixture will fly everywhere.) The macadamia nut cream at this stage will be quite soft and easy to spread into the prepared tart case.

Spoon the macadamia nut cream into the tart case and, using a small spatula, spread the nut cream evenly to just under the rim of the pastry. The macadamia nut cream will rise during cooking and settle after baking, and a small margin is needed to allow for the rising of the cream so that it doesn't overflow.

Preheat the oven to 180°C (360°F).

Rest the filled tart in the refrigerator for about 20 minutes before baking. This will relax the pastry, and also settle the nut cream so that it doesn't rise too ➤

quickly. If possible, place the filled tart case onto a tray when baking so that it can catch any spills and enable the cook to easily turn the tart around.

Once the tart has rested, scatter the frozen fruits over the surface of the nut cream, patting them gently into place. There is no need to push them down hard into the nut cream as they will naturally sink a little as the cream heats up and softens again.

Place the bourdaloue tart on the middle shelf of the preheated oven and bake for about an hour. Turn the tart after 30 minutes.

After an hour the bourdaloue should be a uniform golden colour although the centre of the tart may look uncooked. Test the centre of the tart with a skewer—if it comes out clean the bourdaloue is ready. It will firm up as it cools. Bring the plum jelly or apricot conserve to the boil with a tiny amount of water and use it to glaze the tart.

Davidson's
Plum

Also known as ooray or sour plum

The Davidson's plum has been called by Tim Lowe 'the Queen of Australian rainforest "plums"', in homage to its exquisite, but extremely sour, taste. The plum looks rather like a native version of the familiar blood plum in size, shape and rich colour. Like the blood plum, the ratio of flesh to stone is high. The Davidson's plum has two flat seeds that, together, are about the same size as the domestic plum. Its flavour differs markedly from the domestic plum in the strength of its sharp acidic taste.

The Davidson's plum grows in limited habitats, and is quite rare. Large bunches of plums form in winter, and are preceded by small pink flowers. The leaves of the Davidson's plum are pinnate, which means that the leaf is segmented into a number of smaller leaflets, and the whole leaf resembles a frond. They are also coarse in texture and covered with fine hairs. The skin of the plum may also have these fine hairs, and may need to be peeled. The trees can be found in specialist native nurseries as the large fronds and drooping bunches of plums are highly ornamental. If you find a Davidson's plum tree in the wild, please refrain from harvesting the fruit—these trees are quite rare, and must not be interfered with. The Davidson's plum sauce or dressing that you may see on restaurant menus is made from fruit gathered from cultivated trees.

TO GROW

Davidsonia pruriens

Distribution: Found in limited rainforest areas in northern NSW and far northern Queensland.

This small, slender native of tropical and subtropical rainforests grows to between 6 and 10 m with a regular crown of frond-like leaves and new pink growth. The leaves are large, coarse and pinnate. The plant only occurs naturally in two areas: north-eastern Queensland and north-eastern NSW. The NSW variety will tolerate cool conditions, but will do best in humus-rich soils where there is warmth and moisture. (There are healthy specimens in the Royal Botanical Gardens in Melbourne.) Both the tropical and subtropical varieties can be very slow-growing. The Davidson's plum is appropriate as a specimen tree for small suburban gardens in the warmer parts of Australia. Two or more plants will probably give better fruit production than a solitary specimen.

Propagate from seed. Remove the small, flat seeds from the pulp and sow immediately.

To harvest

Davidson's plums ripen during the winter months. The fruit is ripe when it the skin is a deep purple in colour and the flesh inside a deep, dark red. It is relatively easy to harvest as it conveniently grows in clusters that hang down from the branches.

STORING DAVIDSON'S PLUM

As with most of the bush fruits, the Davidson's plum can be successfully frozen in its whole raw form with no special preparation.

TO COOK

The sharp, acidic Davidson's plum is deliciously tangy and well suited to sauces, jams, dressings and desserts. It is a most versatile fruit and can be treated in much the same way as blood plums in recipes, but modified to compensate for its strength of flavour and acidity.

The whole Davidson's plum is quite a large bush fruit, and weighs around 50 g (with stone). A cup of cleaned Davidson's plums weighs 130 g, and is equal to three cleaned fruit.

Davidson's plums share the characteristic that is common to so many of our bushfoods in that they are intensely flavoured and, therefore, a little goes a long way. When comparing them to the humble blood plum, be aware that in a recipe using 3 to 4 blood plums per serve, only 1 Davidson's plum is required for the same flavour effect. In some recipes, the flavour you want can be achieved with very little of the native fruit, but the volume of fruit in the recipe may then be too low and the sauce or the pie filling will be too dry and won't work. In this instance, simply add some domestic dark plums to the recipe. We usually work with half Davidson's plums and half blood plums. The Davidson's plum will not lose its fabulous colour when cooked, nor will the flesh break down into a mush. We have never found it necessary to peel the plums; the fine hairs have not been evident in the plums that we have used, so if making a sauce, use the fruit whole and purée to a fine texture. The resulting sauce may be sieved if desired. The tangy Davidson's plum is ideal for sauce-making and suited to both savoury and sweet applications.

Goes with

Wild rosella, despite its tartness, and riberry, are two bush fruits that complement the Davidson's plum. Native cinnamon does too, and fresh ginger.

Davidson's Plum Sauce (Savoury)

Both this and the sweet plum sauce can be made in advance and gently reheated. This piquant, savoury sauce should be served hot with poultry such as chicken or turkey, or with veal or pork.

To make 3 cups (750 ml)

6 Davidson's plums (about 260 g), stones removed and finely chopped
1 cup (250 ml) water
2 cups (500 ml) orange juice
¼ cup (50 g) castor sugar
2 sticks cinnamon
a pinch of chilli powder
2 teaspoons (10 g) freshly grated ginger
a pinch of native (black) pepper
½ cup (125 ml) port

In a medium-sized stainless-steel saucepan, combine the plums, water, orange juice, sugar and cinnamon sticks. Place over a medium heat and gently simmer for 20 minutes.

Remove from the heat, discard the cinnamon sticks and purée the sauce.

Return to the saucepan and add the chilli, ginger and pepper. Add the port and simmer gently for a further 5 minutes or until the sauce reaches a smooth consistency. This sauce will have a sweet-and-sour flavour with the tartness of the plums dominating.

SHORTS

- Substitute Davidson's plum for lemon aspen in the Lemon Aspen Dressing (see page 33) and adjust to taste. Use in salads.

- Davidson's plums work well as jams—substitute the quandongs in Quandong Jam (see page 22) for Davidson's plums.

- Pour Davidson's plum coulis over ice-cream.

- Toss equal quantities of Davidson's plums and blood plums in sugar and almond meal and bake in a pie as in Quandong Lattice Pie (see page 24).

Davidson's Plum Sauce (Sweet)

This sauce may be served hot or cold over pancakes, crêpes, waffles and ice-cream or with fruit, nut or curd tarts.

To make 3 cups (750 ml)

6 Davidson's plums (about 260 g), stones removed and finely chopped
1 cup (250 ml) water
2 cups (500 ml) orange juice
¼ cup (50 g) castor sugar
2 sticks cinnamon
1 cup (250 ml) port
½ cup (125 ml) honey

Follow the instructions for the savoury sauce until the purée stage (see page 84).

Return the sauce to the saucepan. At this stage, add the port and honey, and simmer gently for a further 5 minutes or until the sauce has the desired smooth consistency.

Duck Breast with Davidson's Plums

To serve 6

1 tablespoon (25 ml) canola oil
6 x 200 g duck breasts, skin on
3 cloves garlic, crushed
1 large onion, finely diced
¾ cup (185 ml) fresh orange juice
¾ cup (185 ml) port
¼ cup (80 ml) honey
a pinch of salt
a pinch of native (black) pepper
a pinch of mixed spice
9 Davidson's plums (about 320 g), stones removed and thinly sliced
1 tablespoon (20 g) cornflour, dissolved in a little water

Preheat the oven to 60°C (140°F).
Heat the oil in a large, heavy-based pan (stainless steel or cast iron is best) and place the duck breasts, skin-side down, into the pan. (Do this in batches.) Cook on one side for 2–3 minutes, turn over and cook for a further 2 minutes. Don't overcook. Remove from the pan and keep warm in the oven while you prepare the sauce.

Drain the excess oil from the pan, being careful to retain the duck juices. Return the pan to a low heat and add the garlic and onion, and cook gently until the onion is tender. Add the orange juice, port, honey and seasonings, stirring to dissolve the honey. Add the thinly sliced plums to the sauce and gently simmer for a further 5 minutes.

Turn up the heat a little and quickly stir in the cornflour mixture and cook out for no more than a minute.

Slice the warm duck breasts and lay on the serving plate. Pour the sauce over the breasts and serve immediately.

Appleberry

The botanical name *Billardiera* is given to this plant in honour of the famous French botanist Jacques de Labillardière, who visited these shores in the late–eighteenth century. There are over twenty species of *Billardiera* or appleberries, some of which bear edible fruit. The two main edible appleberries are the common appleberry and the sweet appleberry.

Both plants are pretty, twining creepers that have slim leaves, but different coloured flowers; pale yellow in the common appleberry and bluish-mauve in the sweet. Both clamber over and around other shrubs, and climb by twining around the main stems of their host plant.

Both fruits are small, about 1 to 3 cm long, and sausage-shaped. The fruit of the common appleberry is a dull forest green in colour with a slightly fuzzy surface that is a little like Kiwi fruit. The sweet appleberry has a smoother surface, and the berries turn an almost maroon colour when ripe. Many bush fruits are referred to colloquially as 'berries' but very few actually are in the botanical sense. The appleberry, however, is a true berry, as is the native raspberry. The seeds are immersed in the fleshy pulp under the skin. Each fruit can contain at least 50 or more seeds.

Indigenous Australians have always eaten appleberries; as is when ripe, and roasted when unripe. According to botanist Joseph Maiden's record of 1898, the common appleberry was also one of the first fruits to be appreciated by the European settlers.

TO GROW

Billardiera scandens (common),
B. cymosa (sweet), *B. longiflora* (purple)
Distribution: Shady forests and rainforests,
particularly in southern Australia from
Mount Gambier to Victoria and Tasmania.
Also coastal rainforests up to southern
Queensland and south-west WA.

These essentially temperate-zone plants
occur in many states and in many
conditions, except the very dry, so a semi-
shaded spot suits well. They are hardy, and
adapt well to cultivation, making an
attractive light screen on trellises or fences.
The soil should be warm and well drained,
but the plants will adapt to most sandy, or
even clay, soils, as long as they are watered
regularly. They also do well in pots. When
obtaining a plant, look for a local kind as it
will perform the best. Local plants may
show some variation in flower colour.

The *B. scandens* can be propagated from
seed, which must be fermented before it is
sown. To achieve this, squash the ripe fruit
in a bowl and add a little water. Leave this
for several weeks, and when it starts to
ferment, pour the mass into a sieve and
wash off the flesh. Sow the remaining
seeds. They can take up to six months to
start growing, often germinating the spring
following the sowing. Cuttings can be
taken at any time, although they are
sometimes difficult to strike. The young
appleberry plants grow very rapidly, and
usually fruit in the first year. *B. cymosa*
germinates readily from fresh seed in five
weeks or so.

Relations

B. longiflora, or the purple appleberry, has
a rather dry taste and occurs in cool, wet
forests. Some *Billardiera* species do not
have edible fruit, just capsules that held
the seeds.

To harvest

Appleberries flower from around October
to January, and the fruits start to ripen
from December to July. It is not
uncommon for a plant to have both
flowers and berries forming at the same
time. The fruit of the common appleberry
should not be eaten until it is completely
ripe (translucent and very soft). The
common appleberry should be allowed to
fall to the ground indicating that it is fully
ripened. Once it reaches this stage, collect
it quickly before you lose it to the birds.
The fruit of the sweet appleberry is ripe
when it develops its reddish hue. These
berries may be picked straight from the
plant.

STORING APPLEBERRY

Appleberries, particularly the common appleberry, will not keep for
extended periods, even in the refrigerator, so it's best to freeze them. As
the berries ripen over quite a period of time, you'll need to store them as
they ripen until you have a usable amount for cooking. Don't wash the
fruit, simply wipe over any that are soiled and freeze whole. Appleberries
freeze well, and thaw out without losing their structure.

TO COOK

Appleberries perform very well as a cooked fruit as they hold their shape, texture and colour very well. Their exotic cousins, the raspberry and strawberry, are unable to match the appleberry in all of these respects as they often break down when cooked. While the appleberry does not have the high water content of these fruits, it is still juicy to eat. The whole fruit should be used as you would any berry.

The common appleberry has quite a subtle flavour reminiscent of stewed apples with a touch of Kiwi fruit and the sharpness of grapefruit. As I try to describe these flavours so that they become recognisable to our palates I realise how far we must go before we can say 'It tastes like appleberry', and won't try to compare it to something else. The sweet appleberry has a pleasantly sweet aniseed flavour. Both fruits are quite tasty raw, or can be used to make sauces for pork, veal and chicken. They are too subtle in flavour to mix with the more robust red meats and ill suited to fish or seafood. They are good in baked desserts, particularly in pies, tarts, muffins and fruit scones, or scattered through vegetable and fruit-based salads. Add them to the more usual berries for an interesting berry salad. Appleberries are quite small: they are on average around 2 g each, so there are 50 appleberries, give or take a few, to 100 g, and about 65 (weighing about 125 g) to the metric cup. As they are not an intensely flavoured fruit you will need to use reasonable amounts of them in your cooking. It may be useful to think of the appleberry's flavour as being similar in strength, but not in taste, to the apricot.

Goes with

Other bush fruits such as the lilly pillies, muntries and quandong will complement appleberries.

Season appleberries with native mint and the native peppers. Keep away the very strong-flavoured bushfoods such as wild limes, lemon aspens, wild rosellas and bush tomatoes—these will simply overwhelm the appleberry.

Appleberries will succeed with European fruits such as apples, nashi pears, Kiwi fruit, bananas, peaches and berries.

Medallions of Pork with Appleberries

To serve 6

3 teaspoons (15 ml) canola
oil

1 x 1.2 kg pork fillet, cut into
12 medallions

1½ onions, finely chopped

1 Granny Smith, peeled,
cored and chopped

a pinch of salt

a pinch of native (black)
pepper

1½ tablespoons (70 g) honey

¾ cup (190 ml) cream

¾ cup (90 g) ripe
appleberries, fresh or
frozen

Preheat the oven to 60°C (140°F).

Using a large skillet, heat the oil and sauté the pork medallions in batches until just cooked. Remove the pork and keep warm in the preheated oven.

Using the same pan and retaining the pan juices, add the onion, apple, salt and pepper, and cook until the onions and apple are tender. Then add the honey, cream and appleberries, and simmer for a further 5 minutes.

Return the pork medallions to the pan and coat each one with the appleberry sauce. Place the medallions on the plate and carefully spoon the remainder of the sauce over the meat, ensuring that most of the appleberries are visible on the top.

Serve this rich dish with some freshly steamed warrigal greens tossed with warm balsamic vinegar and some long-grain rice, or with a crisp green salad and new potatoes.

SHORTS

• Make an appleberry pie with equal amounts of Granny Smiths and appleberries.

• Stuff chicken breasts with appleberries and wild rice.

• Scatter sliced appleberries over prosciutto and shaved ham.

• Make an appleberry and berry salad.

Native
Tamarind

Most cooks in Australia today would equate tamarind with Asian cuisines, as it features heavily in Malaysian, Thai and Indonesian cookery. In the far north of Australia, from the Kimberley region to Arnhem land, there are stands of these introduced trees, the legacy of Indonesian fishermen who came in pursuit of the sea cucumber or trepang (also known as bêche-de-mer). Indigenous people from these areas use the introduced tamarind pulp to make a tonic to combat colds as it is high in vitamin C, but not as food. The introduced tamarind is in fact the true tamarind *Tamarindus indica*, which originally came from the African continent. The *Diploglottis cunninghamii*, the native tamarind, is unrelated to the true tamarind and is actually related to the lychee.

The native tamarind is an impressive tree in its natural environment of subtropical rainforests on the eastern seaboard of Queensland and NSW. It is a tall, slender tree and its first branches often occur very high on the trunk. The huge leaves spread out from the top like large fronds, and the fruit forms high up in this canopy.

The fruit is slightly reminiscent of the lychee, having an outer casing which houses the fruit flesh. This outer casing splits open when the fruit ripens. The texture of the flesh is also quite lychee-like—it is a smooth, firm pulp. The fruit is actually the aril, the out-growth of the seed stalk which largely encloses the inner seed. The seed is large in proportion to the flesh and the overall fruit is small—about 1 to 1.5 cm wide. The colour of the native tamarind fruit is a vivid light orange. The fruit is delightfully tart, with a hint of mandarin, and quite juicy.

TO GROW

Diploglottis cunninghamii
Distribution: Widespread in Queensland and NSW coastal rainforests.

The native tamarind is a medium to tall subtropical rainforest tree, growing from 10 to 15 m high. It has very large pinnate leaves, meaning that the leaf is separated into a number of smaller 'leaflets' arranged evenly along the stalk. The tree looks as though it has fronds sprouting at the end of the branches, as each leaf can be up to 60 cm in length. The native tamarind will start to fruit after 2 to 3 years. The tree requires fertile, well-drained soils, a protected position and, given its rainforest origins, reliable watering. It makes a very attractive, tall and exotic-looking specimen tree in a lightly shaded site. In more open positions it tends to spread more, and will succeed in mild coastal districts. It has been grown as far south as Melbourne, although it can be very slow-growing and is frost sensitive. The native tamarind can also be grown as a very attractive—but smaller—tub plant. The plant can be propagated from seed, which should be sown fresh.

Relations

D. campbellii, which is known as the small-leaved tamarind, also has an appetising, but sour, red fruit. This species used to be more widespread, but its habitat has been cleared to a large extent, and it now only grows naturally in northern NSW and south of Brisbane. It is attractive as an ornamental, and as a preservation measure would be worth planting in parks and gardens. *D. berniana, D. bracteata, D. diphyllostegia* and *D. smithii* also have edible fruits, although a few may be too acidic for some palates.

To harvest

The fruit of the native tamarind forms very high on the tree. Once the tree has matured, harvesting the fruit from the tree is almost impossible as it doesn't have many low branches. Wait for the ripe fruit to drop to the ground before gathering. Once the fruit is ripe, the outer casings will have already split, so be quick to gather them up before they rot or ants invade. Fruit bats are also fond of native tamarinds, so don't expect a huge and bountiful harvest—the local wildlife may have well and truly beaten you to it.

STORING NATIVE TAMARIND

Once the native tamarinds are gathered, it's best to freeze them. Before placing in freezer bags, clean the fruit by removing the large brown seed and the outer casing. Once frozen, the native tamarind will keep for months. The native tamarind can also be preserved in a light sugar syrup if preferred.

TO COOK

Goes with

Native tamarind, like lemon aspen, is a very tart, acidic fruit with a strong flavour. This intensity of flavour should be respected. It has a delicious taste like a very sharp and refreshing mandarin, so is well suited to dishes that feature fish, shellfish and white meats. The high acidity of the tamarind also makes it suitable for saucing rich meats such as pork, lamb and duck. The fruit is quite small: 90 cleaned native tamarinds weigh about 100 g, and 1 metric cup of fruit is equal to 120 cleaned native tamarinds (or 130 g). Don't underestimate the fruit's intensity; a cup of cleaned native tamarinds is sufficient to provide the definitive flavour for a sauce for at least 8 to 10 serves of meat or fish. Native tamarinds don't require much processing before they can be added to sauces. Just a rough chop will suffice, or leave them whole, but be aware that they will be strong on the palate. When making and straining a sauce, use a few cleaned native tamarinds as garnish—they are attractively small and their colour is striking.

Native tamarind makes excellent jam and cordial. In 1895 the Queensland Government botanist Frederick M. Bailey exhorted his fellows to encourage the use and development of Australian native plants, both as fruit trees in their own right and for root stock for their less hardy exotic relatives. He was enthusiastic about native tamarind and commented that the 'juicy fleshy aril of sharply acid flavour [is] well suited to jam and jelly. Preserves have a delicious flavour'. A tamarind jam or jelly is beautiful in colour, tangy and well suited to savoury applications such as the base of a glaze for poultry or lamb. Use native tamarind in desserts such as curds, sweet jellies, sauces and sorbets.

As the native tamarind is a sharp, acidic fruit, don't combine it with the other highly acidic fruits such as lemon aspen, wild rosella or the limes. It won't suit the piquant bushfoods either, so avoid bush tomatoes. Native tamarind will be complemented by the native peppers, lemon myrtle and native thyme in certain savoury applications. Wattleseed and kurrajong baked into breads, scones and pancakes provide a base for native tamarind jams and jellies. A well-balanced amount of native tamarind is delicious with quandong in sauces and preserves.

Ginger, lemongrass and chilli can all be used successfully with native tamarind.

Stir-fried Prawns with Native Tamarind

To serve 6

1.2 kg fresh green prawns,
  for 30 tails
3½ teaspoons (20 ml) canola
  oil
½ cup (75 g) native
  tamarind, chopped
6 spring onions, chopped
3 cloves garlic, chopped
2 small or 1 large red
  capsicum, chopped
2 teaspoons (10 g) fresh
  ginger, peeled and grated
a pinch of salt
a pinch of native pepper
generous ½ cup (125 ml)
  dry white wine
200 g warrigal greens

Peel and clean the prawns and cut along the back to open and butterfly the meat.

Heat the oil in a wok on a high heat until very hot and add the chopped ingredients. Toss and cook for 2–3 minutes.

Add the prawns, salt and pepper, and wine, and cook for a further 2–3 minutes, tossing frequently.

Wash and lightly steam the young warrigal greens and make a bed in the centre of a large dinner plate.

To serve, arrange the prawns and vegetables on the warrigal greens and drizzle over the remaining pan juices.

Pork with a Native Tamarind Stuffing

This stuffing is also good with poultry.

To serve 6

6 x 150 g pork fillets
olive oil for brushing

Native Tamarind Stuffing
½ cup (60 g) native
  tamarind, finely chopped
12 prunes, finely chopped
1 large onion, finely chopped
1 tablespoon (25 ml) olive oil
a pinch of salt
a pinch of pepper
1 tablespoon honey
¾ cup (55 g) bread crumbs
1 x 55 g egg

To make the Native Tamarind Stuffing, gently fry the native tamarind, prunes and onion in the oil until the onion is tender. Add the salt, pepper and honey, and remove from the heat. Stir in the bread crumbs and egg to form a stuffing.

Preheat the oven to 160°C (325°F).

Make an incision along each pork fillet to make a pocket. Fill each pocket with the stuffing.

Brush the surface of the pork fillets with a little oil and bake in the preheated oven for about 20 minutes or until cooked to your liking. The pork fillets can be served whole, or sliced into thick medallions for a more elegant presentation.

Chargrilled or Barbecued Baby Chicken with Native Tamarind and Ginger Sauce

The sauce can be made in advance and reheated when needed.

To serve 6

6 x 350 g baby chickens
1 tablespoon (25 ml) olive oil

Native Tamarind and Ginger Sauce
2 teaspoons (10 g) unsalted butter
1 large clove garlic, crushed
1 tablespoon (25 ml) soy sauce
1 tablespoon (40 ml) honey
1 tablespoon (25 g) castor sugar
¾ cup (190 ml) fresh squeezed orange juice
1 tablespoon (15 g) finely grated fresh ginger
¾ cup (100 g) native tamarind, seeded and chopped
2–3 stalks fresh coriander, finely chopped

To make the Native Tamarind and Ginger Sauce, melt the butter in a medium-sized pan and gently cook the garlic until just softened. Add the soy sauce, honey, sugar, orange juice and ginger, stirring until the honey and sugar have dissolved. Add the chopped native tamarind and coriander, and allow to simmer for 10 minutes. Remove from the heat and set aside until ready to serve.

If possible, have your poultry dealer bone the chickens for you, leaving the leg bones and wing bones intact, but not attached to the body of the bird. Otherwise follow the following instructions: place the chicken, breast-side down, on a chopping board. Split along the backbone, pull the wings and the legs apart from the carcass. Pull each side of the bird away from the backbone and flatten the birds out butterfly-style. Using a small, very sharp knife, remove the ribs, breastbone, top of the internal wing bones and thigh bones.

Brush the birds with oil on both sides and chargrill or barbecue, breast-side first, for about 8 minutes. Flip them over and cook the other side for a further 7 minutes or until the birds are tender. Take care not to cook them for too long; this will keep them tender and juicy.

Serve the chickens with the hot native tamarind and ginger sauce poured over them.

SHORTS

- Substitute tamarind jam for marmalade in a brandied marmalade sauce to serve over ice-cream or with steamed puddings.

Muntries

Also known as muntari, munthari, monterry, muntaberry, emu apple

Muntries are a terrific little bush fruit—they are so delicious picked fresh from the plant that you'll have to fight off the kids first before you can harvest any. I'm a firm believer in having our children fully involved in as many bushfood activities as possible, so that they can learn to see their land as a provider.

Muntries taste like fresh apples with a sweet sultana finish, and even look like a tiny apple. They have tiny seeds, are about the size of a large pea, reddish green in colour, with a soft downy skin a little like a peach's. They grow in tight clusters along the branches. The pretty white flowers bloom over spring and early summer, and are similar to flowering gum blossoms. The muntries plant is a prostrate spreading shrub which has been successfully domesticated for use as a rockery plant.

Muntries were a precious Koori food plant for such tribes as the Bunganditj of south-western Victoria and south-eastern SA. In late summer and early autumn Koori tribes and clans would gather to feast on the ripe muntries, often taking large amounts of fruit-laden branches back to their camps. Muntries were so important to the southern coastal tribes that they could be classed as a seasonal staple, and any excess fruit was not wasted but pounded into cakes, dried and stored for the leaner winter months, or traded with other tribes for items such as axe heads. They were also valued by the early European settlers as it made excellent jams and tarts.

TO GROW

Kunzea pomifera

Distribution: Coastal and inland sand dunes near the Victorian–South Australian border. Inland to the Victorian Mallee and desert regions, and the South Australian Coorong region.

Muntries are a vigorous prostrate shrub reaching 2 to 3 m across in favoured sites, which occur in sandy or limestone soils on coastal and inland regions.

They have small, rounded leaves and pretty, scented white flowers that grow in tufts, making them an attractive and hardy groundcover that will succeed in many well-drained soils and conditions. Muntries will tolerate salty conditions and strong winds, and although they grow well in many sites they seem to require alkalinity and full sun to fruit. They should do well in a tub in full sun and are certainly well suited to rockeries.

The seeds are very small and fine, but not difficult to germinate. Collect by storing the fruit in a dry place; the seeds will soon drop out. If you come across a good fruiting stock, cuttings may be taken at most times of the year from fresh, firm growth.

To harvest

Muntries ripen in the late summer and early autumn when conditions are warm and mild. The fruit conveniently grows in dense little clusters along the spreading branches and can be very prolific. They are easy to pick and the plant may be trained along supports to make access easier still.

STORING MUNTRIES

Muntries and quandong are the only southern 'seaside' fruits that the Kooris of the area dried for keeping. The fruit should be picked and removed from the stem, then either dried on a clean sheet in full sun in an airy place, or by a drying machine. The fruit can also be frozen with no loss of quality or flavour. This method is better as it provides more options for cooking. Simply pick over the fruit to discard the stems and bruised fruit, place loosely in freezer bags and freeze.

TO COOK

Muntries have a delicious apple–sultana flavour that is retained with cooking. However, their pretty colouring of soft green tinged with deep red does not fare as well. Unfortunately, with the application of heat over a prolonged cooking time, the fruit changes colour to a rather muddy brown. For maximum colour, if using muntries in sauces, prepare them quickly just before serving. In every other way the fruit performs very well. Its structure remains sound and it doesn't break down as some fruits do.

Muntries are small, on average only about 1 cm in diameter, and 100 g of muntries is equal to 230 individual fruits. That's 2300 per kilogram, and 100 g muntries is equal to a full metric cup. Muntries are not highly acidic or as intensely flavoured as many other bushfoods are. They can be readily incorporated into many recipes where apples are traditionally used. Their delicious flavour is perfect with meats such as pork, chicken and duck, and despite their colour change, muntries are popular in jams, chutneys and relishes. They make a delicious addition to vegetable or fruit-based salads in late summer when they are available fresh.

Muntries and apple pie, muntries strudel and muntries tarts are popular and easy to make. Add muntries to your favourite muffin recipe or bake them in cookies, tea breads and cakes. For the best results add the muntries while they are frozen. Muntries may be pickled or preserved in a light sugar syrup.

Goes with

Muntries will be quite happy alongside the native mints and peppers and can be an attractive partner for cumbungi in certain applications, such as a soup or salad. They will make an interesting combination with appleberries, particularly the sweet appleberry.

Wattleseed, bush bananas, native cucumber, kurrajong and the nuts and lilly pillies will all work well.

Don't use muntries with piquant fruits such as bush tomatoes or the highly acidic fruits like lemon aspen and limes, as these would overwhelm them.

Muntries Sauce

Use this sauce wherever you would use a classic apple sauce. The addition of native mint to the tart apple–sultana flavour of muntries gives it a zing.

To serve 6

1 large onion, finely chopped
olive oil
a sprig of fresh native or
    standard mint, finely
    chopped
1½ cups (150 g) muntries
    berries, fresh or frozen
1½ cups (375 ml) apple juice
¾ cup (190 ml) fresh cream
a pinch of salt
a pinch of pepper

Lightly sauté the onion in a little oil until soft. Add all other ingredients, reduce the heat and gently simmer for about 10 minutes. Serve immediately.

Muntries Muffins

These muntries muffins are an interesting alternative to the more standard blueberry or banana muffin. They are quick and easy to make, and the apple–sultana flavour is a pleasant contrast with the richness of the brown sugar.

To make 24 muffins

3 cups (450 g) plain flour
2 teaspoons (10 g)
    bicarbonate of soda
1 teaspoon (5 g) cinnamon
¾ cup (150 g) unsalted butter
⅔ cup (100 g) brown sugar
1 cup (300 g) honey
1 x 55 g egg
1½ cups (375 ml)
    unsweetened apple juice
2½ cups (300 g) muntries
    berries, frozen or very fresh

Preheat the oven to 150°C (300°F).

Sift the flour, bicarbonate of soda and cinnamon together into a large mixing bowl.

Using a whisk (either manual or electric), cream the butter, brown sugar and honey until pale and fluffy. While still beating, add the egg. Add the apple juice and muntries, and whisk well.

Gradually incorporate the dry ingredients into the mixture, stirring well between each addition. Grease or spray a muffin tray and spoon the muffin mixture into each mould. Dot a few muntries on the top of each muffin and bake in the preheated oven for 30 minutes, then turn up oven to 160°C (325°F) for a further 10–15 minutes.

Roast Loin of Pork with Native Mint and Muntries Stuffing

This stuffing is also perfect for lamb, poultry and other rich meats and makes a good main course, hot or cold, or picnic item.

To serve 6

1 x 1.5–2 kg boneless loin of pork
salt and native pepper
canola oil

Native Mint and Muntries Stuffing
1½ cups (150 g) muntries, fresh or frozen
1 large onion, finely diced
canola oil
200 g fine pork mince
1 teaspoon (2 g) dried or 2 teaspoons (5 g) fresh native mint
½ teaspoon ground native pepper
1 x 55 g egg
1⅓ cups (100 g) bread crumbs

To make the Native Mint and Muntries Stuffing, first thaw the muntries if they are frozen.

Gently pan-fry the onions in a little oil until tender. Combine the pork mince, native mint, pepper, egg, bread crumbs and muntries to form a stuffing.

Preheat the oven to 180°C (360°F).

Lay the pork loin skin-side down and pack the prepared stuffing into the meaty side. Carefully form the pork into a tight roll and tie with kitchen string at 3 cm intervals. Rub the surface of the loin with salt and pepper and a little oil.

Roast on the middle rack of the preheated oven for an hour, and then for a further 1–1½ hours at 160°C (325°F).

When the roast is done and the juices run clear from the meat (test with a skewer), remove from the oven and let it rest, loosely covered with foil, for about 10–15 minutes. Carve into medallions and serve hot with Quandong, Port and Chilli Sauce (see page 23) or allow to cool, and slice thinly.

Muntries and Muesli Cookies

These biscuits will keep for at least a week in an air-tight container. This recipe works best with frozen or very fresh muntries.

To make 30 cookies

2½ cups (500 g) unsalted butter

2 cups (330 g) brown sugar, firmly packed

4 x 55 g eggs

2 teaspoons (10 ml) vanilla essence

2 cups (280 g) self-raising flour

1 teaspoon (5 g) salt

3 cups (160 g) wheatgerm

1¼ cups (100 g) desiccated coconut

1¼ cups (125 g) rolled oats

6 cups (180 g) cornflakes or 11–12 cups good quality muesli

4 cups (500 g) frozen or very fresh muntries

Preheat the oven to 160°C (325°F). Lightly grease an oven tray and line with baking paper.

Cream the butter and sugar until light and fluffy.

Beat the eggs with the vanilla and slowly add to the butter mix. Add the remaining ingredients, except the berries, until well mixed through, then add the berries.

If the berries are frozen, don't allow them to thaw before using as they will cook too quickly and dry out. Leaving them frozen slows their cooking time and they will still remain juicy at the end.

After adding the muntries, use a standard ice-cream scoop to portion the mix and place the balls of cookie mix on the prepared tray. Bake in the preheated oven for approximately 20 minutes.

Let the cookies cool and firm up on the tray before transferring them to an airtight container.

S H O R T S

- Lightly dust a chicken fillet in plain flour and pan-fry each side for 3 minutes. Add the Muntries Sauce to the pan with the chicken, and gently simmer until the chicken is tender. Pour the sauce over the chicken and serve.

- Try an interesting variation on a classic Waldorf salad by substituting muntries for apples and macadamias for walnuts.

- Make a refreshing muntries smoothie with muntries, yoghurt, ice-cream, coconut cream and a little native mint.

- Try fresh or dried muntries in your morning muesli or folded through yoghurt.

Nut

Bunya Nut

Also known as bunya bunya nut. Common usage has shortened this to bunya nut

Bunya pines are most frequently found in public parks and gardens, where they are valued for their striking appearance. These isolated plantings are a poor substitute for what we have lost; many stands of the trees have been sacrificed to the timber industry. The beautifully grained timber of the pine was, and still is, highly valued by carpenters, builders and wood workers.

Bunya nut in its shell

Bunya pines are toweringly tall, with wide girths. Aboriginal tribesmen would carve steps into the sides of the trees to harvest the cones since the limbs and branches were too high to reach and climb in the traditional way. The cones do fall naturally in late summer to autumn however, so take care not to camp under a bunya pine then!

The pine cone can weigh up to 10 kg in a good season, and the nuts, which look rather like very large pine nuts, are encased in large, elongated woody shells within the cone. When shelled, they have a firm, waxy texture, especially if opened fresh from the tree. The shell is lined with a chocolate-brown fibre, much like the pellicle on the chestnut. This fibre usually remains in the shell when you remove the nut, but don't worry if a little is left on the nut, it's edible in small amounts. A good nut is creamy beige in colour with some darker patches, and firm, with no black spots or squishiness. Bunya nuts from the northern trees are usually larger and meatier than those from the south. The flavour is similar to an earthy chestnut, but with quite a different texture, and it is starchy and high in complex carbohydrates.

Bunya pines hold the rare distinction of being the only 'owned' property in Aboriginal culture. Each tribe owns a particular stand of trees, the care and harvesting of which have been passed down through the generations. The nuts are an important ceremonial as well as nutritional food for Aborigines, and there are many accounts of such 'bunya' feasts and the role they played in Aboriginal society. Bunya nut season was also a time to fatten up before the onset of the cooler months.

The nut was eaten raw, roasted, or pound into a meal and formed into cakes that were baked in bunya pine ashes.

TO GROW

Araucaria bidwillii

Distribution: Bunya pines once grew widely throughout the mountains of Queensland and northern NSW. Significant stands still exist in Queensland, in the aptly named Bunya Mountains.

The bunya pine often reaches heights of 50 m in its natural state but when cultivated it may only reach a height of 30 m. It has very spiky leaves and long branches that radiate from the trunk. Older trees have a very distinctive domed shape.

The tree is too large for the average suburban garden but would suit larger gardens, hobby farms and farm plantations. It is very slow-growing, and maturity and the production of nuts may take over 15 years. It is definitely a tree that you plant for your children to reap the rewards.

Although it is a tropical to subtropical plant and appreciates warmth and reliable watering, it is quite hardy and frost-tolerant, and therefore grows well in the southern states of Australia.

The plant should be grown from seed, but it is not easy to germinate. It has two growth sequences: one from the seed to a tuber, and months later, a second growth spurt, when the tuber begins to grow. It can be difficult to stimulate either sequence and it's probably easier to obtain established plants from specialist native or fruit tree nurseries. Although not widely available, most of the larger native nurseries stock or know where the trees can be found.

To harvest

Like many bushfoods, bunya nuts are at their best every alternate (or even three-year) season. The female cone is the fruiting one and ripens over the summer months. It is usually ready for harvest from January to March. The cones form high on the tree and unless the harvester is extremely agile and an experienced tree climber (as the boughs on a mature fruiting bunya pine are very high up), it's probably wise to collect the cones when they ripen and fall to the ground. The cone is very large and green in colour, and the bunya nuts (usually 30-plus per cone) are held firmly inside. A sharp knife will usually get the nuts out of this husk without too much trouble.

STORING BUNYA NUTS

Bunya nuts are plentiful in a good season. They can be eaten raw when ripe and fresh, but if you want to keep them they are best frozen after harvesting. This is necessary as the nut will deteriorate in its shell; mould may invade, and the nuts will blacken and become mushy. Even if no mould appears the nuts can dehydrate and become dry and mealy. To freeze, cut the nuts out from the cone and freeze them whole in their wooden shell.

TO COOK

Bunya nuts can be eaten raw, if from a very fresh cone, or cooked, but first you need to get rid of the hard shell. They can be shelled raw but it is quite difficult. Boiling the nut first softens the shell for easier opening, cooks the nut and also rehydrates it if it has been kept for some time (within a fortnight of harvesting the nut will dry out and become quite hard).

To shell and cook: Boil the nuts for 20 to 25 minutes. Place the shell large-end down on a chopping board (perhaps on a tea-towel to steady it). Insert a small, strong paring knife into the very top of the shell, which is the softest part. Being very careful not to cut yourself, bring the knife firmly down to the base of the nut. Pull the shell open and extract the two halves.

The cooked nut has a wonderful waxy texture and is now soft enough to slice, cut or purée (although you will need a fairly heavy-duty food-processor for the latter).

Boiled bunya nuts can be puréed and blended with a light sugar syrup. This will help stabilise the nut and it will keep, refrigerated, for about 10 days if required. Once the nut is in this form it can be added to desserts such as mousses, bavarois or creams.

The raw nut has a drier, harder texture that is better for processing into a meal for baking in breads or cakes. Once prepared bunya nut meal can be kept in a tightly sealed container for a month.

The Bunya wood imparts a delectable flavour to smoked meats or fish. This is only advisable if the tree that the wood is taken from is quite mature and its survival is not threatened in any way.

Goes with

Bunya nuts are versatile and will harmonise with many of the bushfood flavours. In a savoury recipe, they will be complemented by bush 'herbs' such as the peppers, mints, thyme and lemon myrtle. Bunya nuts also team well with cumbungi, wattleseed, native yams and tubers. Sugarbag, while not a bush fruit as such, is divine when used with the bunya nut.

Try bunya nuts with vegetables such as leeks, potatoes, sweet potatoes and pumpkin. Some salad greens also work well.

In desserts, chocolate and caramel complement the earthy chestnut-like flavour.

Chicken Breast with Bunya Nut and Bacon Stuffing

This stuffing also works well with turkey.

To serve 6

6 x 200 g chicken breasts
1 tablespoon (20 g) plain
   flour
1 tablespoon (25 ml) olive oil

Bunya Nut and Bacon Stuffing

1 tablespoon (25 g) unsalted
   butter
1 onion, finely diced
3 rashers bacon, finely diced
1⅓ cups or 15 (225 g),
   bunya nuts, boiled and
   shelled (see page 105)
a pinch of salt
a pinch of native (black)
   pepper
¾ cup (80 g) grated cheddar
2 x 55 g eggs, beaten

To make the Bunya Nut and Bacon Stuffing, heat the butter in a medium-sized skillet and cook the onion and bacon until the onion is tender. Finely chop the bunya nuts and place in the pan with the onion and bacon. Add the salt, pepper and grated cheese, and stir until the cheese melts.

Remove from the heat and briskly stir in the eggs, mixing well. Allow the stuffing to cool.

With a sharp knife, make an incision in each chicken breast to form a pocket for the stuffing. Put the stuffing into the pockets. Dust the stuffed chicken breasts in the flour. Heat the oil and sauté the chicken for 10 minutes on the first side. Turn the breasts and cook for a further 5–10 minutes.

These stuffed chicken breasts are delicious with a Wild Rosella Sauce (see page 45). The tartness of the wild rosella provides an interesting counterpoint to the rich stuffing.

SHORTS

- Boiled bunya nuts puréed with a little cream are a good alternative to traditional starches such as potatoes or rice (you will need a fairly heavy-duty food-processor). Add bunya nuts to casseroles instead of potatoes or serve creamed bunya nuts instead of mashed potatoes.

- Boil some bunya nuts for about 20 minutes then eat them straight from their shells while still hot, with a little salt.

- Use ground bunya nuts in place of almond meal in a cake.

- Add some interest to your next fudge by adding some bunya nuts.

Bunya Nut and Sugarbag Bavarois with a Malt Whisky Custard

Sugarbag is the honey from native bees and has a wonderfully bittersweet flavour that is quite different from honey from introduced bees. If you can't find it substitute with a good-quality Tasmanian leatherwood honey. This dessert can be made a day in advance. You will need 10 dariole moulds or 1 x 25 cm (10 in) plastic or stainless-steel cake ring.

To serve 10

Bavarois

1½ cups (375 ml) milk
2 teaspoons sugarbag or
  1 tablespoon (40 g)
  leatherwood honey
10 egg yolks
generous 1½ cups (400 g)
  castor sugar
1¼ tablespoon (25 g)
  powdered gelatine
3¼ cups (800 ml) thickened
  cream
1⅔ cups (200 g) bunya nuts,
  (10 nuts) boiled, shelled
  and finely diced (see page
  105)

Malt Whisky Custard

2½ cups (600 ml) milk
6 egg yolks
scant ½ cup (100 g) castor
  sugar
¼ cup (65 ml) malt whisky or
  good quality scotch

To make the Malt Whisky Custard, bring the milk to the boil in a medium-sized saucepan. Combine the egg yolks and sugar in a large bowl and, with a balloon whisk, mix until creamy.

Remove the milk once it comes to the boil and slowly pour into the egg mixture, taking care to whisk all the time so the eggs do not scramble.

Pour the mixture back into a clean saucepan and place over a low heat, stirring constantly with a wooden spoon until the custard starts to coat the back of the spoon. Remove from the heat and strain through a fine sieve into a clean bowl. Cool in the refrigerator and whisk gently occasionally to distribute the heat. When lukewarm, add the malt whisky and allow to cool completely. The custard will thicken slightly when completely cold.

To make the Bavarois, bring the milk and the honey to the boil in a large saucepan.

While waiting for the milk, place the egg yolks and sugar in large bowl and, using a balloon whisk, mix until thickened and creamy. Once the milk comes to the boil, remove from the heat and slowly ladle it into the egg and sugar mix, whisking gently all the time.

Pour the mixture back into a clean saucepan. Stir constantly with a wooden spoon over a low heat until it starts to coat the back of the spoon. Once the mixture starts to thicken, remove from the heat and strain through a fine sieve into a clean bowl. Place in the refrigerator to cool, whisking occasionally to distribute the heat and keep the texture silky smooth.

Stir the gelatine into some cold water until it is completely dissolved and add to the lukewarm custard.

Whip the thickened cream until the whisk starts to leave trails in the mix, being careful not to overwhip. ➤

Fold the cream through the mixture, followed by the diced bunya nuts, making sure they are well distributed.

At this stage the bavarois should be of a pouring consistency. Pour into the prepared moulds and set in the refrigerator for at least 2–3 hours.

To serve, spoon about 6 teaspoons of the whisky custard on the side of a medium-sized plate. Dip the dariole moulds, in a bowl of hot water for about 6–8 seconds. Gently invert the mould to release the bavarois. Do this carefully over the serving plate and don't be afraid to turn it out onto your fingers first before placing it on the plate. If it is difficult to unmould, gently slip a sharp fine-bladed knife up one side of the mould to break the seal. (If using a cake ring: run a clean tea-towel under very hot water, wring out excess moisture then wrap around the cake ring.)

Bunya Nut and Ginger Soup

To serve 6

1 tablespoon (25 g) unsalted butter
2 cloves garlic, crushed
2 onions, chopped
4 medium-sized desirée potatoes, peeled and diced
1 tablespoon (15 g) peeled and finely grated fresh ginger
1¾ cups (300 g) boiled, shelled and minced bunya nuts (about 25 nuts)
a pinch of salt
a pinch of native (black) pepper
4 cups (1 litre) Chicken Stock (see page 182)
½ cup (125 ml) thickened cream

Melt the butter in a large saucepan and cook the garlic and onion until tender. Add the potato, ginger, bunya nuts, salt, pepper and stock, and bring to the boil.

Lower the heat to a simmer and boil until the potato is well cooked, about 20 minutes. Remove the soup from the saucepan and allow to cool a little before blending to a purée. Once blended, return to the saucepan and reheat the soup. Stir in the cream, bring back to a good simmer, and serve.

Macadamia

Do Australians need a more object lesson regarding the value of our indigenous foods than the macadamia? The American agriculturists virtually hijacked the macadamia from Australia, despite the fact that it was identified early on by Australian colonialists as valuable. As early as the nineteenth century, loggers were not allowed to fell the macadamia, and by 1900, local botanists were signalling that this tree should be cultivated for its wonderful nut. By this time, however, the Americans had already taken seeds to Hawaii for plantations and made the macadamia their own. It wasn't until 1963 that the first commercial macadamias were planted in Australia, and from that time on, the macadamia industry has become a multi-million dollar one for this country. Unfortunately, in international markets we still lag behind the American producers.

The macadamia is but one edible nut that is native to Australia, and along with the bunya nut, candlenut, red bopple nut, native cashew and native peanut was an important Aboriginal food. Macadamias are high in energy and fat and have a very high oil content—if you light one, it will burn off its oil for 5 to 10 minutes.

The macadamia tree is a subtropical rainforest specimen with hard green leaves, dense spikes of white flowers in winter and spring, and very smooth, hard-shelled nuts that form in small clusters. Like other rainforest nuts, the macadamia's high oil content nourishes the seedlings, giving them a better chance of survival on the forest floor.

I remember buying fresh macadamias when they first became available back in the seventies, and trying to shell them. I tried a hammer first but the nuts just bounced all over the place. I was eventually successful after steadying the round nut on a nest made from a tea-towel and whacking them with a brick.

TO GROW

Macadamia integrifolia

Distribution: Coastal, subtropical rainforest NSW and Queensland border area.

Macadamias are small to medium trees that grow to 12 m, although in their native rainforests they can exceed this height. They are a dense tree and are very suitable as a specimen plant. They need a steady water supply and grow well in most good soils in milder climates, but need protection from harsh winds and frosts. The tree can take many years to develop, and won't bear until its third to fifth year, especially in cooler climates.

Propagation is usually from seed, although professional propagators can graft good forms. Although the capsule is very hard, macadamias germinate readily. Sow the nuts into deeper pots in warmer weather. Growing from seed often means that the quality and quantity of nuts can't be guaranteed—a quality purchased plant may be the better option.

Relations

M. tetraphylla or the rough-shelled macadamia is the only other macadamia with an edible nut that doesn't need extensive processing, however the tree is quite rare. Many of the cultivated macadamias are hybrids between *M. integrifolia* and *M. tetraphylla*. Some species bear fruit toxic to humans so cultivate only the two listed here.

To harvest

The nuts are usually ready to harvest a year after the previous year's flowering. When the macadamia nuts are ready, some will split open and fall from the tree. A good, mature macadamia tree may bear up to 100 kg of nuts in season, although this quantity varies significantly with climate and local conditions. The nuts are easy to pick from the tree.

STORING MACADAMIA NUTS

If the nuts are left in their very hard shells they can be kept for at least 12 months without spoiling. Once shelled, the nuts will keep for some months in an airtight container.

TO COOK

Most cooks are used to purchasing macadamias that are already shelled, roasted or raw, and ready to use. If you do aquire them in their shells however, you can now buy a special macadamia nut cracker from specialist nut or food shops.

The nut is extremely versatile. Once shelled, it can be eaten raw or oven-roasted to bring out the fabulous flavour in the oil. It is best used raw if you want to cook it in cakes, biscuits and puddings, for example, the ubiquitous chocolate chip cookie is delicious with the inclusion of chopped macadamias. Use oven-roasted nuts in ice-creams and mousses, namely dishes without a second cooking process.

Substitute macadamia nut meal in recipes that call for almond, hazelnut or other nut meals. The flavour can be very rich with straight macadamia nut meal so use a blend of macadamia and almond meals. I adore some of the French nut-based desserts and tarts, and the macadamia can easily be used in many of these recipes.

SHORTS

- Replace the frangipane in a Pithivier (a superb puff pastry envelope) with macadamia nut cream (see page 79). The cream is placed on a puff pastry base, covered with another circle of pastry, sealed around the edges, decorated and baked. It's a simple procedure with a stunning result, especially if made with macadamias.

- Try macadamia pie instead of pecan pie.

- Coarsely ground raw macadamias are wonderful in stuffings and in crusts for meat dishes.

Macadamia Nut Crust for Loin of Lamb

To serve 6

1 x 1.2 kg boned loin of
  lamb with flap, trimmed
  (ask your butcher to bone
  out and trim)
4 tablespoons (150 g)
  wholeseed mustard
2 teaspoons (5 g) native mint
1 cup (100 g) very finely
  chopped macadamias
  (almost a meal)
2½ tablespoons (50 g)
  wattleseed, roasted and
  ground (see page 167)
1 teaspoon (5 g) salt
1 teaspoon (2 g) native
  (black) pepper

Preheat the oven to 180°C (360°F).

Lay the loin 'fat'-side down on a large board and pull the flap away. Spread half the mustard and half the mint along the inside of the loin and pull the flap back. Roll the loin back into its original shape and tie with butcher's string at 2 cm intervals to secure. Spread the remaining mustard along the top of the loin.

Combine the macadamias, wattleseed, salt and pepper and the remaining mint and press into the mustard to form a crust around the loin.

Place the loin crust side up on a baking tray and bake for 35 minutes if you like your lamb pink, or 45 minutes if you prefer it cooked through. Rest the loin in a warm place for 10 minutes before carving.

This lovely roasted lamb in a crust would be great served with Wild Lime Sauce at the side (see page 13).

Macadamia Nut and Honey Tart

To make 1 x 22.5 cm
(9 in) tart

300 g Sweetcrust Pastry (see
  page 184)
1¼ cups (250 g) unsalted
  butter
1½ cups (250 g) firmly
  packed brown sugar
¼ cup (50 g) castor sugar
½ cup (125 ml) honey
2 cups (200 g) macadamias,
  coarsely chopped
¼ cup (60 ml) cream

Roll out the pastry to fit the 22.5 cm tart tin, trimming off any overhang. Bake blind (see page 184), and set aside to cool.

Using a heavy-based, medium-sized saucepan on a low heat, melt the butter with the brown sugar, castor sugar and honey. Stir constantly until the butter has melted and the sugars have completely dissolved. Allow the mixture to come to the boil and cook for 2–3 minutes, taking care that the sugar does not catch. Fold the macadamias and cream through the mixture and cook for a further 1–2 minutes. Remove the saucepan from the heat and while the filling is still hot, pour into the prepared tart case. Smooth the mixture evenly into the tart with a spatula if necessary.

Place the filled tart in the refrigerator to chill. The filling will set firm and be easy to cut.

Drizzle melted chocolate over the top in thin lines in a lattice pattern or decorate with long chocolate curls.

Macadamia Lavoche

Lavoche is a wafer-thin 'crispbread' that can be served with soup, dips, cheese and pâtés. It will keep for a week if stored in an airtight container.

To serve 6

2½ cups (345 g) plain flour
2 teaspoons (10 g) salt
2 teaspoons (10 g) castor sugar
2 tablespoons (50 g) unsalted butter
2 teaspoons (10 ml) milk
3 tablespoons (60 ml) water
1 egg yolk
½ cup (50 g) finely chopped macadamia nuts
2 teaspoons (10 g) sesame seeds

Mix together the flour, salt, sugar and butter. Once the butter is well distributed throughout the dry ingredients, add the milk, water and egg yolk, and work until a firm dough is formed. Cover the bowl and rest the dough for at least an hour in the refrigerator.

Line a baking tray with baking paper. Preheat the oven to 160°C (325°F).

Roll out the dough as thinly as you can. The finished lavoche should only be as thick as a corn chip, so work quickly, taking care not to overwork. Cut the lavoche into long triangles and carefully place on the lined baking tray.

With a pastry brush dipped in water, lightly brush the surface of the lavoche and sprinkle with the chopped macadamia and sesame seeds. Bake in the preheated oven until the tops are a light golden brown.

Leaf
Stem
Tuber

Portulaca

Also known as pigweed, purslane, poor man's spinach, munyeroo and by various other Aboriginal names depending on region

Portulaca grows extensively over most of Australia, from the coast to the outback. It's a relative of the Portulacaceae plants that are found all over the world, and is an ancient food not only in Australia but also in the early cultures of India and Iran. The plant was used by Australian colonials as a spinach substitute, particularly in remote areas, hence one of its common names—poor man's spinach. Today the plant is widely used as a salad leaf or vegetable and, in some countries, has been developed into specialised varieties that reflect the desired leaf size and colour.

In the Australian wild the plant is a low-growing and sprawling succulent, with bright green, oblong-shaped leaves, that produces prolific bunches of small yellow flowers in summer. These are followed by seed pods that hold up to 10,000 tiny black seeds.

The entire plant is edible—the leaves, seeds, flowers and even its roots, and is a good source of essential minerals, protein, fibre and water. The outback Aborigines found that Portulaca made an excellent paste as its stems and leaves contain a mucilaginous substance; when they are ground together the water which is released reacts with this substance to form a sticky gelatinous paste. This sticky paste was rolled into balls and eaten, or dried and reconstituted for use as needed. The cakes would also be cooked on hot stones.

The seeds can be collected and ground and used in breads or damper.

Because the whole portulaca plant contains oxalic acid, it can be poisonous if *large* amounts are consumed (meaning if you eat nothing but portulaca all day long!).

Portulaca also has medicinal properties. It is high in vitamin C and was valued by the Aboriginal people as an antiscorbutic remedy. It is also potassium-rich, and acts as a cooling diuretic for urinary-tract inflammation and bladder diseases. As well as being useful against scurvy, and painful urination, it can also be applied as a poultice to burns, scalds and skin diseases.

TO GROW

Portulaca oleracea

Distribution: Widespread across the continent, particularly in central Australia.

P. oleracea makes an excellent and useful ground cover as it grows quickly and can form dense mats, but becomes weed-like if not carefully watched.

Portulaca grows well throughout the country where there is reliable moisture, and is very adaptable. It works well as an early colonising plant on disturbed soil, and will even do quite well in salty depressions and other inhospitable places. The plant does, however, need a well-drained site. The seeds from the portulaca will germinate readily.

Relations

Large pigweed or *P. intraterranea* is another edible pigweed.

To harvest

Once portulaca becomes established it can form a thick mat of vegetation which may be harvested at any time. Take care, however, when the plant is flowering. Pick the portulaca stems when they are at least 6 to 7 cm long to protect the younger shoots, and make sure that you leave some of the leaves at the base of the stem so the plant can sprout from this point. This is also an effective way of keeping the plant under control, as it can readily spread into areas where it is not wanted.

The seeds can be harvested a few weeks after the plant has flowered (over summer is best). The seeds are ready for collection when they have turned a straw colour. Follow the example of the Aboriginal people and lay the stems laden with seed over a surface that will catch them as they dry and fall. It only takes a few days for the seeds to completely fall from the stems. These seeds can then be used freshly ground and baked into a damper, or stored for future use.

STORING PORTULACA

Portulaca leaves are best used on the day they are picked. The leaves and stems may be stored in a sealed plastic bag in the bottom of the refrigerator and will last for a few days. You could try making a seasoned paste from the leaves and drying it as the Aborigines do, but this is more an interesting exercise than an efficient storage system in an urban context. The seeds may be harvested and stored in a clean airtight glass container in a dark place, where they will keep for many months.

TO COOK

Goes with

Portulaca can be used in a salad, in a savoury vegetable dish or as an interesting vegetable alternative in other dishes. It needs little preparation, and retains its colour after cooking. The entire leaf is usable. The slimmer portions of the stem can also be used. The thick parts of the stem are edible, but are sometimes a little tough.

Steaming or cooking in the microwave is the best way to conserve the plant's nutritional properties, although blanching it as a green vegetable has become a common technique. Keep the lid off when blanching so that the oxalic acid doesn't condense and drip back into the pot. Like many bushfoods, portulaca has an acidic and slightly bitter flavour edge, with a distinct tomato flavour. Outback Queenslanders often refer to it as the 'tomato plant'. Although the leaf structures of both plants are absolutely different, it may be instructive to place portulaca in the same flavour category as tomatoes and other salad plants such as endive or radicchio.

The raw portulaca leaves, while tasty and a little tart, have a slightly slimy feel in the mouth despite their crunchy texture. This is because of the mucilaginous quality in the plant's composition, and varies from plant to plant. Wash the portulaca very well before use, and if it's still a problem, blanch the leaves and cool them again before using.

The seeds from the portulaca are hard and have an oily texture. To date there has been no simple way to mill these seeds to produce a flour. The Aborigines used to hand-grind the seeds to obtain a fine flour, which is difficult and tedious work.

Portulaca has often been referred to as the poor man's spinach and the 'tomato plant', so use them as your flavour cues. The leaves are best seasoned with the aromatic bush herbs such as native thyme, native pepper and lemon myrtle. Bush tomato would add to the portulaca's own innate bitterness and should be avoided.

Wendy's Portulaca Pie

Wendy Phelps and her husband David operate Longreach Bush Tucker, which has been involved in research into and the growing of many bushfoods since 1988. This is a simple dish to prepare and can also be baked as a baby quiche and served as finger food. The serving platter could be garnished with a spray of portulaca in bloom.

To make 1 x 25 cm tart

500 g Shortcrust Pastry (see page 183)
2 cups (150–200 g) fresh portulaca
2 teaspoons (10 g) unsalted butter
1 small onion, diced
4 rashers bacon, diced
4 x 55 g eggs
½ cup (125 ml) milk
½ cup (50 g) grated mozzarella

Preheat the oven to 160°C (325°F).

Roll out the shortcrust dough to fit your quiche dish or pie plate.

Trim the portulaca, discarding any large stems and keeping the finer ones. Blanch them until just tender with the lid off, drain and set aside.

Melt the butter in a small pan and quickly sauté the onion and bacon. Whisk the eggs with the milk and add the onion, bacon and portulaca.

Sprinkle half of the grated cheese on the base of the pie plate, pour in the filling and cover the surface with the remainder of the cheese.

Bake in the preheated oven for 40 minutes until the crust is golden.

SHORTS

- Try portulaca as a steamed vegetable seasoned with a little native thyme and olive oil or as a salad with a Lemon Aspen Dressing (see page 33) or Lemon Aspen Mayonnaise (see page 33).

- Use portulaca in dishes that rely heavily on a green vegetable component such as spanakopita (Greek filo triangles), quiche or savoury tarts. Try a portulaca, ham and cheese pie or a portulaca pesto.

- Portulaca pickles well for use as an antipasto, or use it fresh as a garnish.

Samphire

Samphire, like portulaca, is an ancient food plant that is found throughout the world. In Europe, *Sarcocornia stricta* is often known as sea fennel or Peter's cress, and is used by the British and French as a cooked vegetable or pickled in vinegar like gherkins. In the early years of white settlement in Australia, samphire, seasoned with other herbs, was used by the British to combat scurvy and hunger.

Samphire is so redolent of the sea. I live by the bay in Melbourne and am very familiar with a *Sarcocornia* subspecies that grows on the rocky outcrops that jut into the sea all the way down the coast of the Mornington Peninsula. Our local version is quite small and clings in small clumps to the rocks, but I have seen superb large specimens that have colonised rocky ledges in quite large masses on ocean coasts.

Samphire is an interesting-looking plant. Its succulent, smooth-skinned stem is segmented along its length, and varies in colour from a deep olive green to a deep red, and the colour changes with the seasons. As the samphire is often immersed under the salty tide, the flavour of the stem is salty, and something like snake beans. Because of its salt tolerance, samphire is being used in the Mallee and Wimmera areas of Victoria to combat soil degradation from salinity caused by the rising water table in agricultural areas that have suffered from too much irrigation and overwork. Unlike the samphire subspecies found in tidal mudflats, coastal marshes and mangrove swamps, some samphire, especially the older stems, can have a woody core. You will need to discard these pieces before cooking.

TO GROW

Sarcocornia quinqueflora

Distribution: Coastal and inland, all states except NT.

Samphire is a succulent that grows from 5 to 20 cm in length on coastal flats and salt marshes, and will grow well in areas with high salinity. It has fleshy, leafless stems that are segmented like a long sequence of beads, and a twiggy habit. Small flowers appear in spring. It is a useful plant in salt-affected areas with poor drainage, and also does well in dry rocky soils. This plant is easy to strike both by cuttings and division.

To harvest

Samphire is at its best for picking between November to March. After this, especially in the southern states, the samphire dies down and becomes thinner and smaller in size and is less prolific.

STORING SAMPHIRE

It's best not to freeze samphire. It will keep for a few days in an airtight plastic container or in a jug of water as you would keep parsley. Samphire pickles beautifully, and when its at its peak in summer, preserve it in a light pickle for use throughout the year.

TO COOK

Use samphire as a vegetable and also as a salt substitute.

Pick through the samphire and snap off any woody sections and/or discard the stem as you would asparagus. Use only the succulent fleshy stems. Because of its saltiness and its close association with the sea, samphire is perfect to serve with fresh fish and seafood. I usually leave the stems in their original state before cooking and serving. The saltiness is not as evident in the thinner younger stems. Samphire growing in a non-saline area may not be as salty. If the salty flavour is too strong, leach the samphire by blanching it before use. As a precaution, suggest to your guests that they may not need table salt for a dish that has samphire in it. Steaming is an excellent way of cooking samphire—it leaves the stems in a good firm condition, and the flavour intact. As a guide for incorporating samphire into recipes I have found that a very generous handful of samphire weighs about 100 g.

Goes with

Lemon myrtle, lemon aspen, wild lime, warrigal greens, wild thyme, native pepper and native mint can all be used with samphire. It will not be complemented by the lilly pillies, wild rosella or the rainforest plums.

SHORTS

- Steam the samphire stems and quickly finish in a little butter, cream and pepper, or serve with a squeeze of lemon and a little cracked black pepper or melted Wild Lime, Ginger and Coriander Butter (page 11).

- Good, firm stems can be used as a salad or vegetable with delicious dips or dressings such as the Lemon Myrtle Dressing (see page 143) or Lemon Aspen Mayonnaise (see page 33).

- Use samphire as a bed for baking fresh fish. Lay a good thick bed of samphire on the bottom of an oven tray or dish and the fresh fish fillets on top. Squeeze over some lemon juice, sprinkle with ground lemon myrtle and native pepper, add a splash of white wine and cover with foil and bake.

- Try a seafood stir-fry with samphire or add into any stir-fry.

- In some cuisines, samphire is pickled and used as a gherkin substitute. Pour enough good vinegar, such as a Lemon Myrtle Vinegar (see page 139), into a sterilised jar to cover the samphire and season with some mountain pepper (in whole leaf form) or pepperberries. Seal and leave to pickle for at least three months. Use this in antipasto or in sandwiches with smoked salmon or tuna and cottage cheese.

Leaf Stem Tuber

Warm Samphire Salad

To serve 6 (entrée size)

1 large bunch samphire
(about 150 g or about the
same amount as you would
use for an asparagus
entrée)
1 red capsicum
1 green capsicum
1 yellow capsicum
1 Spanish onion, sliced
1 tablespoon (25 ml) olive oil
cracked black pepper to taste
Lemon Myrtle Dressing (see
page 143)

Set up a steamer over boiling water and add the samphire. Steam until the samphire is just tender but still retaining some crispness, about 6 minutes. When ready, refresh quickly in some ice-water to stop the cooking process. Drain the samphire and set aside.

Slice the capsicums into long, thin strips the same length and width as the samphire.

Heat the oil in a wok or shallow frying pan and quickly toss the vegetable strips in the oil and sauté until tender.

Add the cooked samphire at the end to warm through and season with the cracked black pepper. Don't season with salt as the samphire will have plenty of 'salty' flavour.

Just before serving, drizzle the salad with the lemon myrtle dressing.

Samphire Pesto

This light pesto can be tossed through pasta or stirred through hot rice. Spread it on chicken or fish before baking. Use it to flavour a dip or mayonnaise.

To make 3 cups (750 ml)

a large handful (100 g)
samphire
2 tablespoons (100 g)
roasted pine nuts
a pinch of salt
a pinch of ground native
(black) pepper
1½ cups (350 ml) olive oil
2 tablespoons (50 g) freshly
grated parmesan

Wash and dry the samphire. Place in a food processor with the pine nuts and process to a paste.

Add the salt and native pepper, and slowly pour in the oil with the motor running. Once all the oil has been incorporated, add the parmesan.

The pesto should be a smooth but loose, paste-like texture so adjust with oil if necessary. When the pesto is ready, pour into a sterilised jar. It will keep in the refrigerator for a few months.

Steamed Crab with Samphire

To serve 6

6 large sand crabs or blue
  swimmer crabs
a large handful (100 g)
  samphire
2 tablespoons (40 ml) olive
  oil
2 tablespoons (30 g) freshly
  peeled and grated ginger
6 garlic cloves, peeled and
  crushed
native (black) pepper to taste
zest and juice of 3 limes
⅔ cup (150 ml) dry white
  wine
Lemon Aspen Mayonnaise
  (see page 33)

Rinse the crabs well to remove any sand, grit or seaweed, and steam them whole for 5 minutes. Leave the steamer clean and ready to steam the samphire.

Heat the oil in a wok over a high heat, and add the ginger and garlic. Toss briefly, and add the crabs. Cook for a further 3 minutes, tossing occasionally to distribute the flavours.

Add the native pepper, lime zest and juice, and wine. Cover with a lid and cook for 2 minutes.

Place the samphire in the steamer and steam until it is tender and about the same texture as asparagus.

To serve, place the crabs with all their cooking juices on a platter with the steamed samphire on the side. The only way to really enjoy crab is to eat it with your fingers, so provide large finger bowls of hot water with a slice of lemon in them and lots of napkins or a bib for each diner. Serve with a big basket of crusty bread and some lemon aspen mayonnaise.

Native Mint

The dried native mint leaf

Australia has a number of plants which for culinary purposes we call native mint. Although I also like to cook with river mint (*Mentha australis*), We've chosen to focus on 'mint bush' (*Prostanthera rotundifolia*) in this book, as it really is very common in parks and gardens around the country.

The native mint bush has very small rounded leaves that smell and taste distinctly of mint, even though this plant is not a true mint. In spring it has long stems of soft mauve blossoms. The flavour of the leaf is decidedly minty, but it has a secondary peppery taste that is aromatic and very pleasing. It can be used with great success in both savoury and sweet dishes. Once the mint bush is established, it can grow to quite a height and size and will provide you with far more mint than you could ever hope to use. As with lemon myrtle leaves, it's great to have lovely big bunches of native mint hanging to dry as the fragrance is wonderful.

There are a number of *Prostanthera* species so make sure you get the right one. Some, while edible, are far too strong and are unpalatable, such as the *P. incisa*. *P. striatiflora*, or streaked mint bush, is a northern plant that is used only as a medicine plant, and is poisonous to eat. It is found in central and northern regions of NT and is steeped in boiling water to make an inhalant for sinus congestion. When cooled, the liquid can be used as a soothing wash for those suffering colds and flu. The dried and crushed leaves of this plant are also used as a poison to stun game birds up to the size of an emu! Aborigines would leave behind branches of the plant at waterholes to signal that the water had been poisoned.

TO GROW

Prostanthera rotundifolia

Distribution: NSW and Victoria.

P. rotundifolia is a delightful ornamental shrub, and strong-growing, often reaching heights of 2 m in optimum sites. The leaves are small, round and green, and have a strong minty scent. It is not a true mint, but related to the *Westringia*. The flowers are mauve to purple, and occur all over the bush; good specimens are completely covered when they bloom in spring. The plant occurs naturally in cool, moist gullies. It grows in high rainfall districts such as the Great Dividing Range of south-eastern Australia and Tasmania.

Mint bushes are adaptable to the garden, although regular watering will improve health and size, and rich heavy soils will promote growth. Tip pruning is required after flowering, which keeps the plant from becoming straggly. It is suitable as a hedge, in the background or specimen position, particularly for locations near living areas where the leaves can be brushed past. It will probably not succeed in warm, subtropical regions. This species is hardy in cold and frost areas, although it requires good drainage. Plants are not long-lived (between 7 to 10 years), but they are easily propagated from cuttings. Cuttings strike easily, between 3 to 6 weeks, in mild weather, though they should not be taken when the plant is flowering.

Relations

Most high rainfall *Prostanthera* species have strongly scented leaves. Some plants are less appropriate for cooking since the perfume is not sweet, but strong and medicinal-smelling. Try to choose plants that have the best fragrance. *P. ovalifolia* occurs in NSW and Queensland, and has a pleasant smell and taste. Its leaves are longer than *P. rotundifolia*. *P. incisa*, also from NSW and Queensland, has small minty leaves, but they are too strong and medicinal-smelling for culinary use. All three are available from native nurseries, and grow best in cool, moist situations.

To harvest

Once the native mint bush is established it may be harvested at any time.

STORING NATIVE MINT

Once you have a native mint bush established in your garden you'll never need to store fresh mint ever again. However it's a good idea to dry some leaves for both the fragrance that will waft through your home as the mint dries, and also for culinary purposes. Dry the mint by hanging it upside-down in bunches in an airy spot that is out of direct sunlight until the leaves are brittle but still retain some colour. If you dry it too much, the leaves will fall off the branches and will be brown rather than green in colour.

Leaf Stem Tuber

TO COOK

Native mint, fresh and dried, is a strong-flavoured herb, so use it with discretion. It has a more complex flavour than common mints—apart from the expected mintiness it has an aromatic, slightly peppery flavour that develops on the palate. Be careful when adding to your dishes as the flavour develops over time and intensifies. Err on the side of too little rather than too much. It is perfect with traditional accompaniments such as lamb, veal and chicken, and makes a mean mint sauce.

Goes with

Native mint goes with lots of bushfoods—wild lime, lemon aspen, lilly pillies, wild rosella and so on. Be guided by your palate, and let your imagination fill in the gaps.

SHORTS

- Mint flowers make a lovely garnish for desserts or cakes. If making a jelly place a small sprig of native mint in the jar with the fruit jelly. Its mintiness will gently flavour the jelly.

- Fold a tiny amount of dried mint through a sponge mix (a scant quarter teaspoon for one sponge) for a most unusual minty and tasty flavour. We prepared this sponge as a base for a pistachio and wild lime mousse dessert that was served at the gala ball for the centenary celebrations of Australian rules football. I doubt that the MCG would have had much bushfood in its hallowed halls in the course of the first hundred years, but hopefully that'll change now!

- Native mint does suit the flavour of wild lime in particular: try a wild lime and native mint curd.

- Native mint is also pleasant in tea. Steep some leaves and use it as a base for a sorbet or ice-cream.

- Try dried native mint in tiny amounts baked through biscuits. It's lovely with chocolate too.

Native Mint Dressing

To make 1 cup (250 ml)

2 teaspoons (4 g) fresh native
  mint leaves
⅔ cup (165 ml) salad oil
  such as canola
⅓ cup (80 ml) white wine
  vinegar
1 tablespoon (25 ml)
  sweetened apple juice
¼ teaspoon salt
a pinch of native (black)
  pepper

Finely chop the native mint leaves. This will help release the mint oils in the leaves and flavour the dressing.

In a bowl whisk together the oil, vinegar, apple juice, salt and pepper. Add the native mint, and allow to steep for at least 30 minutes, longer if possible. Pour the dressing into a clean jar with a tight-fitting lid and shake well to combine the ingredients.

Braised and Minted Veal Shanks

To serve 6

3 kg veal shanks
¾ cup (100 g) plain flour
olive oil for browning
4 garlic cloves, crushed
2 cumbungi or leeks, cleaned
  and sliced
3 sticks celery, sliced
2 potatoes, peeled and finely
  diced
1 heaped teaspoon (4 g)
  native mint, dried and
  ground
1 teaspoon (4 g) native
  (black) pepper
½ teaspoon salt
zest and juice of 1 lemon
2 cups (500 ml) Veal or
  Chicken Stock (page 182)
1 cup (250 ml) cream

Preheat the oven to 160°C (325°F).

Dust the veal shanks lightly with the flour. Heat up the oil in a large heavy-based skillet and quickly seal and brown the shanks on all sides. Transfer the browned shanks to a large casserole or baking dish, and cover with the garlic, cumbungi, celery and potato. Season with the native mint, native pepper, salt and lemon zest.

Pour the stock, lemon juice and cream over the shanks and cover with a lid or wrap tightly with foil. Place the prepared shanks in the preheated oven for 2–2½ hours. When ready, the shanks should be redolent of rich and minty fragrances, the meat will be falling off the bone, and the sauce deliciously sticky.

Serve the shanks in a large bowl with couscous, rice or crusty bread. Provide finger bowls and plenty of napkins.

Native
Pepper

Dried mountain pepper leaf

The native *pepper trees or shrubs that are used for culinary purposes are from the* Tasmannia *genus of the Winteraceae family. This family of plants is one of a group associated with the ancient Gondwana supercontinent, and is now represented in various species on the modern continents and islands that formed from its demise.*

Two peppers have been popularised by the bushfood movement: the Tasmannia lanceolata *from the south, especially Tasmania, and now known as mountain pepper, and the* T. insipida *that grows along the eastern seaboard, now called Dorrigo pepper.*

For recipes in this book that call for native pepper, either mountain or Dorrigo pepper may be used. Each has its disciples—some swear that the mountain pepper is far more aromatic and flavoursome, and the adherents of Dorrigo pepper will convincingly extol its virtues. They are both wonderful, and add great distinction to recipes where pepper is a definitive ingredient.

Mountain Pepper

Also known as native pepper

The mountain pepper is not related to the true pepper, which is actually an Indonesian vine that has close relatives in Australia. It has the spiciness and heat of pepper, and also a significant aromatic flavour. A mountain pepper tree is easily identified by its distinctive crimson-coloured young stems and branches, and shiny dark green leaves that smell spicy and peppery when crushed in the hand. The leaves are long and slender, slightly broader at the base and taper away (see opposite page). The tree bears a small, yellowish-creamy flower that is also deliciously hot and spicy when in bud. This is followed by glossy, black and fleshy pepper fruits, commonly known as pepperberries, which are about the size of a small pea and contain a cluster of small black seeds in the centre.

European use of the mountain pepper tree can be traced back to the nineteenth century when the bark was used to supplement supplies of bark from a South American relative of the tree that was used as a herbal remedy, known as winter's bark.

T. lanceolata or mountain pepper was mentioned by a former director of the Sydney Botanical Gardens, J. H. Maiden, as a tree with potential as a pepper or allspice substitute, and for its resemblance to winter's bark. The flavour of the leaf is

Pepperberries

pungent, and its intensity is heightened when the leaf is dried. The spicy and aromatic qualities of the leaf dominate initially, followed by the biting heat; the delightful savoury tang lures the palate into familiar territory, only to assail it seconds later with an intense hot pepper burst.

Apart from being an important bushfood ingredient, mountain pepper is also enjoying some success as an essential oil. It's being used as a confectionary flavouring and several international food and fragrance houses are carrying out trials with a view to wider use. Let's hope that Australians discover the worth of this wonderful plant before it goes the way of the macadamia.

Despite being a common south-eastern Australian species, the mountain pepper, particularly in pre-settlement days, does not feature in recorded knowledge of Aboriginal foods or medicines.

TO GROW

Tasmannia lanceolata
Distribution: Tasmanian and Victorian rainforests and wet mountain gullies (to 1200 m) and in similar situations at high altitudes in parts of NSW as far north as the Hastings River.

The mountain pepper tree in the wild grows in moist, cool, high altitude forests. It prefers humus-rich, well-drained soil and part shade. The tree is moderately fast-growing and if regularly watered and cultivated under ideal growing conditions, can grow from 4 to 5 m. It is very frost hardy. The plant is dioecious, which means that the male and female reproductive structures are on separate plants. You'll need one of each to produce a fruiting tree. The mountain pepper may be propagated from seed or cuttings. The seeds should be extracted from the pepperberries and sown immediately, although they can take many months to germinate. Cuttings should be taken once the new spring and summer growth has hardened off. They strike easily, albeit at times slowly.

Relations

T. insipida, known as Dorrigo pepper, comes from NSW, Queensland and NT. It also has hot spicy leaves and fruit.
T. xerophila, commonly known as alpine pepper, is a smaller, bushier plant that grows in alpine regions and is said to have even hotter leaves and berries. Another spicy, hot plant is *T. purpurescens* or broad leaf pepperbush that hails from the high altitude regions of north-eastern NSW. All of these species are highly ornamental and will do well in cooler districts with good rainfall.

To harvest

Pepperberries ripen and usually are harvested from March to May. The pepperberries are relatively easy to harvest as the trees are generally not too tall. If harvesting the flowers, take only what you need of the buds so that you do not reduce the crop of pepperberries. Mountain pepper leaves can be harvested any time from a *mature* tree, not from a young plant that is sending out new growth.

STORING MOUNTAIN PEPPER

The best way to store mountain pepper leaves is to dry them as you would other leaf herbs. Lay them out flat or tie the branches into bunches and dry. Ensure that you have the leaves in an airy position, preferably away from direct sunlight. Once dried, store the leaves in airtight plastic bags or an airtight container and they will keep indefinitely with minimal flavour loss. The leaves may of course be used fresh.

Pepperberries can be frozen whole in sealed freezer bags or kept in salt—either pickle the pepperberries in a solution of brine or layer them with coarse table salt in a sealed container. Again the fruit will keep well for months with its zing well and truly intact. Once dried, pepperberries resemble common peppercorns, and can be used in pepper grinders.

TO COOK

The information here also applies to Dorrigo pepper, which is similar in taste and use.

Mountain pepper leaves and pepperberries contain a large number of the volatile flavour and fragrance compounds also found in other species that are commonly used in the spice and essential oil industries. However, mountain pepper leaves also have unique compounds such as a high concentration of the pungent polygodial. (According to Chris Read from Diemen Pepper in Tasmania, purified extracts containing the compound have been shown to act against a range of bacteria, fungi and yeast isolates.) Polygodial also delivers the sharp, hot taste so loved by the human palate and, together with the other fragrant and volatile compounds in the mountain pepper, produces the unusually flavoured spice.

As with so many bushfoods, mountain pepper has an intensity of flavour that must be respected. Many recipes in this book recommend mountain or native pepper as a substitute for black pepper. Finely milled white or dark peppers are not comparable to mountain pepper; the closest equivalent lies in the very coarse grounds of cracked black pepper. Where possible, use mountain pepper as suggested—it has more complex flavours to contribute to the dish being prepared.

The best way to use mountain pepper leaf is to dry the leaf and mill it into a fine powdered form or break it into larger flakes. It can be used in cooking as you would common white pepper, but keep in mind its additional strength. If substituting mountain pepper in a favourite recipe, use about half the quantities of white pepper.

The mountain pepper leaf should be added to the dish towards the end of the cooking process for the best flavour results. It loses its pungency when added at the beginning. For example, if cooking a casserole, add it during the final 30 minutes of cooking.

On the other hand, add the pepperberries to the sauce or dish *early* in the cooking process so that some of the heat is dissipated. Try them fresh first to get an idea of their intensity.

Mountain pepper will complement almost any bushfood discussed in this book if used primarily in a savoury application. It works well with European and Asian ingredients. Be guided by the application of common pepper to determine complementary flavours for mountain pepper.

Pickled Mountain Pepperberries

Allow the pepperberries to ripen and when you have harvested more than you can use, pickle some in this light brine and you will have them available in your pantry all year round. The pickled pepperberries will keep for at least 6 months if stored in a cool, dark place.

To fill 1 x 1 litre jar

2 cups (230 g) fresh
  mountain pepperberries
2 cups (500 ml) water
½ cup (125 ml) white wine
  vinegar
1 onion, finely diced
2 teaspoons (10 g) salt

Place the cleaned mountain pepperberries in a clean, airtight glass jar.

Combine the water, vinegar, onion and salt in a medium-sized saucepan and place over a medium heat and bring slowly to the boil. Adjust the heat and allow to simmer for 5 minutes.

Pour the brine over the pepperberries and when the liquid has cooled, seal the jar tightly. Allow to sit for at least 4–6 weeks before using.

SHORTS

- The dried pepperberry can be popped into a standard pepper grinder and used as you would peppercorns. Be careful that you don't use too much—pepperberry is much hotter than normal pepper.

- The flower buds are an interesting addition to salads. They can be pickled and used as a caper substitute.

- The complex aromatic flavour and heat of the mountain pepper makes it a perfect addition to curries and chilli dishes.

- The bark from the mountain pepper can be used as an infusion, and will make a pleasant herbal tea.

- Pepperberries are a superb addition to any marinade or pickle solution—they impart great flavour and bleed a soft pink colour into the pickling solution.

Sweet Potato Gnocchi with Dorrigo Pepper, Prosciutto and Parmesan Sauce

This sauce really highlights the delicate sweet potato and pepper flavour of this gnocchi.

To serve 6

Gnocchi
750 g sweet potato, peeled
  and chopped
3 teaspoons (6 g) dried,
  ground Dorrigo pepper
a pinch of salt
3 x 55 g eggs, lightly beaten
2 cups (250 g) plain flour

Dorrigo Pepper, Prosciutto and Parmesan Sauce
1 cup (250 g) cream
1 teaspoon (2 g) dried and
  ground Dorrigo pepper
2 tablespoons (50 g) unsalted
  butter
6 paper-thin slices prosciutto
100 g freshly shaved
  parmesan

To make the Gnocchi, steam the chopped sweet potatoes until they are soft enough to mash. Transfer them to a large bowl, mash, and allow to cool.

Add the pepper, salt, eggs and flour, mixing thoroughly to form a firm dough. If the dough seems a little soft, add a little more flour until the dough is firm enough to work with and is not sticky. Turn out the dough onto a floured board and knead for 2–3 minutes. Divide it into 4 pieces, and roll out each piece into a long sausage. Cut each 'sausage' into 2.5 cm rounds and form them into gnocchi shapes. Dust lightly with flour and mark one side with a fork. Set aside on a floured tray.

Bring a large saucepan of boiling salted water to the boil and gently drop in the gnocchi. When they float up to the surface remove them immediately with a slotted spoon. Place them carefully in a shallow baking dish.

Preheat the oven to 170°C (370°F).

To make the Dorrigo Pepper, Prosciutto and Parmesan Sauce, bring the cream to the boil in a small saucepan. When the cream is boiling, add the pepper. Turn off the heat and whisk in the butter. Pour this mixture over the cooked gnocchi and scatter the shaved parmesan and prosciutto evenly over the surface. Bake in the preheated oven for 10 minutes.

Lemon Myrtle

If I had to choose a tree that encompassed all the advantages of planting, growing, harvesting, cooking and enjoying bushfoods, then the lemon myrtle would be it. A magnificent rainforest plant in its own right, it is also a beautiful specimen tree—bushy with low branches that have long, tapering, deep green leaves and little bunches of small white flowers in autumn. However, the most marvellous feature of this tree is its superb fragrance, which is a blend of lemon, lemongrass and lime. It's a joy to have in the garden, just brushing past the tree will release its scent, and it is especially fragrant after rain.

The leaves, flowers and seeds are all usable in the cook's kitchen, in fresh, dried, whole, shredded, crushed or ground form. The lemon myrtle leaf contains essential oils that give the plant its wonderful perfume and taste. The leaf is a complex blend of citric flavours with a spicy, highly aromatic lemongrass accent.

The lemon myrtle is one of the most valuable and versatile bushfoods identified today. It is currently enjoying enormous success in the hospitality industry where chefs have embraced its flavour with enthusiasm and great creativity.

The lemon myrtle is also the basis of a burgeoning bushfood industry in the Bangalow and Lismore regions of north-eastern NSW. There are a large number of dedicated growers in this rainforest region who have created sizeable plantations of lemon myrtles. In mid-1996, Brian Milgate, of Bushfoods of Australia, Bangalow, had 14,000 trees in cultivation and another 32,000 on order from specialist nurseries. The Australian Rainforest Bushfood Industry Association (ARBIA) in Lismore is embracing organic farming principles in the cultivation of its lemon myrtle plantations.

Offshore, trials into lemon myrtle cultivation are being carried out in China, Indonesia and Thailand.

TO GROW

Backhousia citriodora
Distribution: Subtropical Queensland.

The lemon myrtle is a tall bushy shrub or small tree from the subtropics. It grows to 6 m in cooler districts, but can reach 20 m or taller in the subtropics. It has conspicuous profuse white flowers in autumn. Although frost-sensitive, it is a hardy plant and survives well in the coastal areas of Victoria, SA and southern NSW. In cooler districts, however, it can grow quite slowly. The plant requires a warm and well-drained aspect, and will tolerate full sun to semi-shade positions with good watering. The seed of the lemon myrtle is very fine but germinates well in warm, moist conditions. Many cultivated specimens don't set viable seed, though. Cuttings can be taken at most times of the year but can be very slow to strike, sometimes taking as long as a year to establish.

Relations

B. anisata or the aniseed myrtle is a taller tree from NSW with aniseed-scented and flavoured leaves. *B. myrtifolia* is a shrub from southern NSW and has a nutmeg-scented and flavoured leaf. This species will tolerate cooler climates better than the other *Backhousia* species, although all are adaptable.

To harvest

The leaves from the lemon myrtle may be harvested most of the year, with due consideration given to the establishment of new growth. Usually older leaves, or new growth once it has fully hardened off, are harvested. The leaves should be clean, free of mould and from a plant that has not been treated with any toxic sprays. The flowers and the resulting seed may also be harvested in late winter or spring.

STORING LEMON MYRTLE

If you have one of these magnificent trees you may prefer to use the leaves and flowers fresh. The best way to store the leaves is to air-dry them: simply hang bunches of lemon myrtle in an airy position in your kitchen so that the fragrance can be enjoyed as they dry. For the best results, dry the leaves in a semi-dark position with good air circulation. The leaves will be leached of their flavour and colour, and become too brittle if exposed to direct light, particularly sunlight. This can be done in a bunch or, for a better result, strip the leaves from their woody stems where necessary and lay them flat on an open wire rack such as a cake rack. Once the leaves are fully dried, they can be stored in an airtight container or press-seal plastic bags. Lemon myrtle leaves will keep for at least 6 months with no flavour loss if kept sealed. If the leaves are extensively exposed to air after drying the essential aromatic oils may dissipate and flavour loss will occur. The flowers and seeds may also be dried in this manner.

Leaf Stem Tuber

TO COOK

Goes with

Fresh or dried lemon myrtle makes a delightful herb and seasoning, and readily transfers its superb flavour to the other ingredients being cooked with it. The lemon myrtle leaf is strongly flavoured and aromatic, and if using fresh in a recipe, it is best to shred the leaf very finely. In culinary terminology this is called a chiffonnade.

The dried leaf is probably more versatile. The flavour has intensified with the drying, and an efficient and easy way to incorporate the dried lemon myrtle leaf is to grind it. A mortar and pestle will do, but it is easier to grind the leaf in a blender or a good coffee grinder. If the leaf is finely ground and added to sauces there is no need to strain the lemon myrtle out; all that will be seen is a fine fleck which is quite attractive.

Lemon myrtle performs better in some recipes if it is first infused in hot water. The heat from the water helps the leaf release its essential oils which provide the flavour. In recipes that have a liquid component, add the lemon myrtle to a little of the hot liquid first, rather than directly into the main body of ingredients. For example, when making a mousse, infuse the ground lemon myrtle in the hot liquid with the gelatine, then add this infusion to the cream component of the mousse.

Lemon myrtle is ideally suited to all fish and seafood dishes, and white meats such as chicken, veal and pork. It's also great with vegetables and in Asian-style dishes. Try it in yoghurt or crème fraîche, either in sauces or desserts, and try baking it in biscuits and cakes.

What doesn't go with lemon myrtle is probably more the point. Bush tomatoes, cheesefruit and desert figs would probably not benefit from a partnership with lemon myrtle, but most other bushfoods will be quite complementary if used judiciously.

Lemon Myrtle Vinegar

To make 4 cups (1 litre)
4 cups (1 litre) white wine
   vinegar
2 tablespoons (50 g) castor
   sugar
1 onion, sliced
1 teaspoon (5 g) salt
20 lemon myrtle leaves,
   whole

Dissolve the sugar and salt in the vinegar. Bring to the boil and add the onion and lemon myrtle leaves. Allow to simmer for 10 minutes.

Strain and pour the vinegar into sterilised bottles. They will keep well for quite a while. Refrigerate any opened bottles.

SHORTS

- A chiffonnade of lemon myrtle is lovely over some fresh fish fillets or tossed into a stir-fry. The whole fresh leaf can also be used to wrap around chicken breasts before baking, or to line the cavity of a whole cleaned fish such as snapper or barramundi before steaming or baking.

- I love having big bunches of lemon myrtle drying in the house as it brings the scent of the rainforest indoors. Simply hang the fragrant bunches of leaves in a light, airy spot in your kitchen, or in any room that needs a lift. For an instant natural air freshener, just rustle the drying leaves to release the fragrance.

- Try using lemon myrtle in Asian recipes instead of kaffir lime leaves or to replace lemongrass. The result is delicious. The dish has a lemon–lime characteristic with that something extra.

- Whole lemon myrtle leaves can be added to traditional bouquet garnis for an extra fillip.

- Lemon myrtle tea is terrific pick-me-up, especially if you're suffering from a head cold. The hot lemon-scented vapours are heaven to inhale as you drink the tea.

- Grind some lemon myrtle very finely and incorporate into your favourite shortbread recipe.

- Infuse some finely ground lemon myrtle in some hot water and use it to make a yoghurt sourdough.

- Add ground lemon myrtle to mayonnaise or fold some finely ground lemon myrtle into a hollandaise and serve with steamed asparagus.

Lemon Myrtle Fish Cakes

To make 24 small cakes

1 kg firm fish fillets such as
  flathead, snapper or bream
1 tablespoon (25 g) unsalted
  butter
2 cloves garlic, crushed
1 large onion, finely diced
2 teaspoons (5 g) dried and
  ground lemon myrtle
1 teaspoon (2 g) native
  pepper
1 x 55 g egg, lightly beaten
½ teaspoon salt
1 cup (75 g) fresh
  breadcrumbs
juice of 1 lemon
½ cup (70 g) plain flour
1 teaspoon (2 g) dried and
  ground lemon myrtle, extra
1 cup (250 ml) peanut oil

Finely dice the fish fillets until the flesh is like a mince and place in a large bowl.

Melt the butter in a small pan and cook the garlic and onion until tender. Add them to the fish and stir through. Add the lemon myrtle, pepper, egg, salt, breadcrumbs and lemon juice and mix very well to incorporate and form a firm fish paste. Remove from the heat.

Combine the extra lemon myrtle and flour together in a flat bowl.

Form the fish mince into 24 small cakes and dust all over with the seasoned flour.

Heat the oil in a skillet and fry the cakes for 3–4 minutes until a light golden brown. Cook only a few at a time so that the oil temperature doesn't drop and cause the cake to stew. Lift the cakes from the pan with a slotted spoon and drain away the excess oil by placing on absorbent kitchen paper.

Serve hot with Quandong, Port and Chilli Sauce (see page 23).

Fresh Dates with Lemon Myrtle, Mountain Pepper and Ginger 'Cheese'

To make about 30
hors d'oeuvres

30 fresh dates
2 teaspoons (5 g) ground
  lemon myrtle
1 heaped teaspoon (3 g)
  ground mountain pepper
½ teaspoon (3 g) powdered
  ginger
a pinch of salt
1 cup (200 g) cottage cheese
½ cup (125 g) sour cream

Remove the seeds from the dates by making a slit on one side and carefully lifting out the seeds.

Mix together all the remaining ingredients. Fill the cavity in the dates with the seasoned cottage cheese mixture. Carefully press the two halves of the dates back together to resemble a whole fresh date and serve as a light finger food with drinks.

Lemon Myrtle and Yoghurt Mousse

This marriage of lemon myrtle and yoghurt will please those who don't like their desserts too sweet. Fresh and light, it makes an ideal finish to any meal, and can also be used as a mousse cake filling.

To make approximately 4 cups (1 litre)

1½ cups (675 ml) thickened cream
¾ cup (130 g) castor sugar
1 x 200 g carton plain yoghurt
1 teaspoon (2 g) ground lemon myrtle
1 cup (250 ml) boiling water
1 tablespoon (20 g) powdered gelatine

Whip the cream and sugar until the mixture just starts to thicken and falls from the whisk in ribbons..

Place the yoghurt in a large mixing bowl. Add the sweetened cream and gently blend the two.

Stir the lemon myrtle into the hot water to infuse. Soften the gelatine in the same water until it is completely dissolved. Add a tablespoon of the yoghurt cream mixture to the gelatine and whisk through.

Quickly and thoroughly mix the rest of the gelatine into the yoghurt and cream mixture until it is fully incorporated.

Pour the mousse into a serving dish or mould. Leave it to set in the refrigerator for at least 2–3 hours before serving. This mousse is delicious with a mango or kiwifruit coulis.

Lemon Myrtle and Ginger Tea

This tea can also be made with fresh leaves; simply adjust the quantity to your taste (you'll probably need more). It makes a refreshing summer's drink, served in a large glass jug with lots of ice, some fresh lemon myrtle leaves and perhaps a sprig of native mint and lemon slices. This tea can also form the basis of a sorbet (see page 142).

If you are suffering from a head cold or sinus problems, breathing in the soothing lemon–eucalypt vapours will help clear a stuffy head.

Makes 2 cups (500 ml)

2 cups (500 ml) boiling water
6 whole dried lemon myrtle leaves
4 thin slices fresh ginger, peeled
1–2 teaspoons honey to taste (optional)

Bring the water to the boil in a medium-sized saucepan. Add the rest of the ingredients, lower the heat and simmer for about 5 minutes. Turn off the heat, put a lid on, and let the tea stand for at least 10 minutes so that the lemon oils fully flavour the tea. Strain and serve.

Lemon Myrtle and Ginger Tea Sorbet

To make 1.5 litres

1.5 litres Lemon Myrtle and
   Ginger Tea (see page 141)
1½ cups (450 ml) honey
1 cup (200 g) castor sugar

Bring the tea to boiling point and add the honey and
sugar. Simmer for 5 minutes.

Cool and chill well in the refrigerator. Churn in an
ice-cream machine following the manufacturer's
instructions.

Lemon Myrtle Soused Trout

This dish can be prepared in advance; in fact the flavour improves if done a day before
serving.

To serve 6

3 x 300 g whole smoked
   freshwater trout
scant ½ cup (100 ml) white
   wine vinegar
2 teaspoons (10 g) sugar
a pinch of salt
2 tablespoons (15 g) ground
   lemon myrtle leaves
1 teaspoon (2 g) ground
   mountain pepper

Skin the smoked trout by making an incision along the
back of the fish and peeling away the skin carefully
from each side.

Gently remove each fillet from the backbone and
ribs, taking care to keep the fillets in one piece. Place
the fillets in a shallow dish, rib side down.

Warm the vinegar, sugar, salt and a quarter of the
lemon myrtle until the sugar is completely dissolved.
Allow to cool completely.

Dust each trout fillet with the mountain pepper and
remaining lemon myrtle, and drizzle the cold seasoned
vinegar evenly over the trout fillets.

Cover the dish securely with plastic wrap and leave to
marinate for 1 hour. Collect all the excess vinegar and
juices that have pooled at the bottom of the dish and
repeat the drizzling procedure with these liquids again.
Cover and refrigerate for at least another hour and, if
possible, overnight. Drizzle the trout at least three times
during this period.

Simply serve the soused trout on a bed of the
freshest, crispest salad greens you can find with a
generous dollop of sour cream. For a picnic, serve it on
fresh rye bread.

Lemon Myrtle Dressing

This dressing will keep indefinitely if refrigerated.

To make 4 cups (1 litre)

1½ cups (400 ml) white wine
 vinegar
½ teaspoon salt
2 teaspoons (10 g) castor
 sugar
2 teaspoons (5 g) ground
 lemon myrtle
½ teaspoon ground mountain
 pepper
2½ cups (600 ml) olive or
 preferred salad oil

Combine the vinegar, salt and sugar in a stainless-steel pot and heat gently until the sugar is dissolved. Remove from the heat and add the lemon myrtle and mountain pepper. The heat will help release the natural oils in the lemon myrtle and pepper.

Once the mixture is cool, slowly whisk in the oil. This dressing will separate if left to stand, so give it a good shake or stir before using it on your favourite salad or drizzled over freshly cooked chicken or fish.

Warm Salad of Tasmanian Salmon with Lemon Myrtle Dressing

To serve 6

6 x 200 g Tasmanian salmon
 cutlets
1 teaspoon (2 g) ground
 native pepper
1 teaspoon (2 g) ground
 lemon myrtle
2 cups (500 ml) Lemon Myrtle
 Dressing (see above)
100 g cress leaves

Preheat the oven to 160°C (325°F).

Dust the fish with the native pepper and lemon myrtle. Place on a greased oven tray and bake in the preheated oven for approximately 15–20 minutes.

In a small stainless-steel saucepan, gently warm the dressing through and whisk lightly to mix the ingredients.

To serve, place a small handful of the cress in the centre of a dinner plate. Carefully place the cooked salmon on the salad and gently pour over the heated dressing. Serve with sweet potato chips.

Warrigal
Greens

Joseph Banks and Captain Cook discovered warrigal greens in Australia on their voyage of discovery along the eastern Australian coast, after first sighting the plant on the coasts of New Zealand, and again at Botany Bay on 6 May 1770. They and their crew ate stingray with their greens—surprising because it has taken us over 200 years to offer similar meals at our tables! Banks took seeds from the Australian plants back to the Kew Gardens in England, and from there, distributed seeds to Europe and North America, where warrigal greens were taken up by seed merchants some years later and sold as a hardy summer-growing spinach. Warrigal greens actually preceded macadamia nuts as the first antipodean plant to be commercially sold internationally.

According to Tim Low in *Wild Herbs of Australia and New Zealand*, Banks has a lot to answer for, as 'Banks' liking for New Zealand spinach may have helped decide Australia's fate as a convict colony. When in 1779 he was called before a House of Commons committee to speak upon the suitability of Botany Bay for settlement, he testified that "The grass was long and luxuriant, and there were some eatable Vegetables, particularly a Sort of Wild Spinage". His promise of free greens may have helped swing the vote.'

In the early days of the Port Jackson penal colony, the greens were widely used to allay scurvy. Parties were sent out to search for them and samphire to supplement the meagre rations. In Europe, warrigal greens enjoyed fame in society for some time as a new spinach from the far-flung colony, but unfortunately faded from favour. Warrigal greens, however, are still being grown in parts of France where they are called 'tetragon'. In *Koorie Plants Koorie People*, Beth Gott speculates that the southern coastal Kooris most probably ate the plant as a green vegetable.

TO GROW

Tetragonia tetragonioides

Distribution: Coastal and inland salt marshes and plains mainly in Victoria, Tasmania, NSW, Queensland and SA.

This vigorous fleshy-leaved plant is an excellent ground cover for many different soil types and conditions, being particularly widespread around coastal Australia. The large leaves are rather coarse and leathery. Tiny yellow flowers appear at the base of the leaves at most times of the year.

Warrigal greens have a bright green leaf that glistens, as though it has a fine bead of dew over its surface, due to small glistening cells in its succulent leaves. The leaves are described by botanists as deltoid, which means that they are triangular in shape with sides of equal length, and look a little like an angular pear or an arrow head.

Although naturally occurring in nutrient-deficient sand, the plant will grow more vigorously and produce larger leaves in richer soils. It does best with reliable water, spreading up to 2 m from a single centre and can be trained around taller shrubs. The plant itself is not long-lived, but is easy to propagate and may self-seed.

Propagating from seed gives the best results, though germination can be spasmodic. Sow the whole seed capsules from the base of the leaves making sure that these capsules have not become brown, since the seeds do not seem to sprout as readily then. Each capsule should produce several seedlings.

Relations

T. implexicoma or bower spinach is a scrambling plant common to southern coasts and has edible leaves.

To harvest

Warrigal greens are best harvested in spring and summer. They start to look a bit straggly as autumn progresses into winter and in the colder months the yield is very sparse. They are prolific when in season, and will provide an ongoing supply of greens.

STORING WARRIGAL GREENS

Warrigal greens will keep well in a refrigerator for a few days if sealed in a plastic bag. The leaves can be frozen fresh or blanched, but the leaf structure is affected by the freezing. Cook the thawed leaves before use. If you have a healthy plant or two, storage shouldn't be necessary as the plant will provide a constant supply of fresh leaves over summer, and it's far better to use them in their fresh form.

TO COOK

Goes with

Warrigal greens are a soft-leaved herb, and if eaten fresh, have a slightly succulent feel in the mouth. If the leaves are cooked, this texture changes and it becomes almost identical in texture and colour to the true spinach *Spinacia oleracea*. It has a slight peppery aftertaste.

Despite being unrelated to spinach, warrigal greens also have a high level of soluble oxalates. This means the plant has oxalic acid, which is poisonous to people and animals, but not usually in levels found in vegetables and most plants. Plants with high levels of oxalates have an acidity of taste, sometimes saltiness, especially in the older leaves. If you eat a leaf that is very high in oxalates you will experience an uncomfortable constriction in the throat. For this reason, blanch warrigal greens before eating to leach out the soluble oxalates and saltiness (keep the lid off so the condensation doesn't drip back into the pot). When the warrigal greens are blanched, you will notice a brownish tinge to the water. Discard the water, retaining the leaves.

Rest assured, not all warrigal greens are unpalatable; this very much depends on the soil they grow in and the climatic conditions. There is some research into growing warrigal greens hydroponically to evaluate the effects on the oxalates, and their suitability for commercial cultivation. If you pick the young leaves, the level of oxalates is certainly not discernible. You'll need to eat about 12 cups of leaves per week before the level of the oxalates comes anywhere near dangerous. A good intake of calcium counteracts some of the potentially harmful effects of vegetable oxalates.

Be discerning in the leaves that you pick for salads. Choose only the young light green leaves and nibble on one to determine their edibility. If in any doubt, lightly blanch the leaves, chill and then use as a salad vegetable. As with spinach or silverbeet, warrigal greens can be used in soup, pasta, or simply served as a delicious vegetable. Think spinach, use warrigal greens.

As warrigal greens are clearly a savoury herb, certain bush fruits are precluded from any culinary marriage. For example, I can't quite come to terms with warrigal greens and riberry as a combination. I can imagine, however, steamed warrigal greens with a warm riberry dressing or vinegar. Try to interpret the bushfood flavours that will balance and subtly complement rather than combinations for an unusual effect alone.

Warrigal greens go with native peppers and lemon myrtle. Lemon aspen in a butter sauce or dressing will also work. Try combining warrigal greens with other bush plants like portulaca. The piquancy of bush tomato is an interesting flavour combination, either ground over warrigal greens, or in a dressing or sauce for pasta. Garlic, basil and curry powder will work with warrigal greens.

They are delicious served with poached salmon or chicken, or used as a stuffing for lamb. Other good complementary ingredients include cream, cheese, butter and yoghurt.

Curried Warrigal Greens and Pea Soup

To serve 6

2½ tablespoons (60 g)
  unsalted butter
1 onion, finely chopped
2 teaspoons (5 g) curry
  powder
1 tablespoon (20 g) plain
  flour
1 cup (70 g) warrigal greens,
  blanched and chopped
1 teaspoon (5 g) salt
native pepper to taste
½ teaspoon dried and
  ground native mint or
  1 teaspoon very finely
  chopped fresh native mint
2 cups (250 g) fresh green
  peas, shelled
½ cup (125 ml) dry white
  wine
½ cup (125 ml) cream
3 cups (750 ml) milk

Heat the butter in a saucepan over medium heat and sweat the onion and curry powder for about 10–15 minutes, stirring continually so they don't burn. Add the flour and, while stirring, add the warrigal greens, salt, pepper, mint and peas.

Deglaze the pan with the wine, then gradually add the milk. Slowly bring to the boil and cook for about 15–20 minutes at a gentle simmer. Add the cream and remove the pan from the heat. Purée in a food-processor or blender, and return the soup to the heat. Serve once hot—do not bring to the boil again.

SHORTS

- Toss the Warrigal Greens and Macadamia Pesto (see page 148) through hot pasta, such as the Wattleseed Pasta (see page 170), and top with shaved parmesan.

- Stir the Warrigal Greens Pesto (see page 148) through vegetable soups or spread on bread instead of butter when making sandwiches. Another interesting way to use this pesto is to sandwich it between two slices of eggplant, coat the eggplant in crushed macadamia nuts or almond meal, and pan-fry until golden brown on both sides.

- Poach or oven-bake some fresh Tasmanian salmon and serve on a bed of freshly cooked warrigal greens. Pour some warm Lemon Myrtle Dressing (see page 143) over the fish as well.

- Creamed warrigal greens.

Sautéed Warrigal Greens with Warm Lemon Myrtle Dressing

To serve 6

¾ cup (150 g) unsalted butter
1 kg fresh warrigal greens,
    lightly blanched, leaves
    intact
salt to taste
native pepper or cracked
    black pepper to taste
native nutmeg (or nutmeg
    powder), dried and ground
    to taste
¾ cup (190 ml) Lemon Myrtle
    Dressing (see page 143)

Melt the butter in a large skillet and add the warrigal greens. Season to taste with the salt, pepper and nutmeg, and cook for about 5–6 minutes until the leaves have wilted and changed colour.

In a small saucepan over a low heat gently warm the lemon myrtle dressing, but do not let it get hot.

Put the spinach on a plate and pour over the warm dressing.

Warrigal Greens and Macadamia Pesto

To make 2 cups (500 ml)

1 clove garlic, crushed
½ cup (50 g) macadamia
    nuts, roasted and roughly
    chopped
3½ cups (250 g) fresh
    warrigal greens, blanched
    and chopped
1 teaspoon (5 g) salt
½ teaspoon native (black)
    pepper
generous cup (250 ml) light
    olive oil
¾ cup (100 g) grated fresh
    parmesan

If using a blender or food processor, combine all the ingredients except the parmesan and blend until smooth. Gradually add the parmesan to the pesto, blending each time until the pesto thickens.

You can also make the pesto by hand in a mortar and pestle. Pound the garlic and macadamia nuts together. Slowly add the warrigal greens and seasonings, grinding constantly until a smooth paste is formed. Slowly drizzle in the olive oil and cheese, and mix to thoroughly combine.

Cumbungi

Also known as bulrush

The common bulrush or cumbungi is probably the most easily identifiable of Australian bushfoods. Almost everyone is aware of this aquatic reed with its distinctive rod-like stems, flat, wide, blade-shaped leaves that are 1 to 2 m tall, and its velvety cylindrical cap growing in dams or along creeks and waterways. The cumbungi is an extremely useful plant as its stems, new shoots and pollen are edible. They are not only edible, but are very palatable and versatile 'vegetables'. Cumbungi stems taste similar to leek, but with a slightly peppery and garlic finish. The young shoots are delicate in flavour, reminiscent of hearts of palm or artichokes, and the pollen has quite a nutty flavour. The new shoots of the cumbungi are a true delicacy that are plentiful and easy to obtain, and one that most Australians, certainly non-indigenous Australians, are unaware of.

Cumbungi is one of the many Aboriginal names for the commonly known bulrush that is found throughout Australia. It is so useful and usable that different parts of the plant had different names to identify their purpose. According to Beth Gott and Nelly Zola in *Koorie Plants Koorie People*, Kooris from Lake Boga had three distinct names to identify the rush root, the rush root after harvesting and the same root after cooking.

The cumbungi is a very important traditional Aboriginal plant as it is used both as a food and an important source of fibre, in fact the cumbungi was the most important food plant in the Murray Darling River system. The new shoots were collected and eaten raw as a salad dish, while the fibrous roots were baked and peeled before eating. The Aborigines would eat the tasty starchy centre of the root, and the fibrous root material that remained was used to make string. The stems were harvested in spring when young and used as a vegetable, and would usually be baked or steamed. The pollen, although edible, was not eaten.

TO GROW

Typha domingensis, T. orientalis
Distribution: Grows extensively throughout all Australian states, along the edges and in creeks, rivers, billabongs, dams and lakes.

Cumbungi spreads very quickly, if there is room to expand, in its natural environment of slow-moving waterways or wetlands. It can block drains and soaks, fill small creeks or colonise dams. Although it has considerable potential for invasion, this is a very useful food plant and, in the domestic bushfood garden, would be better confined to large pots submerged in a 'wetland' area or pond.

The best method of propagating cumbungi is by dividing the rhizomes, which may be dug up at any time of the year, and replanting them as they grow new roots very quickly. Seed is released in very large quantities from the female spikes at certain times of the year. These seeds can germinate, but this is often unreliable and unnecessary, when you consider the ease of vegetative propagation. Even detached portions of the stem floating in water may produce new roots.

To harvest

Almost the entire cumbungi can be used, from the pollen to the fibrous stems, to the tender young shoots peeping out of the water. The stems and shoots are best harvested in late spring to summer, from October to January. The pollen can be collected in late spring, although the time can vary depending on the climate. The pollen is ready when large yellow clouds of pollen are released when the male flower is tapped with a finger. The male flower is rod-like and on the stem immediately above the female. The pollen may be collected by running a hand up the flower head. Store the pollen in an airtight container in the freezer.

The stem is cut from the juicy base section of the tall stems. The young shoots from the rhizome can be found at ground level or just under the water. The newer the shoot, the more tender it is.

STORING CUMBUNGI
Once the stems are cut they can be stored in the refrigerator for up to 5 days. Treat them the same way as leeks. For best results, use the young shoots once they are cut. If you have to, keep them well sealed in the bottom part of the refrigerator for a few days. Like any fresh vegetable, they are at their best if eaten immediately after harvesting. The stems and shoots of the cumbungi don't freeze well, so enjoy this plant while it is in season. The pollen can only be effectively stored frozen, as it will rapidly go mouldy otherwise.

TO COOK

The shoots taste absolutely delicious, like artichokes or hearts of palm. They can be prepared with a minimum of effort: steam until tender, and quickly refresh in ice-water if you wish to serve them cold, or toss them while they're hot in a little butter, native pepper and wild thyme. They are also delicious raw, particularly the very young and tender shoots. Wash them well and use as a salad vegetable with other salad ingredients or on their own with a good dressing or mayonnaise. Try any of the bushfood dressings or mayonnaise, or your favourites.

The stems should be well trimmed before use, taking care to discard the outer, more fibrous layers. They should be well cleaned to ensure that no grit or residual water sludge is left. Then treat the cumbungi stems as you would the common leek. If the cumbungi stems or shoots that you have harvested come from a source other than your own dam or water garden, be sure that the water is clean and unpolluted.

The pollen, with its nutty flavour and distinct saffron colour, is plentiful in spring and can be added to flour to flavour and colour cakes, biscuits and breads. While quite nutty in flavour, the pollen can be compared to saffron in cooking.

Goes with

Complementary bushfoods that go with cumbungi shoots and stems include bunya nuts, the native peppers, lemon myrtle, bush tomatoes, macadamias, some lilly pillies, muntries and perhaps ground wattleseed and kurrajong. The cumbungi would not be shown to advantage if prepared with tubers such as the chocolate or vanilla lilies. However the native yams and taro would be suitable.

Other vegetables or seasonings that would complement cumbungi include potato, pumpkin, pepper, caraway seed, tarragon and dill.

Cumbungi and Bunya Nut Soup

This dish combines the stem of the humble cumbungi with the nut from our tallest pine, and is redolent of the crisp, almost garlic-like flavour of the cumbungi and the earthiness of the bunya nut. Because of its hearty flavour and chunky texture, it makes a good main course. This soup may also be puréed for a more elegant presentation, and garnished with slivers of cumbungi and bunya nut.

To serve 6, with leftovers

3½ cups (500 g) bunya nuts
4 (approximately 450 g) cumbungi stems, trimmed
2 teaspoons (50 g) unsalted butter
1 small onion, finely diced
2.5 litres Chicken Stock (see page 182)
1 level teaspoon (5 g) ground bush tomatoes
¼ level teaspoon ground mountain pepper or black pepper
1 sprig river mint or mint, finely chopped
cracked black pepper

Bring a litre of water to the boil in a medium-sized saucepan and add the bunya nuts in their shells. Cook for about 30 minutes. Shell the bunya nuts (see page 105) and finely dice or quickly process them until chopped but not puréed. Set aside.

Clean the cumbungi stems as you would a leek, ensuring that all the grit is removed. Wash well and cut into thin medallions.

In a large heavy-based saucepan or small stockpot over a medium heat, melt the butter and cook the onion until translucent. Pour in the chicken stock and bring to the boil.

Once it comes to the boil, add the sliced cumbungi, bunya nuts, ground bush tomatoes, mountain pepper and river mint to the boiling stock. Turn down to a simmer and cook for approximately 40 minutes.

Serve in wide bowls with a sprinkling of cracked black pepper. Sautéed finely diced bacon is also delicious in this soup. Four rashers will be enough for this quantity of soup.

SHORTS

- Cumbungi and potato soup or chicken and cumbungi pie are two very easy dishes that can be made with cumbungi stems.

- Try a cumbungi shoot salad with native mint dressing.

- Slice some cumbungi as you would leek, and make up a cheesy white sauce. Line a tart tin with puff pastry and top with the sauce and cumbungi. Bake in a 160°C (325°F) until golden brown.

Cumbungi and Avocado Terrine

To make 1 x 18 cm
(about 8–9 in) terrine

6–8 cumbungi stems,
   depending on size
3 medium avocados
a pinch of salt
a pinch of native pepper
juice of 1 lemon
2 tablespoons (40 g)
   powdered gelatine
½ cup (125 ml) hot water
⅔ cup (165 ml) cream
⅔ cup (150 ml) Lemon Myrtle
   Dressing (see page 143)

Clean and trim the cumbungi stems and steam them whole until they are tender, about 15 minutes. Once tender, refresh immediately under ice-water. The cumbungi stems ideally should retain their cylindrical shape. Drain and set aside.

Mash the avocado flesh with a fork, and season with the salt and native pepper. Add the lemon juice to keep it from discolouring.

Dissolve the powdered gelatine in the hot water. Wait for the liquid to clear (about 10 minutes), stirring gently to ensure that all the gelatine has dissolved.

Heat the cream in a small saucepan until it just simmers. Remove from the heat and pour into the dissolved gelatine and mix well. With a whisk or in a blender, combine the avocado and cream mixtures.

Grease or spray a terrine (or log) tin and line all sides with baker's parchment or silicon paper. Make sure a little paper hangs over all sides as this will facilitate the removal of the finished terrine.

Layer the avocado and the cumbungi alternately, starting with a 1 cm layer on the bottom and finishing with the avocado layer. Cover the top layer of the terrine with another piece of paper or plastic wrap and allow to set in the refrigerator overnight.

When ready to serve, gently lift the terrine from the mould by lifting the overhanging papers. If it feels difficult to lift, wrap a tea-towel that has been run under very hot water around the terrine tin for 10–20 seconds. The terrine should come out cleanly.

To serve, use a sharp, thin-bladed knife that has been dipped in hot water to cut nice, even slices from the terrine. Place the terrine flat on the plate and serve with the lemon myrtle dressing.

Cumbungi and Asparagus Salad with Native Mint Dressing

To serve 6

6 good-sized cumbungi stems
24 spears fresh asparagus
6 hard-boiled eggs, quartered
2 handfuls mixed cress leaves
   or greens
a pinch of salt
a pinch of pepper
1 red onion, finely sliced into
   rings
⅔ cup (150 ml) Native Mint
   Dressing (see page 129)

Clean the cumbungi stems by peeling off the outer layers and wash well as you would prepare leeks to remove the sand or grit. Trim the cumbungi and asparagus stalks to the same length.

Lightly steam the cumbungi and asparagus so that they remain crunchy. (They should take about the same time.) Have a large bowl of ice-water ready and plunge the stalks into the water. This will stop the cooking process and ensure that the cumbungi and asparagus remain crisp. Drain the stalks well.

Quarter each cumbungi stem lengthwise so that you have 24 long spears of similar size and shape to the asparagus spears.

Arrange a nest of cress or greens in the centre of the serving plates. Form a pyramid over the greens with alternating spears of cumbungi and asparagus. Place the egg quarters evenly around the plates. Top with the onion rings and season to taste with salt and pepper.

Drizzle the native mint dressing liberally over the salad and serve.

Murnong

Also known as yam daisy, native yam and native dandelion

The murnong was without doubt the most important food plant for the Kooris of southern Australia, particularly in Victoria. White settlers destroyed this previously abundant food supply by overclearing the land and destroying the woodlands where murnong flourished by introducing sheep, cattle and rabbits with their grazing habit.

Murnong was gathered by Koori women using a digging stick, and, according to the squatter Edward Curr, 'At Colbinabbin, (near Echuca), yams were so abundant, and so easily procured, that one might have collected in an hour, with a pointed stick, as many as would have served a family for the day. . . . Indeed, several thousand sheep, which I had at Colbinabbin, not only learnt to root up these vegetables with their noses, but they for the most part lived on them for the first year, after which the root began gradually to get scarce' (sic).

Historical accounts of murnong from the 1840s onwards show that it was once widespread across all regions of Victoria, but most abundant on the open plains. The loss of murnong was a tragedy of the severest degree to the Aborigines of Victoria who depended on it. Millions of murnong all over the plain are now reduced to small patches that must be protected. According to Beth Gott and Nelly Zola in *Koorie Plants Koorie People*, by 1843, close to one and a half million sheep were grazing land that had fed the Koori tribes for centuries.

The tubers were occasionally washed and eaten raw, but would usually be baked in a ground oven. Around Port Phillip, the murnong would be placed on heated stones and then covered with sweet, clean grass and earth. The murnong were cooked until they melted down into a sweet dark-coloured mass called 'minni'. In the western district of Victoria, the murnong would be washed and laid in rush baskets and steamed over a ground oven. They would be placed in the oven at night so that they would be ready for the next morning's breakfast.

Murnong looks very much like the introduced dandelion and has smooth leaves that are not as saw-toothed as the dandelion. The murnong has yellow flowers in spring that droop when in bud, but like the dandelion, exudes from its leaves and stems a milky latex or juice when cut. The tuber is like a small radish but long and tapered like a baby carrot. Both the tuber and the leaves (at certain times) can be eaten.

TO GROW

Microseris lanceolata

Distribution: Southern Australia, mainly in Victoria and SA.

This is probably the most well known of the southern tuberous food plants. It grows in small clumps to 20–30 cm, with a lovely deep yellow flower. Distinguishing characteristics are the flowerbuds, which tend to droop before opening, and the unbranched flower stalk.

The plant flowers in spring and then dies back. Fresh new growth occurs in late autumn.

Murnong grows in open grassy stretches and light forest. It is best suited to a temperate climate and most well-drained soils. It should not be watered in summer, as this may cause the tubers to decay. The old tuber shrivels and dies in autumn and a new one begins to develop.

Propagate murnong from seed. The fluffy seeds should be sown soon after collection in early summer. Viable seed is plump, don't bother with withered ones. The plants must be protected from garden snails and appreciate some organic matter such as a slow-release fertiliser. Some seed sources can be difficult to germinate, and some provenances have larger tubers than others.

Murnong would be useful in a rockery, a large pot or tub, or mass planting.

Relations

There are other forms of *M. lanceolata* which have a tough, branching root system. They are found especially in alpine areas and places with heavier soils. They are edible, but perhaps not as delicious.

To harvest

Murnong should not be harvested in early winter; the new tuber that formed in autumn hasn't filled yet, and the old one is shrivelling and bitter. The best time to harvest murnong is in the spring, when it is in flower. It may be harvested in the middle of summer, but may be difficult to find then as there is little to mark its place when the leaves dry off in the heat. Koori women would not have found this a problem in the bush because of their intimate knowledge of their surroundings, but in our domestic gardens we may need, initially at least, to mark the murnong patch for easy location. The leaves may be harvested, but not in autumn when the plant sends up its first leaves after summer dormancy. The new tuber forms from these new leaves and if picked at this time, the plant cannot regenerate.

STORING MURNONG

Don't store murnong—pick only what you need at the time to avoid nutritional loss.

TO COOK

Unfortunately, due to the difficulty of obtaining sufficient amounts of murnong these cooking tips will be somewhat limited; my murnong patch is still developing. Yet murnong tubers and leaves are quite delectable, and they deserve inclusion in this selection of bushfoods.

The murnong leaves should be picked when young, and make an excellent salad vegetable with a pleasant tang. Don't pick the leaves in autumn, however, or you will jeopardise the new tubers. The tuber can be eaten raw—it is crisp but fairly bland and likely to cause tummy upset and wind, so we don't recommend it. It really only comes into its own when slowly roasted. When slow-cooked (roasted or baked), the murnong breaks down and produces a delicious sweet syrup. Tests on fresh tubers have shown that they contain a level of sugar that increases after roasting or steaming. There is little starch in the tubers and the carbohydrate present, inulin, a simple sugar made up of multiple units of fructose, cannot be absorbed by the human gut until it is broken down. It is primarily the fructose that gives the cooked murnong its wonderful sweetness. If the murnong (and this is true for some other bulbous plants such as the *Arthropodium* species) is not broken down sufficiently during the cooking process, the digestive system will break it down further with colonic bacteria. This can cause flatulence and even distended bellies! (A similar situation occurs with Jerusalem artichokes.)

Another way to successfully cook the murnong tuber is in soups or casseroles. I can imagine murnong gracing our Sunday roasts as a roasted vegetable to serve alongside oven-roasted Mediterranean vegetables, and roasted murnong in place of roasted whole garlic to spread on freshly baked bread. I think we should all plant our own murnong patch and rediscover this ancient and exciting food.

Taro

The Australian taro is similar and related to the taro that is common throughout the South Pacific and Melanesia. Taro is thought originally to have come from Asia but its introduction to the South Pacific, Melanesia and Australia could have taken place thousands of years ago, as various local forms of the taro exist in particular geographic areas. *Colocasia esculenta* has been in Australia long enough for it to have developed its own physiological differences from the taro of New Guinea.

The tuber and leaves can both be eaten but Aborigines of the north did not eat the leaves at all. The tuber was, and still is, an important food. Taro was usually cooked overnight in ground ovens. The method was similar to that used by Aborigines in the south when cooking murnong; the taro would slowly bake overnight and be ready in the morning. Taro has a reasonable level of thiamine and good levels of vitamins C and B, mineral salts and is high in carbohydrates. It's interesting to note that it's now quite a common sight in our local supermarket vegetable department and at the market.

Taro tastes a little like a cross between sweet potato and potato. The leaves are quite palatable when cooked and are sometimes referred to as Tahitian spinach. Taro is very similar to, and should not be mistaken for *Alocasia macrorrhizos*, also known as cunjevoi, which is eaten by the Aborigines after elaborate detoxification processes. There's a difference: cunjevoi has red berries, taro has greenish ones. The leaf stalk of the cunjevoi is attached to the upper edge of the leaf, and the taro's leaf stalk is attached to the back of the leaf about a third of the way from the top on the underside. Cunjevoi has an extremely dangerous poison, and is one of Australia's most poisonous plants. Children have died from just nibbling on the stems. DO NOT grow cunjevoi in your garden.

TO GROW

Goes with

Colocasia esculenta

Distribution: Top end in WA, Queensland and NT.

Taro plants have enormous heart-shaped leaves up to 40 cm long. They are a decorative, lush-looking perennial, and thrive in colonies in damp and swampy, shady places, often protected by the jungle canopy. The richer the soil, the more exuberant they grow. Being more of a tropical plant they are not frost hardy at all. Propagate by division or seed in warm, moist sites. The plant will not tolerate dryness nor exposure to strong winds. Taro grows almost all year round so the tubers can be harvested as required.

Taro can be seasoned with the native peppers and lemon myrtle, native thyme and native mint. It really works with the addition of coconut cream, and chicken and fish are great with taro, especially in curries.

TO COOK

The best and simplest way to enjoy taro is to peel then roast the tubers whole or in as large pieces as is practical and eat them straight from the oven. Taro can also be cut into smaller pieces and boiled like the common potato, but most of the nutritional minerals and vitamins will be lost. After roasting, mash the taro and add it to recipes or add coconut cream for a simple dish. As they are very starchy vegetables, mashing lightens this starch content and makes the taro light and fluffy. It also changes the colour of the vegetable, so don't panic if a slight pinkish tinge creeps in. Mashed taro can also be used in baking. Instead of the infamous pumpkin scone, why not try a true Queensland specialty and make taro scones! The taro leaf can be treated as you would treat spinach and is usually more palatable cooked than raw.

SHORTS

- Try wrapping large pieces of taro in paperbark and oven-roasting them. The paperbark keeps the moisture and the goodness locked in.
- Try taro cooked in a green Thai-style curry with coconut milk and some fresh fish or chicken.
- Taro chips.

Taro Croquettes

To serve 6 large or more,
depending on the size

2 cups taro, peeled and oven
 baked
4 tablespoons (60 ml)
 coconut cream
scant tablespoon (20 g)
 unsalted butter
1 onion, finely chopped
2 teaspoons (10 g) salt
½ teaspoon native (black)
 pepper
1 tablespoon (5 g) flour for
 dusting
egg wash
1 cup (80 g) desiccated
 coconut
½ cup (125 ml) canola oil
Lemon Aspen Mayonnaise
 (see page 33)

Mash the oven-baked taro by hand with a potato masher
for at least 10 minutes. Add the coconut cream little by
little if necessary to keep the taro moist.

Heat the butter in a small pan and cook the onion
until tender. Add to the mashed taro with the salt and
pepper. Mix thoroughly.

Shape the taro mixture into preferred
cake/croquette size and dust with the flour. Dip the
cakes into the egg wash and then coat in desiccated
coconut.

Heat the oil in a heavy-based shallow skillet and
quickly fry the taro cakes until golden, about 2 minutes
on each side. Drain on kitchen paper and keep warm
until the mixture is used up.

Serve with lemon aspen mayonnaise for dipping.

Seed

Wattleseed

Also known as acacia, common name is wattle

Wattle is intimately and immediately identified as Australian. Golden wattle (*Acacia pycnantha*, also known as karrank to the Gunditjmara people of south-western Victoria), widespread in the south-eastern states, is Australia's floral emblem. In the burgeoning bushfood industry wattleseed has probably the highest profile of any of the indigenous foods.

Wattle is also one of the most widely used and useful Aboriginal food plants. Depending on the species, Aborigines eat the seed, either cooked fresh in its pod or dry-roasted and ground on stones to make damper, and also the sweet gums that ooze from the trees. Many species of *Acacia* are used in Aboriginal medicine, such as the southern ironwood and the turpentine tree in the north, and the black wattle and blackwood of the south. Treatments from these trees include the making of antiseptic lotions for cuts, sores and burns, to post-natal smoke treatments to help newborn babies and their mothers. The timber is used to make boomerangs and coolamons.

Some wattles, such as the food wattle mulga *A. aneura*, can be a prolific source of food, yielding up to 100 kg per hectare in the wild. Wattles have high levels of nutrients, and outstrip wheat, rice, and even some meats in proteins and energy.

Being legumes, they have a symbiotic relationship with rhizobia bacteria, which results in nitrogen being fixed from the air so they also have the potential to increase soil fertility and maybe even rehabilitate degraded farm land. Some wattles will continue to produce edible seeds even in drought conditions, and are a great colonising plant for disturbed areas.

Vic Cherikoff from Bush Tucker Supply and Jean-Paul Bruneteau, now of Riberries Restaurant in Sydney, were the first to bring wattleseed to the attention of the food industry in the early eighties. From those early days, wattleseed has developed a strong profile and devoted following, and its appearance on restaurant menus is no longer an oddity. In 1989 we started supplying Qantas Airways with wattleseed bread rolls, and introduced many other bushfoods to the airline industry. It makes sense to serve indigenous foods on our national carrier.

TO GROW

Acacia

Distribution: Australia-wide.

As wattles are one of the most common plants in Australia and there are so many species available we will examine only one in detail here: mulga (*A. aneura*).

This tree grows naturally throughout the arid outback, although not in the Victorian Mallee regions. It is a medium to large shrub or tree (from 3 to 6 m) with thin grey leaves and an open habit. It doesn't flower or fruit until after heavy rain. Once this occurs in spring, seeds are produced in very large quantities. Being a dry-climate plant, mulga does best inland, and is both drought and frost tolerant. Mulga is often infested with a parasitic insect which produces swollen globes on its branches; these 'mulga apples' are edible, and are sweet and juicy.

All wattles are best grown after cracking the hard-coated seed. Soak the seeds in boiling water for at least four hours to allow them to swell up before sowing. Or, individually scratch the coating until you observe a lighter colour. Seedlings should germinate rapidly. This species should not be grown in humid conditions, so don't water the young plants too much.

Relations

Some other wattles that produce delicious seeds or seed pods include bramble (also known as gundabluey or elegant wattle, *A. victoriae*), wirilda (*A. retinodes*), the coastal wattle (*A. sophorae*), and the golden wattle (*A. pycnantha*).

Most wattles seem to be edible, but some can taste bad—avoid *A. ligulata*, for example, as Aboriginal knowledge tells us that eating it will cause one's hair to fall out! Care should be taken to eat only those species that are identified either here or by known experts in standard reference books.

To harvest

Many wattles flower in spring and the seeds ripen during the following summer and autumn. However, wattles bloom at different times in this vast continent, and the seeds ripen accordingly. Harvest depends on whether they are to be eaten fresh as a cooked vegetable or picked as a dry seed. You should be able to pick about 1.5 kg of seed from most wattles. Do not remove the aril (small attachment to the seed), as this is often rich in oil.

STORING WATTLESEED

If necessary the green wattleseed pods may be stored exactly as you would green beans, that is, in the vegetable compartment of the refrigerator. To take advantage of wattle's nutritional benefits, however, it would be far better to simply pick and use as required. The dry seeds can be kept for a very long time in a clean, dry environment, even for decades. Simply roast what you need from the stored seeds as you need them.

TO COOK

Some green pods of wattle taste delicious after they are cooked, but may taste bitter raw. The pods are best steamed or roasted in the oven. Observe these three steps before cooking with wattleseed: oven-roast, grind, then toss in a dry pan over medium heat or infuse.

(1) Place a layer of seeds on a large baking tray and then into an oven preheated to 160°C (325°F). Dry-roast them for about 30 minutes. As they roast and are almost done, they will start to pop, sounding a little like quiet popcorn.

(2) Once roasted, allow the seeds to cool completely before grinding. I find a domestic coffee grinder works best. Wattleseeds are very hard and, unlike kurrajong, you won't be able to grind them in a vitamiser and certainly not with a mortar and pestle. The ground seed may be stored for a time in an airtight container to avoid flavour loss.

(3) Before using the ground wattleseed, either briefly toss the seeds in a dry pan over a medium heat to release the flavoursome oils or infuse them in boiling liquids such as water or milk. Infusion not only releases the oils, but softens the grounds so they become palatable.

If making bread, soften the wattleseeds in boiling liquid, cool, then activate the yeast in the liquid before incorporating into the recipe. If making ice-cream or mousse, prepare a custard-style base and infuse the wattleseed in the milk before adding the eggs. Strain the flavoured milk, and keep the grounds—you might want to incorporate them into the recipe or use them in a biscuit. Wattleseed has so much flavour that you can use the softened grounds in other recipes.

Wattleseed flour, however, is a strong flour and is best used with another flour for the best results in baking. In bread, you'll only need to use about 75 g ground wattleseed to 1.5 kg unbleached flour (i.e. 5% wattleseed). Always add the wattleseed towards the end of the mixing process—it seems to affect the gluten content in the flour and toughen the bread. Wattle flour can be used in breads, muffins, biscuits and cakes, even bagels. In savoury cooking it can be incorporated into sauces and form crusts and stuffings for meat dishes.

Goes with

Wattleseed, like kurrajong, is suitable to use with many other flavours, it just depends on how you use it. Naturally the nuttiness of the wattleseed does make it particularly suited to chocolate and nuts.

Wattleseeds vary significantly in flavour, texture and colour. Some are a very dark brown and others quite golden or mustard in colour. I love coastal wattle, with its rich, nutty and almost fatty flavour for sprinkling on sandwiches and salads. *A. victoriae*, by contrast, is much darker and has a deeper nut flavour with hints of chicory and coffee that make it perfect for baking.

Wattleseed Cream

Use this cream to fill a pavlova or a cake. Jean-Paul Bruneteau of Sydney's Riberries Restaurant uses a similar cream on an emu-egg pavlova. While emu eggs may be a little difficult to find, a good chicken-egg pavlova filled with wattleseed cream is certainly achievable.

To make 600 ml (or enough to fill a standard 8-egg white pavlova)

1 cup (250 ml) water
2 tablespoons (40 g) roasted and ground wattleseed
2 tablespoons (50 g) castor sugar
2½ cups (600 ml) pure or thickened cream

Bring the water to the boil and add the wattleseed and sugar. Let the liquid boil until it has reduced in volume by at least a quarter. Remove from the heat and strain through a fine sieve, reserving the softened wattleseed grounds. Allow to cool.

Whip the cream until firm peaks form (be careful not to overbeat), and gently fold through the wattleseed syrup and the reserved wattleseed grounds.

Try decorating the pavlova with sugar bark. Melt the sugar in a hot oven until it caramelises and starts to 'run'. It's best to do this on a silicon sheet so that the cooled toffee bark can be easily lifted. When it's completely cold, break it into interesting-shaped pieces, and stand them up in the wattleseed cream.

SHORTS

- Bake wattleseed in meringue (but be careful with the quantities—not too much) or in tuiles to accompany ice-creams.

- Make a wattleseed essence or syrup to use in milkshakes, drinks, ice-creams or mousses. A strong wattleseed syrup is delicious poured over pancakes or hot puddings.

- Make an interesting cocktail by shaking wattleseed syrup, a good whisky and a little cream over ice.

- Wattleseed shortbread is my favourite biscuit. Add the wattleseed flour after mixing in the ordinary flour.

- Make a wattleseed and banana cake by adding 3 teaspoons of wattleseed to the flour (quantity to fit a log tin).

- Roasted and ground wattleseed is caffeine-free, and can be used as a coffee substitute.

Wattleseed Blinis

Make baby wattleseed blinis as a base for toppings for finger food, or make larger ones to serve as an entrée topped with smoked salmon, prosciutto or smoked emu.

*To make 36 baby blinis or
12 entrée-sized*

1 tablespoon (20 g) ground
  and roasted wattleseed
3 x 55 g eggs
⅔ cup (150 ml) milk
⅔ cup (150 ml) water
⅓ cup (80 ml) canola oil
2 cups (280 g) self-raising
  flour
2 teaspoons (10 g) castor
  sugar

Heat the wattleseed gently in a dry pan on the stove. This releases the flavour from the seeds and produces a better tasting blini.

Whisk together the eggs, milk, water and oil until well combined. Slowly add the wattleseed and flour to form a spoonable batter. Adjust the texture with milk or flour if necessary.

Allow the mixture to rest for about half an hour to relax the flour and to soften the wattleseed grains.

Place teaspoon (for baby blinis) or generous tablespoon measures (for entrée or luncheon blinis) of the batter onto a lightly greased hot frying pan or solid cooking plate. Cook until small bubbles appear on the surface, then carefully flip the blini over with a spatula and cook the other side.

Serve immediately with a little butter or cool on a rack. Here are some topping combinations.

• Cress, slices of smoked Tasmanian salmon or ocean trout, crème fraîche or sour cream, salmon roe if desired or a little chopped boiled egg, cracked black pepper and chives.

• Warrigal greens, smoked ham or smoked emu slices, avocado, Bush Tomato and Chilli Salsa (see page 7) and snowpea shoots.

• Roasted red capsicums, eggplant, mushrooms, sun-dried tomato, basil and fetta cheese.

Wattleseed Pasta

1 tablespoon (20 g) roasted
  and ground wattleseed
2 tablespoons (50 ml) water
3½ cups (500 g) plain flour
a pinch of salt
5 x 55 g eggs
4 litres water
1 teaspoon (5 ml) olive oil

Soften the wattleseed by combining with the water and heating to a simmer. Remove from the heat and allow to cool. The wattleseed will absorb the water and produce a rich, dark-coloured paste.

Once the wattleseed is ready, combine with the plain flour and salt in a food processor. Add the eggs, one at a time, and the oil, and process quickly until the mixture forms a dough that just holds together.

Divide the dough into three and wrap in a clean cloth or plastic wrap, and rest for at least 30 minutes in the refrigerator before rolling out.

Bring the water to the boil.

Take the dough from the refrigerator, lightly flour and roll it through a pasta machine to the desired thickness. Cut into your favourite pasta shape—fettuccine, tagliatelle and so on. If you don't have a pasta machine, use a rolling pin and roll out the dough on a lightly floured surface to about 2 mm thickness. Using a sharp long-bladed knife, cut the pasta into the size and shape that you like.

Pour a small amount of oil into the boiling water and gently place the pasta ribbons into the pot. Fresh pasta cooks very quickly, so watch it. As a rule of thumb, the pasta is usually cooked by the time most of the pasta rises to the surface.

Take the pot from the heat immediately and drain the pasta. Refresh the pasta in a large quantity of fresh hot water and toss with some cooking oil to coat and keep it from sticking together.

Try this pasta with a Bush Tomato and Chilli Salsa (see page 7) and fresh herbs such as wild thyme, holy basil or native basil, or fresh garden herbs. Or, you could make wattleseed fettuccine and serve it with a sauce made with button mushrooms, field mushrooms and shiitakes.

Wattleseed Bread

To make approx. 40 rolls or 2 loaves

2 tablespoons (40 g) roasted and ground wattleseed
1¾ cups (450 ml) water
15 g fresh or 7 g dried yeast
1 teaspoon (5 g) castor sugar or honey
generous tablespoon (30 g) unsalted butter
5½ cups (750 g) plain flour
1 teaspoon bread improver
2 teaspoons salt
1 x 55 g egg

Boil the wattleseed and water over a medium gas flame and allow to cool.

Activate the yeast in a little warm water with the sugar or honey.

Rub the butter into the sifted dry ingredients (using a dough hook on an electric mixer if possible). Add the yeast mixture and boiled wattleseed. Mix well and knead until smooth.

Place the dough into a clean bowl, cover with a tea-towel, and prove in a warm place until the dough doubles in size.

Divide the dough and shape into rolls or loaves. Prove again.

Preheat the oven to 220°C (425°C). When the bread has risen again, brush the surface lightly with the egg beaten with a little milk or water. Sprinkle some wattleseed on the top and bake in the preheated oven for 15–20 minutes or until golden brown and the base sounds hollow when tapped.

Serve fresh from the oven with Quandong Jam (see page 22).

Wattleseed Ice-cream

To make 1 litre

1 litre thickened cream
2 tablespoons (40 g) roasted and ground wattleseed
6 egg yolks
½ cup (100 g) castor sugar
3 teaspoons (20 g) honey, such as leatherwood

Bring half the cream and the wattleseed to the boil. While the cream is heating, beat the egg yolks and sugar together with a balloon whisk (without fluffing) until thick and creamy. Strain the boiled cream and wattleseed, reserving the wattleseed.

Slowly whisk the cream into the egg mixture and, when completely mixed, pour back into the pot and return to a medium heat, stirring constantly until the mixture thickens and coats the back of a wooden spoon.

Strain the custard and add the reserved wattleseed. Cool over ice or in the coldest part of the refrigerator. When completely chilled, add the remaining cream to the wattleseed custard mix and churn in an ice-cream maker following the manufacturer's instructions.

Kurrajong

Also known as bottle tree, itchy bombs and boab. The Aboriginal name
from the Dharruk people (from Sydney region) has been maintained

Kurrajong seeds

A number of different kurrajong species grow in Australia, ranging from the desert kurrajong *Brachychiton gregorii* to the common or black kurrajong *B. populneus* that is widespread over the ranges and inland plains east of the Great Dividing Range to *B. rupestris* and *B. australis*, common kurrajongs in outback Queensland. The kurrajong has survived land-clearing, especially around homesteads and in paddocks as they are often huge, stately trees that are attractive and also a useful fodder plant for cattle. They often have a very neat trimmed look around the base of the foliage as cattle reach up and eat the lower leaves. Kurrajongs have also been a popular shade tree planted in parks and gardens in urban areas.

The trunk of the kurrajong is quite smooth, stout and rounded. The foliage is dense, and the green leaves are usually tear-shaped, and may be three-lobed.

The kurrajong flowers in spring and early summer, and carries clusters of creamy, bell-shaped blooms with red splotches or streaks on the inside, followed, in mid-autumn, by dark brown, leathery, boat-shaped seed pods about 5 to 7 cm long. Edible, bright yellow seeds covered with very irritating, sharp yellow hairs are encased within. The seeds have a nutty, earthy flavour. A large kurrajong will have around 1000 seed pods or boats per tree, and each boat holds between 15 and 20 seeds.

The kurrajong is an important Aboriginal food as it is high in protein (18 per cent), carbohydrates (about 15 per cent) and fat (25 per cent). The Aborigines would eat them either raw or roasted. Often the seeds would be ground, the husks and irritating hairs winnowed away, and the kurrajong flour formed into cakes and baked.

The clear honey-coloured sap from the kurrajong is also a prized treat, and when rubbed on open cuts and sores is known to encourage healing. The inner bark of the kurrajong is effective as a bandage.

When in seed, kurrajongs attract many native birds—cockatoos, rosellas, choughs and currawongs.

TO GROW

Brachychiton populneus

Distribution: Queensland, NSW and Victoria.

The *B. populneus* grows widely on rocky slopes in NSW and Victoria in open, sunny areas. It is a medium to large shrub or tree (from 7 to 15 m). An *Acacia* or wattle planted nearby is said to improve the quality of the kurrajong.

The kurrajong is slow-growing initially, but propagation by seed is easy. Germinate in pots or sow directly into the ground and keep up a good supply of water. It is lime tolerant.

Relations

In addition to those mentioned in the introduction, the Illawarra flame tree *B. acerifolium*.

To harvest

The seed pods of the kurrajong start to form in autumn and from around mid-May a close eye should be kept on the tree. When about a third of the pods have turned a hard, dark brown and have started to split, they may be harvested. The seed is actually ready when the pods split open, however, they may be picked just before to avoid losing the entire crop to birds. The pods grow in clusters and are carried at the end of branches, and their weight helps bring them within reasonable reach. You should be able to harvest 2 to 4 kg of seed from an established tree. Harvest the ones you can reach easily, either by hand or with the aid of a hook attached to a pole, and leave the pods at the top for the local birds. Once harvested, the seeds need to be removed from the pods and cleaned of their outer husk and the fine yellow hair.

STORING KURRAJONG

Once the seeds are cleaned make sure that they are completely dry before storing. If the seeds seem a little damp, dry them in full sun on a clean sheet for a day—again, watch that the birds don't get to them! Store the dry seeds in an airy, dry environment, and they should keep for months. If preferred the seeds can be roasted and then stored in airtight containers. Don't grind the seeds until you need them as some flavour loss may occur.

Seed

TO COOK

When cleaning the kurrajong seeds always wear rubber gloves to protect your hands and fingers from the needle-like irritant hairs that surround the seeds. If the hairs get into your skin, pick them out as they can be painful.

The seeds must be roasted and ground before use.

Roast the seeds in an oven preheated to 160°C (325°F). Spread the seeds out on a baking tray and place in the oven for about 30 minutes. They will 'pop' a little like popcorn. When the first pops occur, a blue smoke will start to rise from the seeds. Don't panic as this is usual, and indicates that the seeds are almost ready. Roast them to your preferred 'doneness'—the darker the colour, the stronger the flavour. I find 30 to 40 minutes gives about the right brownness and flavour. Some seeds may jump off the tray onto the oven floor so remember to gather them up. Allow to cool completely before grinding.

Kurrajong seeds can also be dry-roasted in a covered pan on the top of the stove. Toss the seeds around regularly to ensure even roasting, allow to cool completely, then grind in a domestic coffee grinder. If you don't have one, use a vitamiser, and only grind small amounts of seed at a time. Due to the kurrajong's high fat content, the seeds can become gluggy if over-processed and if too many seeds are processed at the same time. A mortar and pestle will also break up the seed, but you won't get a loose, powder-like finish.

Kurrajong is a lovely flavour addition to baked products as it is a form of flour in itself. It is delicious in breads, blinis, pancakes, cakes, biscuits and slices. It's also lovely used to dust chicken or fish before pan-frying. It is quite a strong-textured and strong-flavoured flour on its own and is usually more palatable if added to a common flour base at a ratio of 10 to 15 per cent. It can be added to plain white or unbleached flour, wholemeal, light rye or to sourdough. So for a bread recipe that has 1 kg of flour, add 100 g kurrajong.

Goes with

Ground kurrajong is suited to most other bushfood flavours, depending on use. It is particularly delicious with dairy foods, such as milk and cream, chocolate and nuts.

Kurrajong Tempura Batter

To make 2 cups

1 x 55 g egg
½ cup (125 ml) light beer
½ cup (125 ml) water
¼ teaspoon salt
a pinch of native pepper
generous ¾ cup (120 g) rice
  flour
1 tablespoon (30 g) roasted
  and ground kurrajong

In a medium-sized bowl whisk together the egg, beer, water, salt and pepper. Toss together the rice and kurrajong flours and whisk into the liquid until smooth. Set aside to rest at room temperature for 30 minutes.

Dip vegetables such as sliced sweet potato, pumpkin, capsicum or broccoli florets, or fish pieces or prawns into the batter and deep-fry until the batter is a light golden colour. Serve immediately.

SHORTS

- Make kurrajong blinis in the same way as Wattleseed Blinis (see page 169).

- Use roasted, ground kurrajong as a coffee substitute. Use about 2 teaspoons of kurrajong per person and make the coffee in a plunger, dripolator or espresso machine in the usual way. If you don't have any of the above, the kurrajong can be covered with boiling water, allowed to infuse for a few minutes and then strained. It's lovely as a hot drink but also delicious if made up, cooled and then prepared as iced kurrajong 'coffee'.

- Boil the ground kurrajong in a little water, reduce and strain it to form an essence to be added to milk shakes, ice-creams, creams or mousses. If you like, the essence can be sweetened and stabilised by adding sugar and returning to the boil to form a syrup. This syrup keeps for a while in the refrigerator.

Kurrajong Pancakes

The characteristic nutty taste of kurrajong in these pancakes enables them to be used for both savoury and sweet applications. Perfect for a brunch topped with smoked salmon, soft poached eggs or Quandong Jam (see page 22).

To make 6 pancakes

2 x 55 g eggs
1 tablespoon (25 g) castor sugar
a pinch of salt
generous ½ cup (125 ml) water
generous ½ cup (125 ml) milk
2 tablespoons (50 ml) olive oil
1¾ cup (250 g) self-raising flour, sifted
1 tablespoon (30 g) roasted and ground kurrajong
olive oil or unsalted butter for cooking

In a medium-sized bowl, whisk together the eggs, sugar, salt, water, milk and oil until well mixed.

Combine the self-raising flour and kurrajong flour. Slowly add the combined flours to the liquid egg mixture, whisking constantly until it forms a smooth batter. The batter should be the consistency of heavy double cream. Let the batter rest for at least 20 minutes before cooking the pancakes.

Brush a small skillet (about 15 cm across) generously with the oil or butter and place over a medium heat. When hot pour 3–4 tablespoons of the batter into the skillet and cook until the underside is slightly browned, 2–3 minutes. Turn and cook the other side for another 1–2 minutes. Continue until the batter is used up.

To serve, place each pancake on a hot plate and top with a soft-centred poached egg. Place three slices of smoked salmon around each pancake and dollop a little sour cream and salmon roe at the side. Sprinkle cracked black pepper over the dish and serve with a glass of champagne.

Bush
Banana

Also known as doubah, native pear, yuparli

I love the bush banana, and I have put it in the seed section since, as a cook, I find the seeds the most interesting edible part of the fruit. When I first got hold of one I didn't have a clue what to do with it, but a few urgent phone calls to Napperby Station soon solved that problem! Their advice: eat the baby bush bananas whole as they first form; the immature fruits are quite delicious, tasting of peas, squash and zucchini. The larger bush bananas can also be eaten; Aborigines eat the whole fruit after baking it in the hot coals. I must confess, however, that I find the interior of the larger fruits not very edible because of the mass of silky filaments that are attached to the seeds and the relatively thin layer of flesh around the seeds. However, these seeds are wonderful to eat if you detach them from their silky threads. I love them raw or cooked, and they taste like peas fresh from the pod—nothing at all like a tropical banana!

The bush banana is an oval-shaped fruit, a little like a small, smooth-skinned avocado in shape. It is a soft pale green in colour and grows on twining vines that have slender, light green leaves. The flowers are cream to greenish in colour, and bloom in late spring and summer. The pods follow and can grow up to 10 cm if

not picked when young. The fruit is very rich in thiamine and has 2900 mg thiamine per 100 g fruit—ten times higher than any other cultivated food. Aborigines also eat the flowers, which are nectar laden, and sometimes the leaves, roots and tubers of the plant as well.

The photograph shows the inside of a bush banana pod, with some loose seeds.

TO GROW

Marsdenia australis

Distribution: All mainland states; not in Tasmania.

This plant is a gentle climber which likes to sprawl across other bushes or along the ground. Due to its non-vigorous habit, the plant grows well among other plants without covering and strangling them. It grows naturally in the dry parts of all the mainland states, usually near periodic waterways, but is not common in Queensland. It prefers an arid climate and very good drainage. It is drought and frost tolerant and it's doubtful if it would thrive in a humid, coastal site. In a garden situation, it could be trained up a supporting trellis. The pear-shaped pods will split upon maturity, and the released seeds will float away on silky threads. Gather these seeds, which can be sown at most times of the year. However, don't water the seedlings excessively—they are likely to suffer from rot or fungal disease.

To harvest

Pick the baby bush bananas when they are very small if eating whole. Pick the larger bush bananas while they are still green and haven't split—they'll have more seeds.

STORING BUSH BANANAS

Bush bananas don't freeze well but they will keep for a number of weeks under refrigeration without deteriorating.

TO COOK

The most interesting part of the bush banana for the cook is the seed. Remove the attaching silky filaments before using. Each bush banana will yield about 5 g seed. This is a tedious and laborious task but must be done. The cleaned seeds can then be gently steamed as a fresh vegetable or tossed through a stir-fry or pasta. Ground in a mortar or pestle or food-processor (large quantities only), they also bake beautifully, and are particularly delicious in cakes and breads. Try them in a mayonnaise or a pesto. Bush banana seeds make an interesting addition to a stuffing for a rolled loin of lamb. Add them to couscous or risotto, and wherever the flavour of peas are appropriate. I'm currently experimenting with them to make a bush banana tahini.

Goes with

Because of the seeds' light and delicate vegetable flavour, be careful that you don't overwhelm them with other strong-tasting bushfoods. A perfect seasoning for them is a small amount of native mint. The native peppers, native thyme and lemon myrtle all suit bush banana seeds.

Bush Banana Mayonnaise

Freshly steamed asparagus spears or young cumbungi shoots would be perfect with this mayonnaise.

To make 2½ cups (630 ml)

2 teaspoons prepared seed
   mustard
3 egg yolks
a pinch of salt
native (or black) pepper to
   taste
1¼ cup (310 ml) macadamia
   oil
1 cup (250 ml) olive oil
¼ cup (65 ml) Lemon Myrtle
   Vinegar (see page 139)
¼ cup (30 g) bush banana
   seeds, ground

Place the mustard, egg yolks, salt and pepper in the bowl of a food processor and, using a steel blade, process for about 1 minute.

Combine the oils and, with the machine running slowly, dribble in the oils and continue to process. Once the mixture begins to thicken, you can add the oil faster.

When the mixture is fairly thick add the vinegar and the ground bush banana seeds. Add more oil or vinegar to taste.

Bush Banana Tea Bread

Serve this freshly baked with cream and some sliced, fresh tropical bananas sprinkled with a little ground native nutmeg.

To make 1 log or loaf tin

3 x 55 g eggs
¼ cup (65 ml) macadamia nut oil
3½ tablespoons (85 g) castor sugar
1 teaspoon vanilla essence
3 tablespoons (75 g) unsalted butter
2 cups (140 g) cleaned bush banana seeds (about 8 bananas)
2 cups (280 g) plain flour
1 teaspoon (5 g) baking powder
2 teaspoons (10 g) bicarbonate of soda
1 teaspoon (5 g) salt
½ teaspoon (3 g) ground native nutmeg (or nutmeg)

Preheat the oven to 160°C (325°C). Lightly grease the log or loaf tin.

Using a whisk attached to a mixer, beat the eggs, oil, sugar and vanilla essence until light and thick.

Carefully peel the bush bananas and remove the seeds from the core. Reserve the seeds, and finely chop the peeled flesh and fold it through the mix.

Sift all the dry ingredients together and gently fold these through the mixture, adding at least half a cup of the reserved bush banana seeds last.

Pour the batter into a prepared tin and bake on the middle shelf of the preheated oven for approximately 1 hour. Test the tea bread with a skewer to ensure it is baked through. Allow to cool in the tin before removing.

Basic Recipes

Chicken Stock

To make 4 cups (1 litre)

1.5 litres water
1 x 1 kg chicken carcases
1 onion, sliced
1 carrot, sliced
3 sticks celery, sliced
1 teaspoon (5 g) salt
1 tablespoon chopped
   parsley
10 native pepper leaves

Combine all the ingredients except the pepper leaves in a large saucepan and bring to the boil. Skim off any scum that rises to the surface of the stock.

Lower the heat and allow to simmer for about 45 minutes, skimming occasionally to remove any scum that rises to the top.

Add the native pepper leaves, and simmer for a further 10 minutes.

Strain and refrigerate. The stock will keep for a few days.

Veal Stock

To make 4 cups (1 litre)

1.5 litres water
1 kg veal shin and bones
1 onion, sliced
1 carrot, sliced
3 sticks celery, sliced
1 teaspoon (5 g) salt
10 native pepper leaves
½ teaspoon wild thyme

Combine all the ingredients except the pepper leaves in a large saucepan and bring to the boil. Skim off any scum that rises to the surface of the stock.

Lower the heat and allow to simmer for about 45 minutes, skimming occasionally to remove any scum that rises to the top.

Add the native pepper leaves, then simmer for a further 10 minutes.

Strain and refrigerate. The stock will keep for a few days.

Chicken Demi-glace

To make 4 cups (1 litre)

2 litres Chicken Stock (see page 182)
1 tablespoon (25 g) unsalted butter
1 tablespoon (20 g) plain flour

Boil the stock until it is reduced by half to a litre.

Combine the butter and flour to form a paste. Gently cook the paste over a light heat, while constantly stirring, for 5 minutes. Whisk into the stock, and allow to simmer for 10 minutes.

Strain and refrigerate. The demi-glace will keep for a few days.

Shortcrust Pastry

To make 250 g

1¾ cups (250 g) plain flour
¼ teaspoon salt
⅔ cup (125 g) unsalted butter, cubed
2–3 (50–75 ml) tablespoons cold water

Sift the flour and salt into a mixing bowl. Rub the butter into the dry ingredients with your fingertips until the mixture resembles fine bread crumbs. Sprinkle the water over and mix in with a knife and then your fingertips. Knead quickly (or use an electric mixer with a paddle attachment) until the pastry begins to hold together.

Wrap the pastry in plastic food wrap and rest in the refrigerator for at least an hour or until ready to use.

To bake blind, first preheat the oven to 180°C (360°F). Roll out the pastry on a lightly floured surface to fit the tin and carefully line the tin, taking care to press the pastry to the sides. Prick the base of the shell with a fork and line with foil. Fill with baking weights, beans or rice. Bake in the preheated oven until the pastry just begins to brown around the edges and crisp up, about 20 minutes.

Remove from the oven, take out the weights and foil, and bake for another 10 minutes. Cool before filling.

Sweetcrust Pastry

To make 500 g

1¼ cups (250 g) unsalted
  butter
1¼ cups (250 g) castor sugar
3½ cups (500 g) plain flour,
  sifted
3 x 55 g eggs

Lightly cream the butter and sugar in a mixer with a paddle. Add the sifted flour, followed by the eggs, one at a time, beating well between each addition until the pastry begins to hold together.

Wrap the pastry in plastic foodwrap and refrigerate until ready to roll out according to the recipe.

To bake blind, first preheat the oven to 180°C (360°F). Roll out the pastry on a lightly floured surface to fit the tin and carefully line the tin, taking care to press the pastry to the sides. Prick the base of the shell with a fork and line with foil. Fill with baking weights, beans or rice. Bake in the preheated oven until the pastry just begins to brown around the edges and crisp up, about 20 minutes.

Remove from the oven, take out the weights and foil, and bake for another 10 minutes. Cool before filling.

Conversion Tables

Bushfoods

	per 100 g	g per metric cup
appleberries	50 fruits	125 g
bunya nuts (whole)	7 nuts	120 g
bush tomatoes (whole)	200 fruits	110 g
Davidson's plums	2 fruits	130 g
desert figs	600 fruits	110 g
dianella berries	700 fruits	100 g
elderberries	800 fruits	110 g
Illawarra plums	30 fruits	130 g
Kakadu plums	33 fruits	130 g
kurrajong (whole seeds)	750 seeds	160 g
lady apples (flesh)	2 fruits	100 g
lemon aspen	20 fruits	100 g
muntries	400 fruits	100 g
native cucumbers	20 fruits	125 g
native tamarind	90 fruits	130 g
pepperberries (whole)	250 fruits	115 g
quandong (flesh only)	24 fruits	110 g
riberry	200 fruits	110 g
samphire	generous handful	100 g
warrigal greens	varies	70 g
wild lime	100 fruits	140 g
wild rosella	40 flowers	50 g

Ground bushfoods	**g per teaspoon**	**g per tablespoon**
bush tomatoes	5 g	15 g
lemon myrtle	2 g	8 g
native mint	2 g	8 g
native nutmeg	2 g	8 g
native pepper	2 g	8 g
wattleseed	4 g	20 g

Metric units are used throughout this book. The approximate equivalents are as follows.

Dry Weights

10 g	⅓ oz
50 g	1¾ oz
85 g	3 oz
100 g	3½ oz
112 g	4 oz
170 g	6 oz
225 g	8 oz
450 g	16 oz (1 lb)
500 g	1.1 lb
1 kg	2.2 lb

Liquid Weights

1 metric teaspoon	5 ml
½ metric tablespoon	10 ml
1 metric tablespoon	20 ml
1 US teaspoon	5 ml
1 US tablespoon	15 ml
¼ metric cup	62.5 ml
½ metric cup	125 ml
1 metric cup	250 ml
4 metric cups	1 litre

Length

1 cm	⅓ in
2 cm	¾ in
2.5 cm	1 in
5 cm	2 in
10 cm	4 in
20 cm	8 in

Oven Temperatures

100°C	210°F	Very slow	
125°C	240°F	Very slow	
150°C	300°F	Slow	Gas Mark 2
180°C	350°F	Moderate	Gas Mark 4
200°C	400°F	Moderately hot	Gas Mark 6
220°C	450°F	Hot	Gas Mark 7
250°C	500°F	Very hot	Gas Mark 9

Planning a Bushfood Garden

When planting bushfood species, remember that many of them are highly ornamental, and can be easily grown in conjunction with non-bushfood or exotic species.

Many bushfood species may be used in the same ways as more familiar species. Don't assume that they cannot be maintained, shaped or shifted because they are bushfood plants. Note the individual comments about plant use and position in the garden, and use this information to determine where the plant will grow successfully. For example, a background screening plant may not succeed as a specimen out in the open. A rainforest understorey species may not tolerate exposed coastal conditions or the dry inland. A dry climate plant may suffer from fungal infestation if grown in moist humid sites.

Be sure to understand what the plant does as it grows, and its habit. For example, *Araucaria bidwillii* (bunya pine) grows to at least 30 m, and is too large for most small suburban gardens. However, it is a spectacular specimen in a very large garden or farm. *Terminalia ferdinandiana* (Kakadu plum) will not survive in cool climates, unless in a greenhouse. *Tasmannia lanceolata* (mountain pepper)

requires abundant water and a temperate climate. *Correa alba* could be used as a hedge; *Syzygium australe* 'Blaze' can be grown as a potted specimen; *Billardiera cymosa* (sweet appleberry) or *B. scandens* (common appleberry) will succeed as a screen or a trellis.

Not all plants in a natural ecosystem can or will have a use for human beings. However, one can create an 'artificial' ecosystem using entirely Australian food plants. In effect, this is a type of Australian permaculture. And certain sorts of ecosystems can be created to suit certain types of climates.

For example, for a drier climate, try *Brachychiton populneus* (kurrajong), *Santalum acuminatum* (quandong), *Solanum centrale* (bush tomato) and/or *Eremocitrus glauca* (desert lime).

For a cool moist climate, try *Tasmannia lanceolata* (mountain pepper), *Prostanthera rotundifolia* (mint bush) or the *Tetragonia tetragonoides* (warrigal greens).

For a subtropical climate, try *Microcitrus australis* (round lime, wild lime), *Diploglottis cunninghamii* (native tamarind), *Davidsonia pruriens* (Davidson's plum) or *Backhousia citriodora* (lemon myrtle).

These suggested gardens are often highly ornamental and succeed remarkably well. Look for natural combinations of plants if possible, as they often appear very appropriate when combined with one another.

Remember that it may not be practical to harvest many Australian food plants heavily. Some may make better ornamentals than food plants. For example, the *Arthropodium strictus* (chocolate lily) has colourful deep blue or purple flowers and a strong chocolatey fragrance in warm weather. If you eat the tubers when the plant matures, it could be rapidly lost in the garden. But, if tasted carefully and less frequently in a garden, it remains a wonderful ornamental specimen that can last for many years.

There is much significant literature on gardening with native species. Most of these books will have comments relevant to bushfood species, even if the species discussed are not those in this book. Often the family of the species is represented, or sometimes one can examine the comments about certain types of plants, and from this information cross to bushfood plants that inhabit the same ecosystem.

Consult the following as starting points.

- The general SGAP (Society for Growing Australian Plants) publications offer many valuable hints on cultivating Australian food plants. Join the society, and learn about plants as diverse as small ground lilies to vast tropical trees, to attractive water plants. The Australian Food Plants Study Group can offer many hints on growing food plants in your garden, and is continually bringing new and interesting plants into cultivation. See page 202 for the address in your state.

- Refer to the following for further cultivation tips:

David and Patricia Ratcliffe, *Australian Native Indoor Gardening Made Easy*, Little Hills Press, 1991.
Diana Snape, *Australian Native Gardens: Putting Visions into Practice*, Lothian Books, Melbourne, 1992.
Australian Plants Study Group, *Grow What Where*, Thomas Nelson, Melbourne, 1980.
Beadle, N.C.W. et al., *Flora of the Sydney Region*, Reed, Sydney, 1972.
Black, J.M., *Flora of SA*, parts 1–4, Government Printer, Adelaide, 1943–57.
Elliot, Rodger, *Coastal Gardening in Australia*, Lothian, Melbourne, 1992.
— and David L. Jones, *Encyclopaedia of Australian Plants*, vols 1–6, Lothian, Melbourne, 1982.
Society for Growing Australian Plants, Maroondah Group Vic., *Flora of Melbourne*, SGAP, Ringwood, Victoria.

See page 205 for other books which may be of interest.

- In temperate areas, the Southern Bushfood Network offers information on the cultivation and harvesting of southern food plants. Telephone (03) 9416 7150.

Planting Bushfoods

Most plants can be propagated using one of three methods. You can create new plants by seed, cuttings or division. You can also graft plants, however, this will not be covered in this section. To find out about grafting, consult a specialised horticultural handbook. Some general comments on propagation follow. Specialised points are made in the individual plant entries.

SEED

Propagation from seed is used more than any other method of propagation. It is the simplest, and also cheapest way of producing plants, and large quantities of plants can be generated with a small amount of effort.

There is, however, wide variation in the progeny of the plants, and the appearance and taste of the fruit can vary greatly. Some plants must have male and female specimens to fruit, and it is impossible to guarantee the sex of the plant when propagating from seed.

Plants grown from seeds are often more drought hardy than those grown from cuttings, as the root system of a seedling tends to drive deeper into the soil.

Pre-treatment

Many seeds should be sown very fresh. Rainforest plants often have a very short period of viability, and if left for a long period after collection they will no longer germinate. Other seeds can be left for years—wattleseeds, for example, will remain healthy and viable for decades. For the best results, collected seeds should be stored in a glass bottle in a cool, dark and dry place.

Many cool to temperate and alpine plants require stratification. This involves storing the seed in a cold, moist location for several months to simulate the onset of winter. You can leave the seeds in the refrigerator for a period before sowing, or plant the seeds at the beginning of winter. They should start to germinate in spring.

Hard-coated seeds such as wattles, kurrajongs and macadamias seem to germinate best when the hard seed coat has been scratched or cracked. Refer to the relevant entries for instructions, as the treatments are specific to the plants.

Other plants such as the bunya pine and quandongs require different pre-treatment. Detailed instructions on propagation are given in the individual entries.

Temperatures for good germination of the seeds vary, and depend on the natural climate and habitat of the plant. Plants from northern Australia, including those from monsoonal climates, and tropical and subtropical rainforests, require warm or hot moist conditions. The temperature should be consistently over 25°C for good germination. Some plants require temperatures of 30°C or hotter. By contrast, many lilies from southern Australia germinate best between 15 and 20°C. Any warmer and they may rot or not grow until the weather has become cooler.

Containers

Use a clean, sterile flat container with holes to let the water escape when sowing seeds. A margarine or yoghurt container (with holes poked into the bottom), or perhaps a vegetable seedling punnet is suitable for smaller numbers of seedlings. Commercial nurseries use larger containers.

Some Australian plants initiate large, thick taproots when germinating, and it is important to anticipate this by sowing the seeds in a deeper container.

Larger seeds may even be placed directly into jiffy pots in which they will be planted out to avoid transplant shock.

Rainforest species often do not have a deep, penetrating root system, so use a wider flatter pot. Forestry tubes are recommended for wattles and gum trees.

Germination Mixture

It is important that the germination mixture is very well drained. Usually a mixture of sand and peat moss will succeed. You can also germinate seeds in pure propagating sand, commercial seed-raising mix, or standard potting mix. The latter two mixtures can sometimes form a crust on the surface which may prevent the seeds from pushing through. This crust will not appear if the seeds are first covered with a layer of sand or vermiculite.

For best results, the mixture should be clean and sterile. Sterilise the potting mix by heating in a 60°C oven for half an hour.

Sowing

Do not sow seeds too thickly. This causes a lack of aeration among the seedlings when they begin to germinate, and is a prime situation for fungal infestation, which can cause the widespread death of seedlings.

Fine seeds must be only just covered with germination mixture. Coarse heavy seed require a greater depth of mixture. As a rule of thumb, the layer of soil should be no more than twice the thickness of the seed.

Place the seedlings in a lightly shaded protected position. Water using a fine mist whenever the seed-raising mixture begins to dry out. Dry-area plants can be watered less frequently than monsoonal and rainforest species. Clean, well-ventilated conditions are most important.

Germination times vary tremendously; some species germinate within several weeks, others can take one or two years.

Pricking Out

It is important to time the moment of pricking out correctly. Seedlings should be removed from the punnets and transplanted into larger pots when the plants have germinated, and are strong and sturdy, but the roots have not yet developed to a large extent. Pot up the seedlings before the roots twist and coil in the pot, as this creates a weakness in the plants which may cause them to die later.

To pot up the seedling, hold the plant suspended over an empty pot and fill up the pot with potting mix. Alternatively, fill the pot with mixture, and make a hole with a dibbler (a pencil or chopstick). Place the seedling carefully into the pot, pat down to firm up the soil around it, and water thoroughly.

The potting mix should contain a small amount of slow-release fertiliser. Use a low-phosphorus fertiliser for proteaceous plants such as banksias or grevilleas. High quantities of phosphorus added to these plants can cause dieback or leaf burn.

CUTTINGS

Sometimes it is so difficult to germinate from seed that cuttings are the only possible way of propagating plants. Propagation from cuttings allows you to select and grow good, strong plants, since cuttings produce plants that are identical to the parent plant. Different plants from the same species have a wide range of different habits and food tastes, and selection of good fruiting or growing forms is desirable.

Plants that are of the same genetic stock—and therefore identical—are not truly representative of the species, and may be particularly susceptible to certain diseases. To create a healthy population of plants requires taking cuttings from a number of different plants in a locality.

While propagation from seed is strictly seasonal, cuttings can be taken whenever there is appropriate material. Avoid plants that are in flower.

Cutting Mixtures

Cutting mixtures must be free draining and completely sterile. Many propagators use perlite, peat moss and sand, or just pure sand. However pure sand dries out rapidly and requires frequent watering.

Propagating sand can be purchased from most good gardening stores. Sterilise before use by heating in an oven to 60°C (or as low as possible) for about 30 minutes.

Cutting Frames

You can purchase cutting frames from a gardening store, or construct one from rustproof metal. It should have a reliable watering device to keep the cuttings from drying out. Professional propagators use misting jets or an electronic leaf to keep the leaves continually moist. It is also possible to use a timer that waters the cuttings at regular intervals.

Home growers can make a simple cutting frame by filling a pot with cutting medium, inserting some stiff wire into the pot in an arch, and completely covering with a plastic bag. The pot should be deeper than a seedling pot, be clean, and sterile. This method will keep the cuttings moist without a specialised watering system. The pot should be checked regularly to stop the cuttings from drying out.

Cuttings can be taken from firm but fresh growth. A good time of year is after the new season's growth or after flowering. This can be in early or mid-summer in temperate regions. In the tropics growth occurs after the onset of the wet season. However, good cutting material can often be found at most other times of the year.

Tip cuttings are usually the easiest to take. Using a pair of sharp and clean secateurs, cut some small branches from the bush you wish to grow. From these branches, snip about 10 cm of growth (the length of the cutting differs from plant to plant) from the end of the branch. The cut must be made immediately below a leaf node, since this is where the roots will emerge. Remove all the leaves apart from the top third of the cutting. Large-leaved plants may have the top leaves cut in half to reduce transpiration. The cutting should then be placed in the sterilised cutting mixture.

Root hormone is not necessary, however, its use often produces more roots more quickly than untreated cuttings. To use, dip each cutting in root hormone before placing into the pot.

Take care not to fill the pots too thickly with cuttings—too many will reduce air movement and allow fungal spores to spread rapidly.

The length of time plants take to root varies. Check the underside of the pot for roots every two or three weeks. Once roots have developed, pot up each cutting into a separate container with a generous pinch of slow-release fertiliser.

DIVISION

Division has similar characteristics to growing plants from cuttings. It is also vegetative, and thus new plants are identical to the parent.

Division is suitable for clumping plants such as the dianellas, or suckering and running plants such as the *Mentha* spp.

Look at the plant to be divided and find a location where a portion of the plant seems to have a healthy, well-

developed crown and roots. This portion can now be split from the main part of the plant, using either a sharp shovel or a pair of secateurs if the plant is in a pot. Each part should contain plenty of soil and roots. Pot up each portion with a generous pinch of slow-release fertiliser.

GROWING ON AND GARDEN MAINTENANCE

Place newly potted-up plants in a mild, protected site until they become established and introduce them to more exposed locations over a month or two until they harden off. Planting out depends on the speed of growth of the plant. Wattles, bottlebrushes and eucalypts will be ready within 3 months, other plants may take longer. Some rainforest plants are very slow growing and can take a year or two to be ready for planting in the ground.

Don't leave the plant for too long, as root coiling can occur, which reduces the ability of the plant to survive in adverse conditions.

Other Edible Plants

Here are a few other plants to whet your appetite for starting a bushfood garden.

BURDEKIN PLUM

(also known as tulip plum)
Pleiogynium timorense
Distribution: Queensland coastal areas

The Burdekin plum tree bears the most deliciously tart, plum-flavoured fruit. The plums are about 25 cm in diameter and are purplish–red in colour. The tree drops its fruit usually between August and October but the fruit is very hard and astringent when it first falls and needs to be left for a few weeks to ripen. Traditionally the plums are ripened by burying them in clean sand for a week or two, after which they soften and become very palatable. The Burdekin plum makes a great fruit jelly or jam.

CHEESEFRUIT

(also known as Great morinda)
Morinda citrifolia
Distribution: Far north Queensland and coastal NT

When the fruit of this plant is ripe it has an overpowering smell of extremely strong cheese, something like gorgonzola on a very hot day! It is an odd-looking warty fruit that is almost translucent, about 10 cm long and soft when ripe. It's interesting to note that the flowers preceding the fruit are sweet smelling; the fruit only develops its particularly pungent smell when ripe. We have found the most palatable way to use this fruit is to combine it in a salad dressing—it really is delicious in this form.

DESERT FIG

(also known as native fig, small leaved rock fig, rock fig)
Ficus platypoda
Distribution: Arid Queensland, WA, NSW and NT

Desert figs are small trees found on rocky outcrops where water runs off usually into watercourses or waterholes. The fruit is rich in potassium and calcium and is a good source of protein. The warty figs taste pleasantly figgy and sweet and are bright yellow when immature but turn a red, or ochre, colour when ripe. Desert figs have gritty seeds in them which should be removed or strained out for cooking.

DILLON BUSH

(also known as nitre bush, wild grape)
Nitraria billardieri
Distribution: WA, SA, NSW, Vic,
Queensland and NT

Dillon bush is a rather sprawling, spiky
bush that grows in large clumps. It has
small, fleshy leaves and fairly insignificant
flowers but most importantly, bears a heavy
crop of fruit (late summer and autumn)
which varies from dark red to yellow when
ripe. The fruit tastes a little like a salty
grape—a rather pleasant sweet–and–sour
flavour and may be eaten raw or cooked.
Remember to remove the small stone first.

KONKERBERRY

(also known as conker berry, conkle berry)
Carissa Lanceolata
Distribution: Northern Australia including
WA, NT and Queensland

The konkerberry is a luscious little fruit
that is a dark blackish-red in colour and
has a juicy, sweet flavour. In the wild the
fruit sets after rain and has a very short
harvest time. In a garden, with ample
watering, the fruit will ripen at any time of
year.

MIDYIM

(also known as midgen berry)
Austromyrtus dulcis
Distribution: Northern NSW and southern
Queensland

Midyim has a pretty and flavoursome fruit
that appears on the small shrub after
flowering. When ripe, the fruit is a soft,
round white berry that is speckled all over
with tiny red spots. It's a delicious, sweet
fruit with a slightly aromatic flavour.
Honeyeaters, olive backed orioles,
mistletoe birds and crows can often be
found around this plant, feeding on the
berries. The berries can be eaten raw but
also work well in jams and tarts.

SNOWBERRY

Gaultheria hispida
Distribution: Tasmania

The snowberry is a beautiful little fruit
about 1 cm wide. It's a fruit made up of 5
white lobes, yet at the base the colour
changes to a deep pink. The snowberry
ripens from March to June and hence is
good in winter cooking, or simply eaten
raw.

WHITE ELDERBERRY

(also known burne-burne)
Sambucus gaudichaudiana
Distribution: Coastal rainforests,
Queensland, NSW, also temperate Victoria,
Tasmania and SA

The native elderberries are related to the
European elderberries we hear so much of
in elderberry wine and jelly for example.
Where the common European elderberry
is black, Australia has a soft yellow variety,
S. australasica, and a lovely white elderberry
that I'm very fond of, *S. gaudichaudiana*.
The plant is a very attractive shrub that is
low growing with large frond-like leaves

and clusters of tiny white flowers that bloom in spring and are followed in summer by juicy white, translucent berries. Each berry holds about 3 to 4 seeds the same size as currants. The berries are delicious as a fresh fruit, the base of a sauce, or to make into jelly.

CAPE BARREN TEA

(also known as white correa)
Correa alba
Distribution: Victoria, SA, Tasmania and NSW

A native to all south-eastern coastal areas and can be seen along the beaches where it is a hardy, wind-blown plant. Local councils are also fond of planting Cape Barren tea in parks and gardens and street plantings. It's a pretty bush, about 1.5 cm high with soft green leaves that have a silvery underside and a slightly furry feel. The fresh or dried leaves can be used to make a very pleasant tea. It has a gentle flavour, not unlike green tea; like herbal teas you will need to let it infuse a little before drinking.

NATIVE PEPPERMINT

(also known as broad leaf peppermint)
Eucalyptus dives
Distribution: Victoria, NSW

The native peppermint is a sturdy medium-sized tree with broad, soft, grey-green leaves that have a very strong peppermint scent and flavour. The leaves can be used fresh or dry as a flavouring, but use sparingly as they will dominate if you use too much. The crushed, dried leaf makes a refreshing tea.

WILD THYME

(also known as wild basil, sacred balm, holy basil)
Ocimum tenuiflorum
Distribution: Northern Australia, Queensland

Although formally a member of the basil family this herb is frequently referred to in outback Queensland, where it grows naturally, as wild thyme. The taste is highly aromatic and is more akin to thyme than basil. It's a good plant to grow for its perfume. To cook with, wild thyme is great baked into a wild thyme and olive bread, wild thyme and cheese fritters, put through pasta dough, or sprinkled over fresh tomatoes. The leaves can be dried and stored in clean glass jars to retain their flavour.

BULBINE LILY

(also known as native leek, leek lily, wild onion, golden lily)
Bulbine bulbosa
Distribution: Victoria, Tasmania, SA, NSW and inland Queensland

The soft green leaves of the bulbine lily look like onion or very large chive leaves, and its edible tuber tastes distinctly like leek, yet sweeter, and can be eaten all year round. It is high in calcium and iron and carbohydrates and has about an 80% water content. To eat, the tubers should be cleaned, then roasted, baked or steamed. They are also quite pleasant raw and can be grated or thinly sliced in a salad.

Bushfood Suppliers

Ring first to make sure the ingredient you are after is in season.

Victoria

Robins Bush Foods
39 Lothian Street
North Melbourne 3051
Tel (03) 9326 6188
Fax (03) 9326 6114
Stocks all frozen and dried bushfoods. Includes specially made-up preparations such as chutneys, sauces, vinaigrettes, marinades, sweet syrups, cordials, jams and jellies.

The Vital Ingredient
206 Clarendon Street
South Melbourne 3205
Tel (03) 9696 3511
Fax (03) 9696 5549
Distributes products from Robins Bush Foods and Bush Tucker Supply.

Tarnuk Bush Food and Flowers
21 Smith Street
Thornbury 3071
Tel (03) 9416 7150
For Southern Australian raw bushfoods such as warrigal greens, native mint and appleberries.

Rosebuds
233 Williamsons Road
Templestowe 3106
Tel (03) 9846 4142
Selection of products from Red Ochre.

Daimaru
Melbourne Central
211 La Trobe Street
Melbourne 3000
Tel (03) 9660 6666
Selection of value-added foods from Robins, Bush Tucker Supply and Red Ochre.

David Jones
310 Bourke Street
Melbourne 3000
Tel (03) 9669 8200
Selection of value-added foods from Robins, Bush Tucker Supply and Red Ochre.

King Island Products
351 Moorabool Street
Geelong 3220
Tel (052) 216 399

Myer Melbourne
314 Bourke Street
Melbourne 3000
Tel (03) 9661 1111

Coles Supermarkets
Prahran, Rowville, Epping, Knox
*Bushfoods section stocking products from Robins,
Bush Tucker Supply and Red Ochre.*

Coles Supermarkets
Bondi Junction, Castle Hill
*Bushfoods section stocking products from Robins,
Bush Tucker Supply and Red Ochre.*

New South Wales

Bush Tucker Supply Australia
482 Victoria Road
Gladesville 2111
Tel (02) 9817 1060
*Stocks all frozen and dried bushfoods. Includes
specially made-up preparations such as chutneys,
sauces, vinaigrettes, marinades etc.*

Gundabluey Bushfoods
26 Tenterden Road
Botany 2019
Tel (02) 9316 6300
Mobile 018 161 266
Fax (02) 9316 6305
Stocks frozen and dried foods.

Bushfoods of Australia
Dudgeons Lane
Bangalow 2479
Tel (066) 87 1005
Fax (066) 87 1358
Stocks native herbs and spices.

Posh Foods P/L
Unit 9 Ashmore Estate
1a Coulson Street
Erskinville 2043
Tel (02) 9550 6022

David Jones (Aust)
Market Street
Sydney 2000
Tel (02) 9266 5544
Value-added foods, some dried herbs and spices.

ACT

Good Things
43 The Crescent
Queanbeyan 2620
Tel (06) 297 4724

Poachers Pantry
Marakei Nanima Road
Hall ACT 2618
Tel (06) 230 2487
Distributor

Queensland

Bush Tucker Supply
South East Queensland
28 Kennedy Terrace
Paddington 4064
Tel (07) 3368 3615

Longreach Bush Tucker
PO Box 51
Longreach 4730
Tel–fax (076) 58 3873
*Stocks wild orange, wild lime, native
peppermint, kurrajong, wild thyme, portulaca,
bush cucumbers.*

Garozzo Agencies
38 Redden Street
Portsmith
Cairns 4870
Tel (070) 35 3456
Distributor for Robins Bush Foods.

Australian Tropical Native Food Resources
Lake Street
Cairns 4870
Tel (070) 53 7458
Stocks Burdekin plum, lemon aspen, cheesefruit.

The Australian Comestible Co.
36 Harlow Crescent
Noosa Parklands 4565
Tel (074) 74 0883

Gabrielle Cooney
30 Nolan Street
Whitfield 4870
Tel (070) 32 0898

Red Ochre Grill
43 Shields Street
Cairns 4870
Tel (070) 51 0100
Value-added Red Ochre products.

Noel Joliffe
Australian Native Produce Suppliers
Unit 3, 148 Tennyson Memorial Ave
Yeerongpilly 4105
Tel (07) 3217 1999
Fax (07) 3217 1555
Distributor for Robins, Bush Tucker Supply and Red Ochre.

Coles Supermarkets
Kenmore, The Gap, Robina
Bushfoods section stocking products from Robins, Bush Tucker Supply and Red Ochre.

South Australia

Australian Native Produce Industries P/L
87 Harrison Road
Dudley Park 5008
Tel (08) 8346 3337
Fax (08) 8346 3387
Nursery, and stocks Red Ochre products.

Red Ochre Grill
129 Gouger Street
Adelaide 5000
Tel (08) 8212 7266
Fax (08) 8212 6686

Shoalmarra
Tumby Bay 5605
Tel (086) 88 2546
Quandong stockist (dried and processed).

Gourmets Choice
Unit 4, Deacon Avenue
Richmond 5033
Tel (08) 8234 2296

Coast and Country Foods Distributors
Box 641
Port Lincoln 5606
Tel (086) 82 2701

Regency Food Services
27 Taminga Street
Regency Park 5010
Tel (08) 8268 8688
Distributor for Bush Tucker Supply.

Fleurieu Fine Foods
Yankalilla 5203
Tel (085) 58 2436

Coles Supermarkets
Burnside Village, Gawlor
*Bushfoods section stocking products from Robins,
Bush Tucker Supply and Red Ochre.*

Western Australia

Mahogany Creek Distributors
Unit 1, Lot 140 Agett Road
Malega 6062
Tel (09) 249 2866
Distributor for Bush Tucker Supply.
Pat Foods
26 Munt Street
Bayswater 6053
Tel (09) 272 6522

Tasmania

Tasmanian Wild Foods
Pepper Berry Cafe
91 George Street
Launceston 7250
Tel (003) 344 589

Butterfields Tasmania
20 Letitia Street
North Hobart 7000
Tel (002) 31 4214

Coles Supermarkets
Meadow Mews, Glenorchy
*Bushfoods section stocking products from Robins,
Bush Tucker Supply and Red Ochre.*

Northern Territory

Parap Fine Foods
40 Parap Road
Darwin 0820
Tel (08) 8981 8597
*Distributor for Robins, Bush Tucker Supply and
Red Ochre.*

Altitudes Bar and Eatery
1st Floor
Darwin International Airport
Sir Henry Wiggly Drive
Marrara 0810
Tel (08) 8945 1120
*Distributor for Robins, Bush Tucker Supply and
Red Ochre.*

Nurseries and Growing Contacts

NURSERIES

Victoria

Kuranga Native Nursery
393 Maroondah Highway
Ringwood 3134
Tel (03) 9879 4076

CERES Bushfood and Permaculture
Nursery
Lee Street
Brunswick 3056
Tel (03) 9387 4403

Victorian Indigenous Nurseries
    Cooperative (VINC)
Yarra Bend Park
Fairfield 3078
Tel (03) 9482 1710

Bushland Flora
Clegg Road
Mt Evelyn 3796
Tel (03) 9736 4364

Plants Naturally
PO Box 24
Monbulk 3793
Tel (03) 9756 7495

Peninsular Bushworks
16 Hunts Road
Bittern 3918
Tel (059) 83 9649

Goldfield's Revegetations
Bendigo's Indigenous Nursery &
    Wildflower Farm
Dyson's Road
Mandurang 3551
Tel (054) 395 384

St Kilda Indigenous Nursery Co-operative
525 Williamstown Road
Port Melbourne 3207
Tel (03) 9645 2477

New South Wales

Forbidden Fruits
McCauley's Lane
Mullumbimby 2480
Tel (066) 84 3688

Bryant's Native Plant Nursery
Cosy Camp Road
Bex Hill 2480
Tel (066) 28 4323

Dealbata (Cold Climate) Australian
    Plant Nursery
off Bloomfield Street
Dalgety 2630
Tel (064) 56 5043

Newcastle Wildflower Nursery
45 Pacific Highway
Bennett's Green 2290
Tel (049) 48 8576

Mcauley's Lane
Mullumbimby 2480
(066) 84 3688

Limpinwood Gardens Nursery
Limpinwood Valley Road
Via Chillingham 2484
Tel (066) 79 3353
Fax (066) 79 3143
Specialises in rainforest plants and cut and grown selections of bushfood plants.

Terania Rainforest Nursery
Alstonville 2477
Tel (066) 246 033
Wholesale quantities only, rainforest plants.

Possum Creek Native Nursery
PO Box 66
Bangalow 2479
Tel (066) 871 305
Wholesale quantities only, rainforest plants.

Queensland

Edible Landscapes
37 Bangalia Street
Torwood 4066
Tel (07) 3870 3872

Yeppoon Rainforest Nursery
Adelaide Park Road
Yeppoon 4703
Tel (079) 39 3963

Fairhill Native Plants
Fairhill Road
Yandina 4561
Tel (074) 46 7088

South Australia

Australian Native Produce Industries
Native Food Plant Nursery
PO Box 163
Paringa 5340
Tel (085) 95 1611

Munthari Wild Food Plants of Australia
Lot 4–5, Main North Road
Rahynie 5412
Tel–fax (08) 8847 2542

Western Australia

Permaculture and Environment Centre
Lot 40, Farrall Road
Midvale 6056
Tel (09) 274 4995

Zanthorrea Nursery
155 Watsonia Road
Maida Vale 6057
Tel (09) 454 6260

Men of the Trees (MOTT)
Lot 2. Stirling Crescent
Hazelmere 6055
Tel (09) 250 1888

Northern Territory

Ironstone Lagoon Nursery
Lagoon Road
Berrimah 0828
Tel (088) 984 3186
Fax (088) 984 4978

Weowna Native Plant Nursery
Red Cliff Road
Humpty Doo 0836
Tel/Fax (088) 9888 2440

Tasmania

Plants of Tasmania Nursery
65 Hall Street
Ridgeway 7054
Tel (002) 39 1583

SOCIETIES FOR GROWING AUSTRALIAN PLANTS

Victoria

SGAP Victoria Inc
17 Craig Court
Heathmont 3136
Tel (03) 9729 4292; 9728 5891

New South Wales

SGAP New South Wales Ltd
3 Currawang Place
Como West 2226
Tel (02) 9528 2683

ACT

SGAP Canberra Region Inc
PO Box 217, Civic Square
ACT 2608
Tel (06) 231 7055

Queensland

SGAP Queensland Region Inc
PO Box 586
Fortitude Valley 4006
Tel (07) 3341 4272

South Australia

SGAP South Australian Region Inc
29 Tennyson Avenue
Tranmere 5073
Tel (08) 8331 9325

Western Australia

Western Australian Wildflower Society Inc
PO Box 64
Nedlands 6009
Tel (09) 383 1254

Tasmania

SGAP Tasmanian Region Inc.
GPO Box 1353P
Hobert 7001
Tel (002) 29 1710

GREENING AUSTRALIA
....

Victoria

Greg Bain
PO Box 525
Heidelberg 3084
Tel (03) 9457 3024
Fax (03) 9457 3713

New South Wales

Paul Cruickshank
GPO Box 9868
Sydney 2001
Tel (02) 9560 9144
Fax (02) 9550 0576

ACT

Mark Thomas
GPO Box 9868
ACT 2601
Tel (06) 281 8585
Fax (06) 281 8590

Queensland

Bill Stanfield
GPO Box 9868
Brisbane 4001
Tel (07) 3844 0211
Fax (07) 3844 0727

South Australia

Malcolm Campbell
GPO Box 9868
Adelaide 5074

Tel (08) 8207 8757
Fax (08) 8207 8755

Western Australia

Murray Edmonds
1118 Hay Street
West Perth 6005
Tel (09) 481 2144
Fax (09) 481 0024

Tasmania

Don Thompson
GPO Box 9868
Tasmania 7000
Tel (002) 23 6377
Fax (002) 23 6392

INDUSTRY CONTACTS

Brian Milgate's Grower Network
   (Lemon Myrtle)
Australian Native Food Resources
Development P/L
6/63 Ballina Street
Lennox Head 2478
Tel (066) 875 555

ARBIA (Australian Rainforest Bushfood
   Industry Association)
Sibylla Hess-Buschmann, Secretary
PO Box 6407
South Lismore NSW 2480
Tel (066) 89 7433

Australian Native Bushfoods Industry
Denise Hart, Secretary
PO Box 309
Civic Square 2608
Tel 015 519 456

Australian Food and Flora
Caroline Graham, Manager
23 Agery Road
Kadina 5554
Tel (08) 8821 3565

Australian Quandong Industry Association
Danny Matthews, President
PO Box 236
Upper Sturt 5156

References

Aboriginal Communities of the Northern Territory, *Traditional Bush Medicines: An Aboriginal Pharmacopoeia*, Greenhouse Publications, 1988.

Australian Food Plants Study Group newsletters, SGAP.

Australian Plants Study Group, *Grow What Where*, Thomas Nelson, Melbourne, 1980.

Cherikoff, Vic and Jennifer Isaacs, *The Bush Food Handbook*, Ti Tree Press, Sydney, 1989.

Costermans, Leon, *Native Trees and Shrubs of South-eastern Australia*, Rigby, Adelaide, 1981.

Council for Aboriginal Reconciliation, *'Valuing Cultures'*, Key Issue Paper No. 3, AGPS, 1994.

Cribb, A.B., *Wild Food in Australia*, Collins, Sydney, 1981.

Flood, Josephine, *Archeology of the Dreamtime*, Angus & Robertson, Pymble, 1992.

Garnet, J. R. and Elizabeth Conabere, *Wildflowers of South-eastern Australia*, vols 1–2, Thomas Nelson, Melbourne, 1974.

Gott, Beth and Nelly Zola, *Koorie Plants, Koorie People*, Koorie Heritage Trust, Melbourne, 1992.

—and John Conran, *Victorian Koori Plants*, Yangennanock Women's Group, Hamilton, 1991.

Gray, Patience, *Honey from the Weed*, Papermac, London 1987.

Harden, Gwen (ed), *Flora of New South Wales*, 1990-

Isaacs, Jennifer, *Bush Food*, Weldon Publishing, Sydney, 1987.

Jones, D. L., *Ornamental Rainforest Trees*, Reed, Balgowlah, 1979.

Latz, Peter, *Bushfires and Bushtucker: Aboriginal Plant Use in Central Australia*, IAD Press, Alice Springs, 1995.

Low, Tim, *Wild Herbs of Australia and New Zealand*, Angus & Robertson, Pymble, 1993.

—, *Bush Tucker: Australia's Wild Food Harvest*, Angus & Robertson, Pymble, 1992.

—, *Wild Food Plants of Australia*, Angus & Robertson, Pymble, 1991.

Marchant, Neville G. et al, *Flora of the Perth Region*, 1987.

Nicholson, Nan and Hugh, *Australian Rainforest Plants*, vols 1–4, 1992–94.

Sharshewski, Peter and Dr Shawn Somerset, *Kakadu Plum: An Opportunity for the Food Industry*, Queensland Department of Primary Industries.

Skinner, Gwen, *The Cuisine of the South Pacific*, Hodder & Stoughton, New Zealand, 1983.

Society for Growing Australian Plants, *Australian Plants*, vol. 17, no. 138; vol. 16, no. 130; vol. 18., no. 142, SGAP, Sydney.

Society for Growing Australian Plants, *North Queensland Plants*, SGAP.

Wrigley, John and Murray Fagg, *Australian Native Plants*, William Collins, Sydney, 1979.

The Citrus Industry: History, Botony and Breeding, vol 1, University of California Press, 1943.

Index